CONTENTS

PREFACE

The importance of the Essais *of Montaigne in the intellectual tradition that gave rise to the eighteenth-century* philosophes *has long been acknowledged.*[1] *Indeed, over a century ago, the critic Sainte-Beuve briefly sketched Montaigne's philosophical connections with the Encyclopedists. Montaigne's fortunes and influence in France in the sixteenth and seventeenth centuries, and in the period 1812-1852, have already been studied.*[2] *But, for the eighteenth century, we have only Maturin Dreano's history of Montaigne's fortunes; he leaves untouched the question of the essayist's influence in the Enlightenment.*[3] *The present study attempts to fill a part of this gap.*[4]

In the domain of Diderot scholarship, research has of late been occupying itself with the question of the Encylopedist's relationship to modern thought, but it has also been concerned with the problem of Diderot's sources.[5] *A host*

---

[1] Mme. du Deffand remarked: " Montaigne est leur père à tous " (cited in Louis DUCROS, *Les Encyclopédistes* [Paris, 1900], p. 17, which see with regard to Montaigne's relationship to the *philosophes*, pp. 17-29); also Fritz SCHALK, " Einleitung in die Encyclopädie der Französischen Aufklärung ", *Münchner Romanistische Arbeiten*, VI (München, 1936), *passim*.

[2] Pierre VILLEY, *Montaigne devant la postérité* (Paris, 1935); Alan M. BOASE, *The Fortunes of Montaigne; A History of the Essays in France, 1580-1669* (London, 1935); Donald M. FRAME, *Montaigne in France, 1812-1852* (New York, 1940).

[3] Maturin DREANO, *La Renommée de Montaigne en France au XVIIIᵉ siècle* (Angers, 1952).

[4] A contemporary scholar has recently proposed " Diderot and Montaigne " and " Montaigne in the Eighteenth Century " as rewarding subjects of study (Henri PEYRE, in a review of *Diderot Studies III* in the *Romanic Review*, LII, iv [Dec. 1961], 302). The present study was sketched in a preliminary fashion in my unpublished Master's Essay (Columbia University, 1960).

[5] See, for example, Franco VENTURI, *Jeunesse de Diderot* (Paris, 1939); Aram VARTANIAN, *Diderot and Descartes* (Princeton, 1953); Paul VERNIÈRE, *Spinoza et la pensée française avant la Révolution* (Paris, 1954); Alice Green FREDMAN, *Diderot and Sterne* (New York, 1955); Jacques PROUST, *Diderot et l'Encyclopédie* (Paris, 1962).

11

of critics and scholars since the eighteenth century have suggested points of contact between Diderot and Montaigne, but there has been, thus far, no full-scale confrontation of the two writers. Almost thirty years have passed since Jean Thomas, in his elegant little book L'Humanisme de Diderot (2nd ed., Paris, 1938), placed the eighteenth-century philosophe in the Montaignean tradition, drawing numerous parallels between the essayist and the Encyclopedist. These parallels, however, were only incidental to his main thesis, which was to demonstrate the evolution of Diderot's humanism. The present inquiry follows the path indicated by Thomas.

At the outset, it would be well to define the sense in which I use the word "humanism" in the course of this study. Humanism implies a belief that man, although confined to the realm of nature, possesses certain unique qualities which set him apart from the rest of living things. The distinctiveness of man is such that he cannot be explained in purely mechanistic or material terms. He alone has the capacity for judgment and self-reflection, and the power to direct his actions. Humanism, furthermore, since it includes man within nature, thus denies him transcendence, while at the same time affirming belief and faith in the value of individuality.

The reader is warned that I shall not attempt to provide a complete encyclopedia of the ideas of each writer. It does not seem to me of fundamental interest to place side by side all the possible similarities and differences that might be found in two such fertile minds. Nor can the precise boundaries between influence and affinity be defined. The subtitle of this book indicates its scope and its method. Diderot's humanism is to be viewed as an evolving intellectual attitude which ultimately cannot be separated from his techniques as a literary artist. In order to relate Montaigne to this development, I have permitted Diderot's own references to the essayist to establish the structure of the book.

The edition of reference for Montaigne's Essais is, except when noted to the contrary, the one-volume edition of that work by Albert Thibaudet (Paris: Bibliothèque de la Pléiade, 1950). In Chapter I, where Diderot's quotations from the Essais are compared with the original text, first reference will be to the edition of the Essais by Pierre Coste (Paris, 1725), a copy of which is in the collection of the New York Public Library, followed by the Pléiade edition reference. The Coste text, which we may assume was the one utilized by Diderot, is based on the edition of 1595 and therefore exhibits certain variants from the text of the Bordeaux Copy. In all Montaigne references, I have retained the archaic spellings.

Although the standard edition of reference for the works of Diderot is the Œuvres complètes edited by Jean Assézat and Maurice Tourneux (Paris, 1875-77), 20 vols., designated in this study as "A-T", it is being supplemented and superseded by recent editions which are both more accurate and more readily accessible to the reader. I have chosen, therefore, to make use of current editions whenever possible. Minor inconsistencies in Diderot's spelling have been regularized to conform with modern French usage.

I take pleasure in expressing my appreciation to the following members of the Columbia University faculty: to Professor Donald M. Frame, who

12

with sure judgment and unfailing eye guided this study in its successive stages; to Professor Otis Fellows, who provided the initial spark and whose enthusiasm was a continual source of inspiration; and to Professors Diana Guiragossian, Craig Brush, John Nelson, and Howard Porter, for their helpful criticisms and suggestions. I also wish to thank Professor Gita May, of Columbia, who directed an earlier phase of the work, for her kind interest and encouragement. Finally, to my first and best of readers, my wife Sandra, without whom this book could not have been, go feelings deeper than all words.

J. S.

INTRODUCTION

Montaigne et Diderot réunis font plaisir à voir, mais
n'étonnent point. Les préjugés rendent les hommes
ordinaires plus ou moins petits. Les philosophes les
renversent, montant sur ces débris et se trouvant à
même hauteur.

L. S. MERCIER [1]

The popularity of Montaigne's *Essais* in France did not remain
constant during the two-hundred-year period following the book's
first publication. The *Essais* enjoyed a peak of success in the first
twenty-five years of the seventeenth century, falling into disrepute
after the publication of the *Logique de Port-Royal* in 1662, and condemnation by Rome in 1676. This decline in the official approval of the
Essais coincides with the supplanting of Montaigne's fideism by Cartesian rationalism, which exercised a strong influence on Church doctrine
in the second half of the seventeenth century.[2] The impetus for the
eighteenth century's revival of Montaigne comes in 1724 with the
appearance of the first French edition of the *Essais* since 1669, published
in England by Pierre Coste. Reissued in 1725, 1727, 1739, and 1745,
it was the standard edition of the eighteenth century and was pre-
sumably the one utilized by Diderot. Significantly enough, the *Essais*
thus arrive from England, concurrently with the wave of empiricist
ideas from across the Channel. Coste, incidentally, had published in
1695 a translation of John Locke's book on education, and in the 1708
edition of this work, he finds that the *Essais* serve as a pertinent com-

---

[1] Louis Sébastien MERCIER, *Néologie...* (Paris, 1801), II, 59. Quoted in
DREANO, *Renommée*, p. 526.

[2] BOASE, *Fortunes*, p. 209 : " ... in some respects the success of Cartesianism in the second half of the century necessarily coincides with the
discredit of the *Weltanschauung* represented by Montaigne, Charron, and
most of the writers dealt with in this book."

mentary to Locke.[1] The presence of the *Essais* on the Index and a new distinction as a precursor of empiricism help to accredit Montaigne as an ally of the *philosophes* in the battle for emancipated thought.

It should not be thought, however, that the *Essais* had to reënter France on Locke's coat-tails. The time was ripe for a renewal of interest in Montaigne, whose eclipse had been due in part to the success of Cartesianism and the classical aesthetic. The eighteenth century's revival of the *Essais* is symptomatic of its reaction against classicism and Cartesianism. Though the *philosophes* owed much to Descartes, Cartesianism acquired a bad name among them because of its association with Church doctrine. The *philosophes*, therefore, were quick to disclaim any connection with the thought of Descartes and, rather, sought their ancestors among such figures as Bacon, Newton, Gassendi, and Bayle.[2] Montaigne too was involved in their disputes over language, style, composition, ethics, education, philosophy, politics, and religion. In general, however, the eighteenth century was not capable of nor interested in understanding Montaigne as a man of the Renaissance, and chose to use him for its particular ends rather than know him on his own terms. As the century wore on, he was considered in turn an *honnête homme*, a *libertin*, a *philosophe*, and a revolutionary.[3]

Thus the eighteenth-century mind saw in Montaigne chiefly a reflection of itself, and ignored or scorned what was not in accord with its own character. Voltaire, for example, praises Montaigne's ideas—his skepticism, his empiricism, his critique of intolerance and religious fanaticism—ideas which Voltaire affirms are eighteenth-century ideas. But Voltaire does not understand Montaigne as well as he claims, and does not exercise the principle of relativity which he might have learned from the essayist. While establishing exaggerated identities between his time and the sixteenth century, he fails to recognize the infinite nuances in the essayist's ideas which separate him from the *philosophes*. Moreover, if Voltaire is too eager to identify his thought with Montaigne's, he remains scornful of the style and composition of the *Essais*, and pitilessly refuses to admit Montaigne into the company of the truly great on aesthetic grounds. Voltaire steadfastly opposes the dry precision of his own polished style to Montaigne's grossness and barbarous lack of taste.

Rousseau appears not to have been notably concerned with Montaigne's style, and, on the other hand, borrows more of Montaigne's ideas than he readily admits. He is, of course, particularly attracted to the essayist's primitivism, which he equates with his own, and to his

---

[1] *De l'Education des enfants* (Amsterdam, 1708), pp. xxix-xxx. Cited in DREANO, p. 85.

[2] VARTANIAN, *Diderot and Descartes*, p. 34: "Inasmuch as the innatist metaphysics of official Cartesianism was something that the philosophes, as diligent students of Lockean epistemology, rejected and combated, they understandably refused in good faith to style themselves Cartesians." See also BOASE, *Fortunes*, p. 425.

[3] DREANO, p. 552.

16

ideas on education, which he freely borrows. He is critical of Montaigne's skepticism and doubts the sincerity of his self-portrait, but this denigration of Montaigne serves Rousseau's own self-laudatory purpose.[1]

Diderot, like his great contemporaries, is a child of his own century. He chooses to admire that in Montaigne which is in tune with his own temperament, losing sight therefore of much of Montaigne's complexity. Unlike Rousseau, Diderot is not concerned directly with the question of Montaigne's sincerity. Unlike Voltaire, Diderot found in Montaigne a style and an aesthetic which bore strong resemblances to his own. Indeed, he was almost alone in his century in defending the essayist's manner of composition; and in defending Montaigne, he defends himself.

This affinity in style was first noted by Jacques-André Naigeon, Diderot's disciple and editor, who also played an important role in the history of the *Essais*.[2] Thoroughly steeped in the work of his two idols, Naigeon often takes the opportunity to note affinities between them. He discusses, for instance, their digressiveness, and proceeds to explain the inner order that underlies their apparent unconcern with logical method:

Je suis très éloigné de blâmer ce qu'on appelle communément des écarts, soit dans Montaigne, soit dans la plupart des ouvrages de Diderot. Ceux qui en jugent ainsi, prouvent assez qu'ils sont incapables de saisir les rapports plus ou moins éloignés qu'ont entre elles certaines idées ; ils ignorent que ces idées qui leur paraissent si incohérentes, s'enchaînent dans l'entendement du philosophe par des analogies très-fines, très-délicates, qui échappent à des lecteurs vulgaires.

Rien ne ressemble plus à un chapitre de Montaigne, ou à quelques écrits de Diderot, que la conversation habituelle et libre d'une douzaine d'hommes de beaucoup d'esprit.[3]

The disorder of the *Essais* is the result of an art and a method whose principles are hidden : " Personne ne savait mieux que lui ce que sa manière d'écrire pouvait avoir de choquant pour les esprits vulgaires ; il a prévu leur critique, et sans y répondre directement, il a révélé lui-même le secret de sa méthode, et enseigné l'art de lire son livre et de l'entendre." [4] He then quotes the well-known lines from " De la vanité ", the essay which has been so misunderstood even in the present century, and uses them to justify Diderot's " alleged " digressions :

« Je m'esgare, mais plustot par licence que par mesgarde. Mes fantasies se suyvent, mais par fois c'est de loing, et se regardent, mais d'une veue

---

[1] The reader is referred to the relevant chapters of Dreano's study for further details on Montaigne's fortunes in eighteenth-century France.

[2] Naigeon published a posthumous edition of Diderot's works in 1798, and in 1802 he put out the first edition of the *Essais* to be based on the Bordeaux Copy.

[3] NAIGEON, *Mémoires historiques et philosophiques sur la vie et les ouvrages de Denis Diderot* (Paris, 1821), p. 373.

[4] *Ibid.*, p. 375.

oblique. » (III, ix) Ce passage peut servir à justifier les prétendus écarts de Diderot, qui ne sont d'ailleurs ni aussi nombreux, ni aussi hardis que ceux de Montaigne. On voit que dans ces deux philosophes, doués d'une imagination vive et forte, et d'une grande pénétration, ils avaient leur source, ou si l'on veut leur raison, dans l'habitude de méditer profondément les questions dont ils s'occupaient ; dans cette inquiétude d'esprit qui donne le besoin de connaître, et qui les portait, comme par instinct, à chercher dans une matière tout ce qu'on peut y voir ; dans le désir si naturel de s'emparer les premiers des vérités qu'ils trouvaient sur toute la longueur de la route qu'ils avaient parcourue, et qui, ainsi préparées, et pour ainsi dire mûries par leurs recherches et leurs méditations, n'auraient coûté à ceux qui seraient venus après eux que la peine de les recueillir ; enfin, dans cet art si nécessaire et si rare, de ne prendre que les sommités du tout, et de n'offrir au lecteur que des résultats, en supprimant toutes les idées intermédiaires qui les ont produits.[1]

Thus Naigeon, appreciative student of Montaigne and overzealous disciple of Diderot, despite his *parti-pris*, adumbrates many modern critics in his sympathetic understanding of the idiosyncracies of his two favorites. He was the first to perceive the stylistic affinities in their writings and to seek an explanation of these peculiarities in an instinctive habit of mind, a combination of imagination and meditative powers, an ability to synthesize and to perceive subtle analogies.

Sainte-Beuve, discussing the *Entretien avec M. de Saci*, mentions Diderot in the ranks of Montaigne's posterity :

Montaigne... préside non-seulement aux Sceptiques purs (Bayle, Hume), mais à tous les autres qui infirment l'homme et lui contestent son point de vue du *moi* central et dominant : ainsi les Matérialistes empiriques... ; les Athées... ; les Naturistes comme d'Alembert et Diderot, qui, tout en étant dans la bienveillance (d'Alembert), ou dans l'enthousiasme fréquent (Diderot), n'admettent de loi morale qu'une certaine affection, une certaine chaleur muable et propre à la nature de chaque animal ; les Panthéistes et Spinosistes (dont est déjà Diderot), qui, tout en admettant un grand ordre général et une loi du monde, y perdent l'homme comme un atome et un accident, comme une forme parmi une infinité de formes, lui nient sa liberté, et que son mal soit mal, que sa vertu soit vertu absolue. Et notez que ce Panthéisme et Spinosisme, que je range sous Montaigne, comme absorbant la nature humaine et le moi, rejoint pourtant à certains égards le Stoïcisme.[2]

One would indeed have to quarrel with this schematization which, as Sainte-Beuve admits, was only an attempt to " ébaucher le cadre ", but which nevertheless is inaccurate with respect to both Diderot and Montaigne. Once again, however, it will help us to clarify further the

---

[1] NAIGEON, *Mémoires historiques et philosophiques sur la vie et les ouvrages de Denis Diderot* (Paris, 1821), p. 375.

[2] SAINTE-BEUVE, *Port-Royal*, 2nd edition (Paris, 1860), II, 389. For an analysis of the inaccuracies in Sainte-Beuve's portrait of Montaigne in *Port-Royal*, see Donald M. FRAME, " Did Montaigne Betray Sebond ? " *Romanic Review*, XXXVIII, iv (Dec. 1947).

relationship between our two authors. For example, it will be necessary to consider to what extent they " infirment l'homme " and whether indeed human nature and the ego are " absorbed " in the mechanics of the infinite. These are questions, it seems to me, which are at the heart of the *Essais* and of the most personal of Diderot's writings, such as *Le Neveu de Rameau, Le Rêve de d'Alembert,* and *Jacques le fataliste.*

In our own century, the *rapprochements* between Montaigne and Diderot have proliferated at a prodigious rate. Cru noted that Diderot, " like his favorite Montaigne, delighted to make his reading a matter for independent thought and composition ".[1] In 1914 a Viennese scholar viewed the French Enlightenment as the direct descendant of the Renaissance, considering as common characteristics a liberation from Aristotelianism and scholastic method, a sharpened definition of personality, and a new critical sense. He draws parallels between Montaigne's " Apologie de Raimond Sebond " and Diderot's philosophical works, notably the *Pensées philosophiques,* the *Promenade du sceptique* and the *Rêve de d'Alembert,* and finds the importance of Seneca in the works of both writers " more than coincidental ".[2]

In his study of the ethical ideas of Diderot, Pierre Hermand finds it impossible to state with any precision what the influence of Montaigne was in this regard, and his general impression is rather negative : " Aussi bien ne semble-t-il pas qu'il ait fourni grand'chose à Diderot, ni pour la méthode, ni pour les résultats où aboutit en morale l'effort de sa réflexion ",[3] although he states that " Diderot a lu et relu Montaigne avec délices ; et il le lut d'assez bonne heure, car il le cite plusieurs fois dès l'*Essai sur le mérite*... il le cite dans l'*Essai sur Claude et Néron,* et de façon inexacte, ce qui montre qu'il écrit de mémoire ".[4] He is skeptical of the suggestion that Diderot owes his inspiration for the last-named work to Montaigne's " Defence de Seneque et de Plutarque " (*Essais,* II, xxxii), but conjectures that perhaps Montaigne's praise of the cannibals' way of life had some part in the formation of Diderot's anarchic ideal.[5] A possible connection between the essay " Des cannibales " and the *Supplément au voyage de Bougainville* has been alluded to so often by critics that it hardly seems necessary to be so cautious.

---

[1] R. Loyalty CRU, *Diderot as a Disciple of English Thought* (New York, 1913), p. 159. Cf. Naigeon's statement that Diderot may have been influenced by Montaigne's method of using his reading as a springboard for his own free composition : " Le plan de Diderot est beaucoup plus vaste et mieux conçu que celui de l'auteur des *Essais:* en effet ce que Montaigne avoit imaginé *pour subvenir à la trahison de sa mémoire,* Diderot le faisoit pour étendre, pour multiplier la science, et pour détruire les obstacles divers que les préjugés politiques et religieux opposent aux progrès de la raison " (*Encyclopédie méthodique* [Paris, 1792], II, 218).

[2] Karl von RORETZ, *Diderots Weltanschauung* (Vienna, 1914), p. 7. (My translation.)

[3] Pierre HERMAND, *Les Idées morales de Diderot* (Paris, 1923), p. 237.

[4] *Ibid.,* p. 235.

[5] *Ibid.,* p. 236.

The two works belong in the history of primitivism, and since Diderot was familiar with the essay, it does not seem unlikely that it was in the back of his mind.[1]

Hubert Gillot and Jean Thomas are less hesitant than Hermand in ascribing Diderot's developing humanism to the influence of Montaigne. According to Gillot, Diderot " admirait Montaigne sans réserves ".[2] He finds that Diderot saw in Montaigne an ideal mentor who could resolve the conflicting demands of reason and humanity :

> Si, d'instinct, Diderot va à Montaigne comme à un maître de pensée et un précepteur de bien-vivre, n'est-ce pas que la sagesse largement humaine de « Maître Michel » a de quoi satisfaire à la fois les exigences de sa raison, qu'il veut libre de tout préjugé, souverainement maîtresse d'elle-même, investie de tout pouvoir d'examen et de critique, et son idéal d'humanité, ennemie de la contention des Stoïciens, comme de la molle indulgence des Epicuriens, heureuse dans la plénitude et l'harmonie de la nature, confiante en la destinée, énergique et virile ? [3]

Thomas, who seeks to establish Diderot as the true inheritor of Montaigne's humanism, states that of all the books Diderot read, " il en est un qu'il a aimé d'une particulière tendresse, et qui l'a marqué d'une empreinte ineffaçable ; ce sont les *Essais* de Montaigne ".[4] He, like Naigeon, sees a spiritual affinity between the two which is almost unique in the history of French letters : " Depuis Montaigne, aucun écrivain français n'avait été aussi sensible à la complexité des choses. La souplesse et la vivacité de son intelligence lui révélaient, d'un coup d'œil, les aspects opposés de chaque question, tandis que sa curiosité, toujours en tourment, cherchait à embrasser tous les problèmes qui se posent à l'esprit humain." [5] Thomas further suggests that Diderot restored to

---

[1] Emile Faguet comments : " Le chapitre sur les cannibales n'est pas à négliger. Très complaisamment [Montaigne] croit y montrer comment une société sans lois, sans règlements, sans police, vit dans la justice, dans la fraternité et dans la paix. On croirait quelquefois lire le *Supplément au voyage de Bougainville*, beaucoup plus décent et beaucoup plus spirituel " (*Seizième siècle: Etudes littéraires* [Paris, n.d.], p. 401). Compare a contemporary critic : " De la polygamie indienne, [Montaigne] sait pourtant tirer argument contre la conception chrétienne du mariage ; ce que faisant, il annonce toutes ces histoires de sérail ou de polygamie musulmane qui feront les beaux jours et les mille et une nuits de notre dix-huitième siècle, préparant à leur manière libertine les réflexions autrement sérieuses de Diderot dans les *Bijoux indiscrets* ou dans le *Supplément au voyage de Bougainville* " (R. ETIEMBLE, *L'Orient philosophique au dix-huitième siècle*, I [Paris, 1956], p. 56).

[2] Hubert GILLOT, *Denis Diderot: L'Homme, ses idées philosophiques, esthétiques et littéraires* (Paris, 1937), p. xiv.

[3] *Ibid.*, p. 290.

[4] THOMAS, *L'Humanisme de Diderot*, p. 89.

[5] *Ibid.*, p. 43. Ernst Robert Curtius claims Thomas " gives the much-tortured word Humanism an unusual meaning : that of ethical individualism, empiricism, and naturalism. ... According to Thomas, France has had only two ' Humanists ' — Montaigne and Diderot. With this thesis, to be sure,

French letters a taste for synthesis (which again recalls Naigeon's remarks), but synthesis controlled by experience.[1]

Since Thomas, numerous critics have echoed and amplified his insights. According to Jean Pommier, " nul plus que ce disciple de Montaigne n'a eu le sentiment de l'instabilité des choses ".[2] Lester Crocker perceived resemblances between the *Essais* and Diderot's correspondence :

Oserons-nous dire que la *Correspondance* nous fait penser un peu aux Essais de Montaigne? C'est le même style de causerie intime, de sages commentaires mélangés de curieuses anecdotes, d'imprévu venant du manque de suite : on en retire la même impression de saveur et de charme. On croit sentir une certaine affinité entre ces deux grands esprits, malgré les différences de caractère : tous deux esprits réalistes et penseurs profonds, s'attachant par un commun humanisme aux problèmes de la vie et de la destinée humaine ; tous deux possesseurs d'un scepticisme critique qui ne leur permet pas d'adopter les solutions faciles et toutes faites ; tous deux enfin, voyant de tous les côtés des parcelles de vérité infiniment complexe, trop élusive pour la créature bornée qu'est l'homme. Moins profonde que celle de Montaigne, l'œuvre de Diderot est dans un sens plus large. Nous ne vivons plus avec un seul homme, mais avec toute une époque. Montaigne nous admet surtout dans l'intimité de son esprit ; Diderot nous offre aussi l'épanchement spontané et les émotions ardentes de son cœur.[3]

Scholars have not ceased to explore the facets of this native affinity.[4] Otis Fellows states that, " like Montaigne, Diderot was ever intrigued by man's nature, ' divers et ondoyant ' ".[5] Pierre Mesnard remarks apropos of the *Essai sur les règnes de Claude et de Néron:* " S'il eût vécu

---

we do not get very far. What Thomas calls Humanism no longer has anything to do with the great historical manifestations of Humanism, nor with a spiritual and intellectual connection with Antiquity " (" Diderot and Horace ", excursus in *European Literature and the Latin Middle Ages* [New York, 1953], p. 577). To be sure, this is a distortion of Thomas' thesis. Furthermore, it is unfair to Diderot since, of all his great contemporaries, he possessed perhaps the widest acquaintance with the culture of Antiquity. Gillot insists on " cette culture humaniste qui fait de Diderot le dernier des grands Humanistes de l'âge classique " (*op. cit.*, p. 236).

[1] *Op. cit.*, p. 63.

[2] Jean POMMIER, *Diderot avant Vincennes* (Paris, 1939), p. 101.

[3] Lester G. KRAKEUR [Crocker], *La Correspondance de Diderot* (New York, 1939), p. 101. Cf. the following comment on the relation between the *Essais* and the Letters to Sophie Volland : " Diderot y retrouve l'art de se dire, qu'avait enseigné Montaigne, et même étant donné le développement en ce siècle des salons et de la vie sociale, il y ajoute l'art d'exprimer sa société " (Paul LEDIEU, *Diderot et Sophie Volland*, cited in *The Age of Enlightenment*, ed. Otis Fellows and Norman Torrey [New York, 1942], p. 296).

[4] Fritz SCHALK, " Einleitung ", p. 134.

[5] Otis FELLOWS, " The Theme of Genius in Diderot's *Neveu de Rameau* ", *Diderot Studies II*, ed. Otis Fellows and Norman Torrey (Syracuse, 1952), p. 186.

davantage il est extrêmement probable que Diderot eût de plus en plus exprimé sa pensée sous une forme semblable à celle des *Essais* de Montaigne ou du *Dictionnaire* de Bayle." [1] Terming the *Lettre sur les aveugles* an " ' Essai ' à la Montaigne ",[2] Paul Vernière sounds a warning note on how Diderot must be read in order to be correctly understood :

> Il faut lire Diderot sans cesse de scruter son visage, étudier chaque œuvre en méditant sa genèse, sa date et son exacte portée, enregistrer les questions sans prétendre y répondre, et dans chacune des thèses qu'ils propose, déceler dans quelle mesure il y adhère. Seule cette casuistique nous permettra de ne pas être dupes d'une pensée instinctivement fluide, déroutante pour les esprits carrés, et qui ruse comme celle de Montaigne devant la vérité qui se dérobe.[3]

Etiemble asserts that the *Essais* and Diderot's dialogues are " œuvres rigoureuses mais secrètes en leur composition ".[4] Henri Bénac, discussing Diderot's fictional techniques, contends that the novel, for Diderot, " c'est la possibilité, au fond, d'écrire des essais comme Montaigne ". The *Neveu de Rameau* might well have been entitled an *essai* " au sens d'expérience " by Montaigne himself.[5] Further, should one deem *Jacques le fataliste* marred by certain technical weaknesses, " le point de vue change singulièrement si on le considère comme un essai à la manière de Montaigne, essai qu'on pourrait intituler : ' Fatalisme et Humanisme '." [6] In the same vein, J. Robert Loy suggests that Diderot is playing the role of Montaigne in his last major work, the *Essai sur les règnes de Claude et de Néron*, in which he is giving us, " comme son maître bordelais à la fin d'un autre siècle mouvementé, un livre de sagesse, ruminé pendant toute une vie ",[7] and in which " c'est plutôt [le] style de bavardage d'un Montaigne qui l'emporte ".[8] For Gita May, Diderot's style evokes " le manque délibéré d'apprêt et de cérémonie, le tour familier et terre-à-terre du Montaigne des derniers Essais ".[9]

Turning from stylistic matters to the question of philosophic outlook, we note that Loy considers that Diderot's " general feeling for the interpretation of human existence remains much the same, one of *reasoned optimism*. Has more been required or received from Montaigne and

---

[1] Pierre MESNARD, *Le Cas Diderot, essai de caractérologie littéraire* (Paris, 1952), p. 234.

[2] Paul VERNIÈRE, ed. *Œuvres philosophiques*, by Diderot (Paris, 1956), p. 77.

[3] *Ibid.*, p. iv.

[4] *Op. cit.*, p. 18.

[5] Henri Bénac, ed. *Œuvres romanesques*, by DIDEROT (Paris, 1959), p. xv.

[6] *Ibid.*, p. xvii.

[7] " *L'Essai sur les règnes de Claude et de Néron* ", *CAIEF*, XIII (juin 1961), p. 241.

[8] *Ibid.*, p. 242.

[9] *Diderot et Baudelaire, critiques d'art* (Genève-Paris, 1957), p. 93.

Rabelais? " [1]   Georges May finds that Diderot at the end of his life resembles Montaigne in his final period, but his schema is more dynamic than Loy's :

Le passage de l'optimisme systématique des années 40 à la sagesse sceptique et souriante qui fait ressembler le Diderot des dernières années à Montaigne vieux rendait une transition pessimiste dialectiquement néces-saire. ... En 1769, Diderot en est au même point, pourrait-on dire, que l'auteur du troisième livre des *Essais*, son maître. Son voyage, il l'a fait sans s'éloigner des bords de la Seine. Le résultat est le même : il a compris maintenant que la sagesse, loin d'être un état statique et confortable qu'on atteint une fois pour toutes, exige au contraire un effort incessant, une agilité d'esprit permanente ; qu'elle consiste en un équilibre instable qu'il faut constamment corriger et rétablir.[2]

Robert Niklaus, on the other hand, remains convinced of a strong current of skepticism inherited directly from Montaigne, and which he asserts runs throughout Diderot's career, from the *Essai sur le mérite et la vertu* to the *Essai sur les règnes de Claude et de Néron*. He sees this consistently skeptical attitude in the *Lettre sur les aveugles*, which he then takes as representative of his whole work : " Dès la première page le lecteur de Diderot se voit contraint de poser la grande question de Montaigne, il se la pose à nouveau en cours de route pour finir avec Diderot par un , Que sais-je ? ' retentissant." [3] Speaking of *Jacques le fataliste*, Bénac notes " le scepticisme, le sens de la relativité et le natura-lisme qui marquent une influence de Montaigne beaucoup plus nette... que celle de Rabelais qu'on a souvent mise en lumière ".[4]

A recent commentator, linking Diderot with modern philosophers, points out " two basic influences which seem to have molded Diderot's personality : Montaigne's search for truth at the expense of a system, reinforced by Baconian-Newtonian experimental method, and Descartes' principle of matter in motion as an apriori hypothesis, discarding, of course, the Cartesian metaphysical dualism ".[5]

From this brief sampling of commentaries linking Montaigne and Diderot, certain clear bases of comparison emerge. Most of the scholars quoted have followed Naigeon in seeing an intellectual and spiritual affinity, and their characterizations of this affinity are generally con-sistent. What chiefly strikes them is a similarity of mind and method of coping with perceivable reality. Both writers are skeptical, critical ;

---

[1] J. Robert Loy, *Diderot's Determined Fatalist* (New York, 1950), p. 185.
[2] Georges May, *Quatre Visages de Denis Diderot* (Paris, 1951), pp. 97, 154.
[3] " Diderot et le conte philosophique ", *CAIEF*, XIII (juin 1961), pp. 314-315.
[4] *Op. cit.*, p. 893.
[5] Arnolds Grava, " Diderot and Recent Philosophical Trends ", in *Diderot Studies IV*, ed. Otis Fellows (Geneva, 1963), p. 74. One wonders, however, how these two influences (obviously intellectual) served to mold Diderot's *personality*.

their minds are associative and sinuously mobile, fleeing systematizations and absolutes; their style is digressive, uninhibited, " tel sur le papier qu'à la bouche ".

We have, for the most part, not judged the foregoing opinions of scholars and critics, preferring simply to pass them in review, allowing them now to reinforce and now to modify one another. Our intention has been to observe the various ways Montaigne and Diderot have been linked by the critical intuition. The time has come to explore this relationship more fully than previous scholars have done, to determine to what extent, in fact, the *Essais* are important to the maturing Diderot, and to set the limits of such an affinity.

I. DIDEROT, READER OF THE *ESSAIS*

> Je mesure mon enjambée, dirait Montaigne, à celle
> de mon compagnon de voyage.
>
> Diderot (A-T, XIII, 37)

There is abundant evidence to show that Diderot read the *Essais* early in his career and that they were among his *livres de chevet* throughout his life.[1] Diderot mentions Montaigne in his first published work, a free translation of Shaftesbury's *Essay on Merit and Virtue* (1745). Subsequently, we find direct and indirect references to Montaigne in the *Pensées philosophiques* (1746), *La Promenade du sceptique* (1747), *Les Bijoux indiscrets* (1748), the *Lettre sur les aveugles* (1749), the *Lettre sur les sourds et muets* (1751), several articles for the *Encyclopédie*, *Le Neveu de Rameau* (circa 1761, 1762 and later), *Sur Térence* (1765), the *Salon de 1767*, the *Réfutation du livre d'Helvétius intitulé l'Homme* (1773-74), and *Jacques le fataliste* (1773-75). His lengthiest discussion of Montaigne is found in one of his last works, the *Essai sur les règnes de Claude et de Néron* (1778 and 1782). This constitutes an impressive list which, while it is incomplete, includes most of Diderot's important works. Montaigne was thus one of Diderot's most constant companions during his lifetime, and especially in his later years. There is a wide range in the type of reference that Diderot makes to Montaigne : passages in which he merely mentions him by name together in a list with others ; where he quotes him textually ; where he paraphrases him ; where he criticizes him ; where he praises him ; and passages where

---

[1] Maturin Dreano (*Renommée*, pp. 300-312) has gathered together Diderot's references to Montaigne. However, his treatment, in addition to being incomplete, is achronological and contains a considerable number of errors. A chronological procedure allows us to demonstrate the continuity of Montaigne's presence in Diderot's thought as well as to note any possible relationship between the *Essais* and the evolution of Diderot's ideas.

he does not refer to Montaigne directly, but alludes to him by means of borrowings of his expressions.

Despite the evidence of Diderot's early acquaintance with the *Essais*, we can only conjecture as to the exact period of his first encounter with Montaigne. We may perhaps assume that it goes back to the time of his youth in Langres, and that the *Essais* occupied a prominent place in the Diderot family library on the Place Chambeau. Arthur Wilson speculates that by the time the young Diderot renounced his studies for the priesthood and was leading a bohemian life in Paris, he knew by heart the beautiful passage in praise of Paris from the essay " De la vanité " and was in entire agreement with the sentiments Montaigne expresses.[1] And, towards the end of his life, the aging Encyclopedist writes : " Si j'ai le malheur de vivre assez longtemps pour perdre ceux qui me sont chers, Sénèque, Plutarque, Montaigne, et quelques autres, viendront souvent adoucir l'ennui de la solitude où mes amis m'auront laissé." [2] It is significant that Sophie Volland, who for so many years shared intimately in Diderot's intellectual and emotional life, thought it fitting to bequeath him " seven little volumes of Montaigne's Essays bound in red morocco, together with a ring that I call my Pauline ".[3]

Unfortunately, the whereabouts of this edition of Montaigne and of others Diderot possessed are unknown, owing to the dispersal of his library subsequent to its arrival in Russia.[4] Recent attempts to identify the books which were part of Diderot's library have yielded no information about an edition of the *Essais*.[5] A copy containing Diderot's marginal comments would undoubtedly havé been of great value to us, and it is to be hoped that such a document will one day come to light.

Montaigne is quoted three times in Diderot's translation of Shaftesbury, the *Essai sur le mérite et la vertu* (1745). In the Letter to his brother, Canon Pierre-Didier, which serves as a foreword to the work, Diderot quotes textually a passage from Montaigne's essay " De la liberté de la conscience " to illustrate how religious fanaticism, which is more to be feared than atheism, can easily lead to barbarism and the destruction of moral and cultural values.[6] Diderot's reference to the

---

[1] Arthur M. WILSON, *Diderot: The Testing Years, 1713-1759* (New York, 1957), p. 67. See also *Essais*, III, ix, 1089.

[2] *Essai sur les règnes de Claude et de Néron*, A-T, III, 367.

[3] WILSON, *op. cit.*, p. 228. Wilson translates from the original document, which I have not seen.

[4] For a brief résumé of the fortunes of Diderot's library following its transfer to Catherine II, see Arthur M. WILSON, " Leningrad, 1957 : Diderot and Voltaire Gleanings ", *French Review*, XXXI (1957-58), pp. 351-363 ; Herbert DIECKMANN, " Manuscrits de Diderot conservés en Russie ", *Diderot Studies IV*, ed. Otis Fellows (Geneva, 1963), pp. 53-57.

[5] See Jacques PROUST, " La Bibliothèque de Diderot ", *Revue des Sciences Humaines*, fasc. 90 (avril-juin 1958).

[6] A-T, I, 9 ; *Correspondance*, ed. Georges Roth (hereafter referred to as *Corr.*), I, 51 : " Il est certain qu'en ces premiers temps, dit Montaigne, que notre religion commença de gagner autorité avec les loix, le zèle en arma

French civil wars of the sixteenth century is undoubtedly inspired by Montaigne's reflections in the same essay and elsewhere : " Mais rappelez-vous l'histoire de nos troubles civils, et vous verrez la moitié de la nation se baigner, par piété, dans le sang de l'autre moitié, et violer pour soutenir la cause de Dieu, les premiers sentiments de l'humanité ; comme s'il fallait cesser d'être homme pour se montrer *religieux*" (A-T, I, 9).[1]

Together with Montaigne's critique of religious fanaticism should go his condemnation of atheism, " une proposition come desnaturée et monstrueuse ",[2] which Diderot, however, does not quote. He limits himself to the essayist's rebuke of weak-willed atheists :

Il y a des gens, dit-il, qui simulent l'athéisme, à ceux-là il suffit et il vaut mieux leur faire honte de leur athéisme. Si l'on en croit Montaigne, il faudrait en renvoyer la conversion au médecin : l'approche de danger leur fera perdre contenance. *S'ils sont assez fols*, dit-il, *ne sont pas assez forts pour l'avoir plantée en leur conscience. ... Hommes bien miserables et escervellez, qui taschent d'estre pires qu'ils ne peuvent !* (A-T, I, 19 n.) [3]

Now, as Venturi has shown,[4] this entire note, including the allusion to and quotation from Montaigne, is a reworking of a passage from Shaftesbury's *Moralists*. We shall therefore not analyze this passage further, but only note that Diderot sometimes gets his Montaigne via other writers.

There remains one more quotation of Montaigne in Diderot's footnotes to the *Essai sur le mérite et la vertu* which is perhaps the most interesting because it is textually inexact, and seems to be a paraphrase from memory :

Les erreurs particulières engendrent les erreurs populaires, et alternativement : on aime à persuader aux autres ce que l'on croit, et l'on résiste difficilement à ce dont on voit les autres persuadés. Il est presque impossible de rejeter les opinions qui nous viennent de loin, et comme de main en main. Le moyen de donner un démenti à tant d'honnêtes gens qui nous ont précédés ! Les temps écartent d'ailleurs une infinité de circonstances qui nous enhardiraient. « Ceux qui se sont abbruvez successivement de ces estrangetez, dit Montaigne, ont senti par les oppositions qu'on leur a faictes, où logeoit la difficulté de la persuasion, et ils ont calfeutré ces endroicts

---

plusieurs contre toute sorte de livres payens ; de quoi les gens de lettres souffrent une merveilleuse perte. J'estime que ce désordre ait plus porté de nuisance aux lettres que tous les feux des barbares. Cornelius Tacitus en est un bon tesmoing ; car quoique l'Empereur Tacitus, son parent, en eût peuplé par ordonnances expresses toutes les librairies du monde, toutes fois un seul exemplaire entier n'a pu eschapper la curieuse recherche de ceux qui désiroient l'abolir pour cinq ou six vaines clauses contraires à nostre creance." Cf. *Essais*, II, xix, 754.

[1] Cf., for example, Montaigne's comments on the civil wars in *Essais*, I, xxxi and xxxii.

[2] *Essais*, II, xii, 490.

[3] Cf. *Essais, ibid.*

[4] Franco Venturi, *Jeunesse de Diderot* (Paris, 1939), pp. 346-357.

de pièces nouvelles ; ils n'ont pas craind d'aiouter de leur invention, autant qu'ils le croyoient nécessaire, pour suppléer à la résistance et au default qu'ils pensoient être en la conception d'aultruy. » (*Essais*, liv. III, chap. xi) Histoire fidèle et naïve de l'origine et du progrès des erreurs populaires. (A-T, I, 37, note 2.) [1]

Since Venturi has established this note as Diderot's own,[2] let us compare it with the original passage from " Des boyteux " :

> Or les premiers qui sont abbreuvez de ce commencement d'estrangeté, venans à semer leur histoire, sentent par les oppositions qu'on leur fait, où loge la difficulté de la persuasion, & vont calfeutrant cet endroict de quelque piece fausse. ... L'erreur particuliere faict premierement l'erreur publique : & à son tour aprés l'erreur publique fait l'erreur particuliere. Ainsi va tout ce bastiment, s'estoffant et formant de main en main : de maniere que le plus esloigné tesmoin, en est mieux instruict que le plus voisin : & le dernier informé, mieux persuadé que le premier. C'est un progrez naturel. Car quiconque croit quelque chose, estime que c'est ouvrage de charité, de la persuader à un autre : Et pour ce faire, ne craint point d'adjouster de son invention, autant qu'il voit estre necessaire en son conte, pour suppleer à la resistance et au deffaut qu'il pense estre en la conception d'autruy. (*Essais*, Coste, III, xi, 277f. ; Pléiade, 1152.)

We observe that Shaftesbury's translator might well have suppressed quotation marks, for most of the footnote is a paraphrase of the above passage. Diderot seems to have thoroughly absorbed the passage in his mind, so that he appears not to realize that the idea with which he begins the footnote is not his own. Using the present tense as in the original, apparently unaware of his source, he comments on it, elaborates it, and carries it forward as he goes, until it occurs to him to quote Montaigne. In doing so, he substitutes past tenses for the present tense. The whole is an amalgam of quotation, pseudo-quotation, paraphrase, commentary, and amplification.

What may be concluded from these references to Montaigne in the *Essai sur le mérite et la vertu* ? The first two quotations show that Diderot had the text of the *Essais* before him, either in the original or in Shaftesbury's transcription. They present Montaigne in two different lights : now against fanaticism, now against atheism. The third reference indicates that Diderot did not always quote the *Essais* from a text at hand but that he had already read and savored this passage, stored it in his memory, and appropriated it for his own, almost unconsciously. During the early period of his career, as Diderot moves from belief through various stages of theism, deism, natural religion, towards atheism,[3] Montaigne seems to represent the party of reason and modera-

---

[1] Dreano does not mention this passage.

[2] *Op. cit.*, p. 351.

[3] See Aram VARTANIAN, " From Deist to Atheist, Diderot's Philosophical Orientation 1746-1749 ", in *Diderot Studies I*, ed. Otis Fellows and Norman Torrey (Syracuse, 1949), pp. 46-63.

tion, the point of skeptical equilibrium, in which antinomies are sustained in circumspect detachment. Montaigne is Diderot's mentor in this period of search.

Having found the Montaigne of the "Apologie" and "Des boyteux" lurking in the footnotes of Diderot's debut into letters, we meet him again more directly in the *Pensées philosophiques* (1746), the work which has been termed an expansion and development of what was merely latent the year before in his notes to Shaftesbury. The essay "Des boyteux" is still in the back of Diderot's mind and again slight inexactitudes prove that he quotes from memory:

D'où nous vient ce ton si décidé ? N'avons-nous pas éprouvé cent fois que la suffisance dogmatique révolte ? « On me faict haïr les choses vraisemblables, dit l'auteur des *Essais*, quand on me les plante pour infaillibles. J'aime ces mots qui amollissent et modèrent la témérité de nos propositions, *à l'adventure, aulcunement, quelquefois, on dict, ie pense*, et autres semblables : et si j'eusse eu à dresser des enfants, ie leur eusse tant mis en la bouche cette façon de respondre enquestante et non resolutive : *qu'est-ce à dire ? Ie ne l'entends pas, Il pourrait estre, est-il vray*? qu'ils eussent plustost gardé la forme d'apprentis à soixante ans que de représenter des docteurs à l'âge de quinze. »[1]

In *Pensée* xxvi, Diderot's allusion to the above passage takes the form of a brief exchange of dialogue with Montaigne : " Si j'avais un enfant à dresser, moi, je lui ferais de la Divinité une compagnie si réelle, qu'il lui en coûterait peut-être moins pour devenir athée que pour s'en distraire " (*ibid.*, p. 26). *Pensée* xxvii, which consists entirely of the following sentence, appears simply to be an innocent paraphrase : " L'ignorance et l'*incuriosité* sont deux oreillers fort doux ; mais pour les trouver tels, il faut avoir *la tête aussi bien faite* que Montaigne " (*ibid.*).[2] In utilizing Pascal's version of the famous passage, Diderot seems at once to be echoing and replying to both Pascal and Montaigne. He alludes to Pascal's critique of the essayist's supposed indolence, but clearly lets the accent fall on the qualities and not the shortcomings of a mind such as Montaigne's. The serene nonchalance of Montaigne appears more agreeable to Diderot's temperament than Pascal's tragic vision. On the other hand, Montaigne's attitude with regard to what is for him unknowable may be suited to the self-sufficient sage, but the author of the *Pensées philosophiques* is anything but self-sufficient.

---

[1] *Œuvres philosophiques*, ed. Paul Vernière (Paris, 1956), *Pensée* xxiv, p. 24. Cf. *Essais*, Coste, III, xi, 280 ; Pléiade, 1155. In the A-T edition, the passage is rectified to conform with Montaigne's text, as Vernière notes in his edition. Dreano does not include this passage.

[2] Cf. *Essais*, Coste, III, xiii, 330 : " O, que c'est un doux et mol chevet, et sain, que l'ignorance et l'incuriosité, à reposer une teste bien faite ! " (Pléiade, 1205.) Vernière notes : " Mais Diderot utilise la transcription de Pascal : ' L'ignorance et l'incuriosité sont deux doux oreillers pour une tête bien faite ' *(Entretien avec Monsieur de Saci).*" We note in passing that Diderot seems to have been fond of the phrase " tête bien faite". See for example *Corr.*, IV, 154 ; V, 119, 134.

Moreover, for the future Encyclopedist, ignorance and *incuriosité* are not congenial. The very conception of the *Encyclopédie* presupposes " une tête bien pleine " as well as " bien faite ".[1]

In the *Promenade du sceptique* (1747, not published until 1830), Diderot again chooses to be in the camp of the skeptics, the satirists and the critics, rather than that of the dogmatists : " Si vous le prenez sur le ton de Bayle, de Montaigne, de Voltaire, de Barclay, de Woolston, de Swift, de Montesquieu, vous risquerez sans doute de vivre plus longtemps ; mais que cet avantage vous coûtera cher ! " (A-T, I, 185.) Diderot characterizes Montaigne as the standard-bearer of the Pyrrhonists : " Cette troupe n'avait point eu d'étendard, lorsqu'il y a environ deux cents ans un de ses champions en imagina un. C'est une balance en broderie d'or, d'argent, de laine et de soie, avec ces mots pour devise : *Que sais-je?* Ses fantaisies, écrites à bâtons rompus, n'ont pas laissé de faire des prosélytes. Ces soldats sont bons pour les embuscades et les stratagèmes " (A-T, I, 216f.). This light mockery is in contrast to his later defense of Montaigne's manner of composition in the *Encyclopédie* article " Pyrrhonienne ". We may surmise that Diderot was carried away by his allegorical verve, as the tone of the *Promenade* would indicate, or that indeed his understanding of Montaigne had deepened in the interim.

In 1748, in the *Mémoires sur différents sujets de mathématiques*, Diderot forsakes the role of critic and moralist and enters the realm of pure reason. He takes leave of ethics not without regret, however, and not without a note of justification for his previous indiscretions (especially his licentious novel, *Les Bijoux indiscrets*,[2] published earlier

---

[1] In general, the influence of Montaigne appears strong in the *Pensées philosophiques*. There are other reminiscences of Montaigne in the work. The anecdotes dealing with credulity and miracles, paraphrased from Livy and Cicero, recall Montaigne's manner in the essay " Des boyteux ". Indeed, Diderot ends the story of the assumption of Romulus with a phrase borrowed from that essay : " ... cette aventure se *calfeutra*, avec le temps, d'un si grand nombre de pièces, que les esprits forts du siècle suivant devaient en être fort embarrassés " (*Pensée* xlix, p. 41). Cf. *Essais*, III, ix, 1152.

In *Pensée* xxi (p. 21f.), a " professeur célèbre " writes in his notes : " Athées, je vous accorde que le mouvement est essentiel à la matière ; qu'en concluez-vous ? ... que le monde résulte du jet fortuit des atomes ? J'aimerais autant que vous me dissiez que l'*Iliade* d'Homère, ou la *Henriade* de Voltaire est un résultat de jets fortuits de caractères." Montaigne, borrowing from Cicero (*De Natura Deorum*, II, xxxvii), criticizes the Epicureans in like manner : " Si les atomes ont, par sort, formé tant de sortes de figures, ... pourquoy... ne croid on qu'un nombre infini de lettres grecques versées emmy la place, seroyent pour arriver à la contexture de l'Iliade ? " (*Essais*, II, xii, 610.) Montaigne, however, is probably not Diderot's source here.

Towards the close of the *Pensées philosophiques*, Diderot defends himself against the devout : " Il y a longtemps qu'ils ont damné Descartes, Montaigne, Locke et Bayle ; et j'espère qu'ils en damneront bien d'autres " (*Pensée* lviii, p. 46).

[2] In the *Bijoux indiscrets*, there is a reference to the " imagination de Montaigne " (A-T, IV, 224).

that same year) : " Je n'opposerai point à vos reproches l'exemple de Rabelais, de Montaigne, de La Motte-le-Vayer, de Swift, et de quelques autres que je pourrais nommer, qui ont attaqué de la manière la plus cynique, les ridicules de leur temps, et conservé le titre de sages. Je veux que le scandale cesse ; et sans perdre le temps en apologie, j'abandonne la marotte et les grelots, pour ne les reprendre jamais " (A-T, IX, 79). But Diderot was to play the role of jester again and again. His research into mathematics and physics satisfies him only temporarily.

In 1749, Diderot publishes the *Lettre sur les aveugles*, which is concerned with epistemological questions, particularly with the problem of the passage from sensation to perception, and thence to judgment and the formation of ideas. Apart from the lyrical pages devoted to the impassioned cosmological visions of blind Saunderson, the work's originality lies in its dialectical examination of the opinions of Locke and Condillac on the question of whether a man blind from birth and who had recovered his sight would be able to tell visually the difference between a cube and a sphere. The work is a critique of sensationalism, empiricism and innate ideas.

It is pertinent to inquire exactly to what extent Montaigne is an influence in the *Lettre sur les aveugles*. Certainly, the work proves that Diderot, who is at last entering his intellectual maturity, has learned Montaigne's lesson well. He realizes that human complexity resists the seductive but deceptive formulations of the systematic intellect, that indeed all our judgments are relative. From his interrogation of the blind man of Puiseaux and the example of the blind geometrician Saunderson, Diderot perceives the difficulties involved in trying to penetrate the opacities of the world of the blind, whose ideas, for want of a sense organ, diverge from and yet parallel those of normal men. Their ideas of physical objects differ from the norm, but their notions of morality are also different, since all our notions are conditioned by a physical relativity :

Je n'ai jamais douté que l'état de nos organes et de nos sens n'ait beaucoup d'influence sur notre métaphysique et sur notre morale, et que nos idées les plus purement intellectuelles, si je puis parler ainsi, ne tiennent de fort près à la conformation de notre corps. (*Œuvres phil.*, p. 92.)

Que la morale des aveugles est différente de la nôtre ! Que celle d'un sourd différerait encore de celle d'un aveugle, et qu'un être qui aurait un sens de plus que nous trouverait notre morale imparfaite, pour ne rien dire de pis ! (*Ibid.*, p. 93.)

Although it is not likely that there was a direct influence of the " Apologie de Raimond Sebond " on the *Lettre sur les aveugles*, it seems clear that the essay was present enough in Diderot's mind at this period. Montaigne too drew upon his experience with a blind man as evidence for the relativity of knowledge based on sensory perception : " Il est impossible de faire concevoir à un homme naturellement aveugle qu'il

n'y void pas, impossible de luy faire désirer la veue et regretter son defaut " (*Essais*, II, xii, 664). Diderot makes a similar statement about the blind man of Puiseaux :

Quelqu'un de nous s'avisa de demander à notre aveugle s'il serait bien content d'avoir des yeux : « Si la curiosité ne me dominait pas, dit-il, j'aimerais bien autant avoir de longs bras : il me semble que mes mains m'instruiraient mieux de ce qui se passe dans la lune que vos yeux ou vos télescopes ; et puis les yeux cessent plutôt de voir que les mains de toucher. Il vaudrait donc bien autant qu'on perfectionnât en moi l'organe que j'ai, que de m'accorder celui qui me manque.» (*Œuvres phil.*, p. 89.)

Montaigne's personal acquaintance with a blind man has taught him how the blind use words that refer to vision, but without any real awareness of what it is to see :

J'ay veu un gentil-homme de bonne maison, aveugle nay, aumoins aveugle de tel aage qu'il ne sçait que c'est que de veuë : il entend si peu ce qui luy manque, qu'il use et se sert comme nous de paroles propres au voir, et les applique d'une mode toute sienne et particuliere. On luy presentoit un enfant du quel il estoit parrain : l'ayant pris entre ses bras : Mon Dieu, dict-il, le bel enfant ! qu'il le faict beau voir ! qu'il a le visage guay ! Il dira comme l'un d'entre nous : Cette sale a une belle veue : il faict clair, il faict beau soleil. Il y a plus : car, par ce que ce sont nos exercices que la chasse, la paume, la bute, et qu'il l'a ouy dire, il s'y affectionne et s'y embesoigne, et croid y avoir la mesme part que nous y avons ; il s'y pique et s'y plaist, et ne les reçoit pourtant que par les oreilles. (*Essais*, II, xii, 665.)

Similarly, when the blind man of Puiseaux says : " cela est beau ", he is not judging, but merely reporting the judgments of those who see and which are nothing but hearsay to him. " La beauté, pour un aveugle, n'est qu'un mot, quand elle est séparée de l'utilité ; et avec un organe de moins, combien de choses dont l'utilité lui échappe ! " (*Œuvres phil.*, p. 83f.) Montaigne concludes in like manner from the blind man's error : " Que sçait-on si le genre humain faict une sottise pareille, à faute de quelque sens, et que par ce defaut la plus part du visage des choses nous soit caché ? " (*Essais*, II, xii, 665.) These parallels between the two works are not intended to demonstrate any direct influence, as we have already made clear, but merely to show certain affinities between Montaigne's important essay and Diderot's *Lettre*, which Vernière has characterized as an " Essai à la Montaigne ".

Diderot closes the *Lettre* on an apparently profound note of skepticism :

Hélas ! madame, quand on a mis les connaissances humaines dans la balance de Montaigne, on n'est pas éloigné de prendre sa devise. Car, que savons-nous ? ce que c'est que la matière ? nullement ; ce que c'est que l'esprit et la pensée ? encore moins ; ce que c'est que le mouvement, l'espace et la durée ? point du tout ; des vérités géométriques ? interrogez des mathématiciens de bonne foi, et ils vous avoueront que leurs propositions sont toutes identiques. ... Nous ne savons donc presque rien ; cependant combien d'écrits dont les auteurs ont prétendu savoir quelque chose ! (*Œuvres phil.*, p. 146.)

In spite of what Niklaus has termed a "resounding 'que sais-je?'" I believe it would be an error to accept this as Diderot's last word. He is not convinced of the fruitlessness of human inquiry, but rather displays frustration in face of the fact that the scope of his speculations is far beyond the existing state of knowledge and technology. It is for this reason, the urgency of developing modern tools of inquiry, that Diderot will undertake the *Encyclopédie* the following year. There is a playful irony in Diderot's profession of skepticism, which is as Montaignean as the "que sais-je?": "Je ne devine pas pourquoi le monde ne s'ennuie point de lire et de ne rien apprendre, à moins que ce ne soit par la même raison qu'il y a deux heures que j'ai l'honneur de vous entretenir, sans m'ennuyer et sans vous rien dire" *(ibid.).*[1]

Voltaire read the *Lettre sur les aveugles* as soon as it appeared, and glowingly praises the work in a letter to its bold young author. He takes issue, however, with the atheism expressed by Saunderson, and affirms his own deism.[2] In his reply, Diderot insists that "le sentiment de Saunderson n'est pas plus mon sentiment que le vôtre", but he qualifies this statement: "mais ce pourrait bien être parce que je *vois.*"[3] His profession of faith ("Je crois en Dieu") is also modified: "quoique je vive très-bien avec les athées" *(ibid.,* p. 78). He concludes his letter to Voltaire by a flippant disposal of the question:

Il est donc très important de ne pas prendre de la ciguë pour du persil, mais nullement de croire ou de ne pas croire en Dieu : « Le monde, dirait Montaigne, est un esteuf qu'il a abandonné à peloter aux philosophes » ; et j'en dis presque autant de Dieu même. *(Ibid.)*

This is not a direct quotation from the *Essais*, as Diderot admits.[4] It appears, however, to be a combination of two different passages:

... un tas de gens, interpretes et contrerolleurs ordinaires des desseins de Dieu, faisans estat de trouver les causes de chasque accident, & de voir dans les secrets de la Volonté Divine, les motifs incomprehensibles de ses œuvres. ... *Ils ne laissent de suivre pourtant leur esteuf,* et, de mesme crayon peindre le blanc et le noir. (*Essais*, Coste, I, xxxi, 218f. ; Pléiade, II, xxxii, 254.)

Ceux qui l'ont prinse à gauche, ceux qui l'ont prinse à droite, ceux qui en disent le noir, ceux qui en disent le blanc. ... *Voyez l'horrible impu-*

---

[1] Diderot justifies his air of *désinvolture* in the *Lettre* in a way reminiscent of Montaigne : "Et toujours des écarts, me direz-vous. Oui, madame, c'est la condition de notre traité" (p. 140). There is an ironic touch in his remark apropos of Condillac : "Je crains bien que vous ne disiez, en comparant ma critique avec sa réflexion, que vous aimez mieux encore une erreur de Montaigne qu'une vérité de Charron" *(ibid.).*

[2] Voltaire à Diderot, 9 juin 1749 (cited in *Corr.*, I, 74).

[3] A Voltaire, 11 juin 1749 *(ibid.,* I, 75f.).

[4] "Dirait Montaigne." Roth corrects A-T's erroneous "disait Montaigne."

dence dequoy nous pelotons les raisons divines. (*Essais*, Coste, II, xii, 129 ; Pléiade, 486f.) [1]

It is fascinating to observe how these two passages from the *Essais*, which lay dormant in Diderot's mind, coalesce to form something new, so vastly more daring, and yet so Montaignean. Diderot has gone much further than simply combine " esteuf " and " peloter " into one coherent image. One might even say that he has betrayed Montaigne by means of a pseudo-quotation that inverts Montaigne's position, and yet retains the ring of the essayist's style. Animating both passages from the *Essais* is Montaigne's impatience with human presumption to fathom the motives of Divinity. The eighteenth-century *philosophe*, however, is not aware of any such " horrible impudence " ; he can allow himself to speculate freely (keeping in mind the little word *presque*) not only on the mysteries of the universe, but on the very existence of God.

One cannot help thinking, at the mention of hemlock, of Socrates in the closing pages of the *Phaedo*. What is important, of course, is that Socrates took the hemlock in the name of the inviolability of his conscience and not for the sake of his personal beliefs in themselves. Diderot was to find himself in the prison of Vincennes but six weeks after his letter to Voltaire. Decidedly, Diderot preferred parsley to hemlock ; henceforth, except perhaps for some bold pages of the *Encyclopédie* censored by his publisher Lebreton, he will consign his conscience to his desk drawer and to posterity.

The launching of the *Encyclopédie* with the appearance of the Prospectus and preparation of the first volume occupies Diderot in 1750. In the article " Art ", Diderot criticizes Montaigne's conservative attitude towards firearms :

Montaigne, cet homme d'ailleurs si philosophe, ne rougirait-il pas s'il revenait parmi nous d'avoir écrit *que les armes à feu sont de si peu d'effet, sauf l'étonnement des oreilles, à quoi chacun est désormais apprivoisé, qu'il espère qu'on en quittera l'usage.* N'aurait-il pas montré plus de sagesse à encourager les arquebusiers de son temps à substituer à la mèche et au rouet quelque machine qui répondît à l'activité de la poudre, et plus de sagacité à prédire que cette machine s'inventerait un jour? (A-T, XIII, 370f.) [2]

It is the spirit of Bacon which infuses the *Encyclopédie* :

Mettez Bacon à la place de Montaigne, et vous verrez ce premier considérer en philosophe la nature de l'agent, et prophétiser, s'il m'est permis de

---

[1] Italics mine in both passages. Cf. another of Diderot's echoes of Montaigne in the *Salon de 1767* : " [nous sommes] des pelotons de contradictions " (A-T, XI, 58).

[2] Cf. *Essais*, Coste, I, xlviii, 321 : " ... sauf l'estonnement des oreilles, à quoy desormais chacun est apprivoisé, je croy que c'est un' arme de fort peu d'effet, & espere que nous en quitterons un jour l'usage." (Pléiade, 327.)

34

le dire, les grenades, les mines, les canons, les bombes, et tout l'appareil de la pyrotechnie militaire. Mais Montaigne n'est pas le seul philosophe qui ait porté, sur la possibilité ou l'impossibilité des machines, un jugement précipité. Descartes, ce génie extraordinaire né pour égarer et pour conduire, et d'autres qui valaient bien l'auteur des *Essais*, n'ont-ils pas prononcé que le miroir d'Archimède était une fable? *(Ibid.)*

Diderot believes firmly in the progress of technology, to which fact the *Encyclopédie* and its magnificent plates bear witness. It is worth noting that even here when the essayist is not his model, Diderot nevertheless feels the need to reckon with Montaigne, successively complimenting, reproaching, and finally excusing him.

In 1751, the same year that Volume I of the *Encyclopédie* appeared, Diderot refers to Montaigne's manner of composition in the *Lettre sur les sourds et muets*, justifying a brief digression as " une réflexion qui ne serait guère plus déplacée ici que la harangue de l'empereur du Mexique dans le chapitre des coches de Montaigne " (A-T, I, 379). Far from criticizing Montaigne,[1] Diderot cites him here as a precedent for his own lack of adherence to the standard rules of composition. In order to prove that his essay is not as rambling as it seems, he recapitulates in outline form at the close of the *Lettre* all the points he has discussed in the course of the work, in effect demonstrating that the associative method of composition is as orderly as a more consciously methodical procedure.

Like Montaigne, Diderot has only contempt for nobility and purity of linguistic expression when it is at the expense of energy and imagination. He rebels against the classicist's zeal to " refine " and thus impoverish the French language and turns to Montaigne as an example of a writer who, rather, enriched the language, but whose picturesque expressions have since been banished by the purists : " Quelle perte pour ceux d'entre nos écrivains qui ont l'imagination forte, que celle de tant de mots que nous revoyons avec plaisir dans Amyot et dans Montaigne " (A-T, I, 388).[2]

In the *Encyclopédie* article " Pyrrhonienne ", it is significant that Diderot considers Montaigne's Pyrrhonism only as an afterthought, and dwells primarily on the literary qualities of the *Essais* :

Mais parmi les sectateurs du Pyrrhonisme nous avons oublié Michel de Montaigne, l'auteur de ces *Essais* qui seront lus tant qu'il y aura des hommes qui aimeront la vérité, la force, la simplicité. L'ouvrage de Montaigne est la pierre de touche d'un bon esprit. Prononcez de celui à qui cette lecture déplaît, qu'il a quelque vice de cœur ou d'entendement ; il n'y a presque

---

[1] DREANO (p. 300) states that Diderot was not equally pleased by "tous les hors-d'œuvre des *Essais*. ... Le fameux chapitre : *Des Coches*, si souvent critiqué au XVIIIᵉ siècle, l'a d'abord déconcerté lui aussi. Certaine harangue d'un empereur du Mexique y est ' un modèle de réflexion déplacée ' ".

[2] Diderot makes similar statements regarding Montaigne in the *Essai sur les règnes de Claude et de Néron* (A-T, III, 240, 384).

aucune question que cet auteur n'ait agitée pour et contre, et toujours avec le même air de persuasion. (A-T, XVI, 485.)

Diderot does not find the disorder of the *Essais* disturbing, but feels rather that they accurately represent the workings of the human mind : " Les contradictions de son ouvrage sont l'image fidèle des contradictions de l'entendement humain. Il suit sans art l'enchaînement de ses idées, il lui importe fort peu d'où il parte, comment il parte, comment il aille, ni où il aboutisse. La chose qu'il dit, c'est celle qui l'affecte dans le moment " *(ibid.)*. Nevertheless, there is always a connection between the most seemingly disparate thoughts :

> Quoique rien ne soit si varié que la suite des objets qui se présentent à notre philosophe, et qu'ils semblent amenés par le hasard, cependant ils se touchent tous d'une ou d'autre manière ; et quoiqu'il y ait bien loin de la matière des coches publics à la harangue que les Mexicains firent aux Européens, quand ils mirent le pied pour la première fois dans le Nouveau-Monde, cependant on arrive de Bordeaux à Cusco sans interruption ; mais, à la vérité, par de bien longs détours. Chemin faisant, il se montre sous toutes sortes de faces ; tantôt bon, tantôt dépravé, tantôt compatissant, tantôt vain, tantôt incrédule, tantôt superstitieux. Après avoir écrit avec force contre la vérité des miracles, il fera l'apologie des augures ; mais, quelque chose qu'il dise, il intéresse et il instruit. (*Ibid.*, p. 486.) [1]

We note that Montaigne's sincerity, intellectual honesty, and artless naïveté appeal to Diderot ; and, perhaps more than anything else, he appreciates Montaigne's ever-changing many-sidedness and the brilliance of his associative mind. Apart from justifying the essayist's seeming lack of logical order, Diderot has concerned himself but little with Montaigne as a skeptic philosopher, and makes no mention of the " que sais-je ? " or the " Apologie de Raimond Sebond ". The essayist gives way to Bayle as the standard-bearer of skepticism : " Mais le scepticisme n'eut, ni chez les Anciens, ni chez les modernes, aucun athlète plus redoutable que Bayle " *(ibid.)*. Diderot drew very heavily on Bayle's dictionary for countless *Encyclopédie* articles ; it is clear that he recognized in Bayle a proponent of modern critical techniques who made Montaigne appear quaint indeed. However, Diderot considers skepticism as practiced by Bayle to be a destructive principle, Bayle's aim being to humiliate man and make reason subservient to faith.[2]

---

[1] Diderot seems to have been fascinated by the structure of " Des coches ". In addition to the passage in the *Lettre sur les sourds et muets* and the above quotation, he recounts the sequence of topics during a spirited conversation at the Baron d'Holbach's as follows : " Comme rien ne ressemble mieux à un rêve que la conversation de deux ou trois hommes bien éveillés, qu'on arrive tous les jours à Cusco par le coche de la province de Champagne, nous tombâmes sur la question des germes préexistants " (*Corr.*, IX, 94).

[2] Cf. Diderot's remarks on Bayle and his use of reason in the article " Manichéisme " (A-T, XVI, 69) : " La raison, selon lui, est un principe de

In dealing with other *Encyclopédie* articles which have been attributed to Diderot by his various editors (Naigeon, Belin, Brière, Assézat-Tourneux), we shall adopt the prudence of Jacques Proust.[1] Let us first consider those articles which, in addition to " Pyrrhonienne ", have been positively identified as Diderot's.

Discussing the character of Diogenes in the article " Cyniques ", Diderot praises Montaigne's style : " C'était, dit Montaigne, dans son style énergique et original qui plaît aux personnes du meilleur goût lors même qu'il paraît bas et trivial, une espèce de ladrerie spirituelle, qui a un air de santé que la philosophie ne méprise pas ", and he goes on to paraphrase a passage from " De Democritus et Heraclitus " (A-T, XIV, 263).[2] In the article " Encyclopédie ", Diderot imitates Montaigne's " low and trivial " style : " Lorsque Molière plaisantait les grammairiens, il abandonnait le caractère de philosophe, et il ne savait pas, comme l'aurait dit Montaigne, qu'il donnait des soufflets aux auteurs qu'il respectait le plus, sur la joue du Bourgeois Gentilhomme " (A-T, XIV, 440).[3] Apropos of Aristotle, Montaigne is briefly mentioned in the article " Grecs " : " Montaigne a dit de celui-ci, qu'il n'y a point de pierres qu'il n'ait remuées " (A-T, XV, 66).

The brief article " Imposture " must be credited almost entirely to Montaigne, for, following a short definition of the term, Diderot passes imperceptibly into a fairly close paraphrase of the opening paragraphs of Montaigne's essay " Qu'il faut sobrement se mesler de juger des ordonnances divines ", of which he seems to have been especially fond :

Mais le vrai champ et sujet de l'imposture sont les choses inconnues. L'étrangeté des choses leur donne crédit. Moins elles sont sujettes à nos discours ordinaires, moins on a le moyen de les combattre. Aussi Platon dit-il qu'il est bien plus aisé de satisfaire, parlant de la nature des dieux que de la nature des hommes, parce que l'ignorance des auditeurs prête une belle et large carrière. D'où il arrive que rien n'est si fermement cru que ce qu'on sait le moins et qu'il n'y a gens si assurés que ceux qui nous content des fables : comme alchymistes, pronostiqueurs, indicateurs, chiromanciens, médecins, *id genus omne*, auxquels, je joindrais volontiers, si j'osais, dit Montaigne, un tas d'interprètes et contrôleurs des desseins de Dieu, faisant

destruction, et non pas d'édification : elle n'est propre qu'à former des doutes, à éterniser les disputes et à faire connaître à l'homme ses ténèbres, son impuissance et la nécessité d'une révélation, et cette révélation est celle de l'Ecriture." Also (*ibid.*, p. 82) : " Son grand but, du moins à ce qui paraît, était d'humilier la raison, de lui faire sentir son impuissance, de la captiver sous le joug de la foi."

[1] *Diderot et l'Encyclopédie* (Paris, 1962), p. 507 : " Jusqu'à preuve du contraire, les seuls articles que nous sommes en droit d'attribuer à Diderot sont ceux que les éditeurs de l'*Encyclopédie* ont signalés par un astérisque, et les articles anonymes qui se trouvent contenus dans les divers choix de textes de Diderot présentés par Naigeon." This renders doubtful the authenticity of a great number of articles included in A-T.

[2] Cf. *Essais*, Coste, I, l, 335f. ; Pléiade, 341.

[3] Cf. *Essais*, Coste II, x, 90 : " Je veux qu'ils donnent une nazarde à Plutarque sur mon nez." (Pléiade, 449.)

état de trouver les causes de chaque accident, et de voir dans les secrets de la volonté divine les motifs incompréhensibles de ses œuvres ; et quoique la variété et discordance continuelle des événements les rejette de coin en coin, et d'orient en occident, ils ne laissent pourtant de suivre leur esteuf, et de même crayon peindre le blanc et le noir. (A-T, XV, 189.) [1]

In the absence of quotation marks, and in the disguise of modern spelling, the reader remains totally unaware that the admissive " dit Montaigne " applies to the entire passage. Diderot closes the article with a phrase copied from the same essay : " Les *imposteurs* qui entraînent les hommes par des merveilles, en sont rarement examinés de près ; et il leur est toujours facile de prendre d'un sac deux moutures." [2]

There remain a number of references to Montaigne in minor articles that cannot be attributed with certainty to Diderot. As the possibility nonetheless exists that he may have written them, we shall make brief mention of them here.

In the article " Caraïbes, ou Cannibales ", there appears the following remark : " Ils ont plusieurs femmes qui ne sont point jalouses les unes des autres, ce que Montaigne regard comme un miracle dans son chapitre sur ce peuple " (A-T, XIV, 28). The author's memory has been treacherous here, however, for Montaigne wrote to the contrary : "Les nostres crieront au miracle : Ce ne l'est pas ; C'est une vertu proprement matrimoniale, mais du plus haut estage " (*Essais*, Coste, I, xxx, 216 ; Pléiade, I, xxxi, 252).

Montaigne is quoted in " Ondoyant ",[3] and his judgment of Jean Bodin is given in " Politique " (A-T, XVI, 342). We find a comment on his style in " Vigueur " : " Il y a peu d'auteurs qui aient plus de *vigueur* dans le style que Montaigne " (Brière, XX, 350). In " Pire ", there is a reminiscence of the passage from the " Apologie de Raimond Sebond " which Diderot had quoted in a footnote to the *Essai sur le mérite et la vertu* : " Il y a des hommes qui croient au fond de leur cœur, et qui font tout pour paraître incrédules ; ils sont *pires* qu'ils ne paraissent ; d'autres au contraire sont incrédules au fond de leur cœur, et ils affectent la croyance commune ; ils tâchent de paraître meilleurs qu'ils ne sont " (A-T, XVI, 294).[4] The short article " Nonchalance " indicates a somewhat ambiguous reaction to the *Essais* : " Il s'échappe des ouvrages de Montaigne une *nonchalance* que le lecteur gagne sans s'en apercevoir, et qui le tranquillise sur beaucoup de choses importantes ou terribles au premier coup d'œil " (A-T, XVI, 148f.). Perhaps Diderot found in Montaigne an equilibrating antidote to his own restless spirit.

---

[1] *Essais*, Coste, I, xxxi, 218f. ; Pléiade, I, xxxii, 254. Cf. above, p. 33.

[2] Cf. *Essais*, Coste, *ibid.*, p. 219 : " ... s'ils n'ont un peuple du tout à leur mercy, ils lui font assez aisément sentir que c'est prendre d'un sac deux moultures, & de mesme bouche souffler le chaud & le froid." (Pléiade, *ibid.*, p. 255.)

[3] *Œuvres*, ed. Brière (Paris, 1821-23), XVIII, 22f.

[4] See above, p. 27. Cf. *Essais*, II, xii, 490 : " Hommes bien miserables et escervellez, qui taschent d'estre pires qu'ils ne peuvent ! "

If by Diderot, the *Encyclopédie* article " Recueil " (included in the Brière edition of his works, but not in that of Assezat-Tourneux), would throw light on his work habits and the whole question of his rewrites of Montaigne. It would also explain, in some measure, why attempts to glean marginal comments from the books presumed to have belonged to his library have not always met with success.[1] In the absence of Diderot's personal copy of the *Essais*, and of a *recueil* like the one he proposes as a model in this article, it is fortunate at least that we have the article itself, which gives as a sample entry a passage drawn from Montaigne. The article defines a *recueil* as

un registre ou une collection raisonnée de toutes les choses dignes de remarque, qu'un homme a retenues dans ses lettres ou dans ses études, tellement disposées que, parmi un grand nombre de titres et de sujets de toute espèce, on puisse trouver facilement celui qu'on cherche, et y avoir recours dans l'occasion. ... Les recueils... sont... des espèces de magasins où l'on dépose les meilleurs et les plus beaux endroits des auteurs, afin de les avoir toujours prêts pour s'en servir. (Brière, XIX, 170f.)

The suggested method of ordering the passages in the *recueil* and of setting up a topical index is that used by Locke, but Diderot gives two examples of his own " méthode d'écrire des chapitres " : the first is from the *Essais*, the second from the *Caractères* of La Bruyère. There is a significant difference, however, between the two examples. The Montaigne passage, as Brière notes, is " entièrement défiguré ",[2] while the La Bruyère quotation is an exact rendering of the original.

One might speculate about the possible reasons for this. Did Diderot transcribe the passage from the *Essais* from memory, or did he willfully paraphrase from the original text ? The exactitude of the La Bruyère passage, a word-for-word copy of the original, eliminates the possibility of simple negligence. The most logical explanation—whether Diderot had the *Essais* before him on his desk or not makes little difference—is that Diderot felt the need to paraphrase Montaigne rather than quote

---

[1] See WILSON, " Leningrad, 1957...", p. 353. Wilson comments : " Possibly Diderot read so hastily and impressionistically that he had no impulse... to make marginal comments." Cf., however, Georges May, editor of Diderot's marginal comments on Hemsterhuis' *Lettre sur l'homme et ses rapports*. May states that Diderot is a born *glossateur*, and underlines the importance for Diderot of this means of creation, that of using another's book as a springboard for his own thought. It is again evidence of Diderot's propensity for dialogue. (HEMSTERHUIS, *Lettre sur l'homme et ses rapports, avec le commentaire inédit de Diderot*, ed. Georges May [New Haven, 1964], pp. 12f.)

[2] Cf. *Essais*, Coste, III, viii, 162f. ; Pléiade, 1036f. The " disfigured " passage is long and does not exhibit significant differences from the original, with the exception of the following phrase : " Quels vices n'éveillent pas les disputes, dit Montaigne, *étant presque* toujours commandées par la colère ? " The italicized words have been added to the original. Diderot and his age thrived on conflict ; so this comment of Montaigne's is omitted from his paraphrase : " Ainsi Platon, en sa republique, prohibe cet exercice aux esprits ineptes et mal nays."

him exactly. It is not simply a question of eliminating certain archaisms in spelling and syntax, but of somehow making the passage his own, which is, after all, the proper method of note-taking. The " disfigurements " in the passage from " De l'art de conférer " quoted in the article " Recueil " are minor changes which tend to simplify, and to clarify, while preserving Montaigne's " spirit ". This was a fashion of the age, which produced a quantity of collections designed to " improve " on the style and composition of the *Essais* while distilling their " essence ". Diderot shares to some extent this ambivalent attitude towards Montaigne in taking liberties with his *moyen français*, though he has immeasurable respect for his use of language. In any case, we have reason to suspect that he continually referred to his edition of the *Essais* and that he kept in a *recueil* many such paraphrased passages " afin de les avoir toujours prêts pour s'en servir ".

In 1758, in his *Réflexions sur le livre de l'Esprit*, Diderot compares Helvétius with Montaigne, both of whom are fond of paradox :

> Il n'y a rien qui veuille être prouvé avec moins d'affectation, plus dérobé, moins annoncé qu'un paradoxe. Un auteur paradoxal ne doit jamais dire son mot, mais toujours ses preuves : il doit entrer furtivement dans l'âme de son lecteur et non de vive force. C'est le grand art de Montaigne, qui ne veut jamais prouver, et qui va toujours prouvant, et me ballottant du blanc au noir, et du noir au blanc. (A-T, II, 272f.)

This passage is interesting for the light it casts on Diderot's art. We recall that Diderot had termed the style of Montaigne " artless " and naïve. Now it would seem that this aspect of the *Essais* is, on the contrary, the result of Montaigne's consummate art as an " auteur paradoxal ". Here is an example of the eighteenth century's choice of Montaigne as a tactical ancestor in its search for the " furtive " methods of expression which the political climate of the age made necessary. In the *Encyclopédie*, Diderot finds it essential to be an " auteur paradoxal ", to present the proofs and leave the conclusions implicit so as to " furtively enter the reader's mind ". But paradox is, for Diderot, not only a means of taking the censor unawares. It is to be an essential element of his mature dialogues and works of imaginative fiction ; that is, it becomes an artistic principle. Today we would be more likely to speak of " irony " and " ambiguity " as artistic principles rather than use the term paradox, which belongs to the vocabulary of logic. I find it not unlikely that for Diderot the word " paradox " possessed this power of extension into the realms of art. Perhaps it will not prove unfruitful in this regard to look for Montaigne's influence.

According to Herbert Dieckmann, Montaigne's *Essais* are one of Diderot's important sources for his essay *Sur Térence*,[1] which deals with questions of aesthetics. Diderot differentiates between " taste ", a

---

[1] H. DIECKMANN, " Diderot : *Sur Térence*, le texte du manuscrit autographe ", *Studia Philologica et litteraria in honorem L. Spitzer* (Berne, 1958). Dieckmann dates the work 1765, rejecting A-T's date of 1762.

civilized virtue which is the refined, elegant fruit of centuries of artistic development; and " verve ", a passionate demon that may take possession of those whom nature has marked as born artists. Speaking of Terence's relative lack of " verve ", Diderot gives as an example of this quality

> un Cannibale amoureux qui s'adresse à la couleuvre et qui lui dit : « Couleuvre, arrête-toi, couleuvre ! afin que ma sœur tire sur le patron de ton corps et de ta peau, la façon et l'ouvrage d'un riche cordon que je puisse donner à ma mie ; ainsi soient en tout temps, ta forme et ta beauté préférées à tous les autres serpents. » [1]

This quotation of the love song from the essay " Des cannibales " is not exact. Let us compare the original :

> Couleuvre, arreste toy, arreste toy, couleuvre, afin que ma sœur tire sur le patron de ta peinture, la façon et l'ouvrage d'un riche cordon, que je puisse donner à m'amie ? [sic] ainsi soit en tout temps ta beauté & ta disposition preferée à tous les autres serpens. (*Essais*, Coste, I, xxx, 217 ; Pléiade, I, xxxi, 252.)

Diderot does not repeat " arrête-toi " ; he substitutes " corps " and " peau " for " peinture ", and " forme " for " disposition ". These changes, which at first view appear quite negligible, are nevertheless significant. They show that Diderot feels so sure of his Montaigne that he quotes him from memory without bothering to seek verification, indicating a close familiarity with his subject. Moreover, the inexactitudes which result suggest certain differences between Diderot and the essayist. In this passage, for example, Diderot's alterations serve to freeze the serpent's movement. In Montaigne's text, the repeated " arrête-toi " expresses forcefully the gyrations of the snake, which in its movement becomes a pattern of colors lacking definite shape. In Diderot's mind the snake has, in a sense, arrested its movement through the substitutions mentioned above.[2] The snake—which in Montaigne's text was in movement, formless, and, as it were, potential —has, in Diderot's version, acquired a concreteness, a more palpable reality, although it has become more static. We thus observe Diderot's different sensitivity to plastic values. Apart from these textual differences in Diderot's quotation, what are the implications for Diderot's aesthetics ? Though he agrees with Montaigne on the essentially natural

---

[1] *Œuvres esthétiques*, ed. Paul Vernière (Paris, 1959), p. 62.

[2] See " Lexique de la langue des *Essais* " (Vol. V of the so-called " Edition Municipale " of the *Essais*), prepared by Pierre Villey and Grace Norton. Four general meanings are given for *disposition:* (1) *pouvoir de disposer;* (2) *direction;* (2) *arrangement;* (3) *bonne ordonnance; manière d'être;* (4) *qualité de ce qui est dispos; agilité.* Although Villey considers *manière d'être* the proper meaning in this context, it is evident that for Montaigne the word is charged with latent movement.

(Montaigne would have said *naïf*, in the sense of " unlearned ") quality of the poetic gift, he insists on the higher value of tempering it with what we can only term a classical conception of taste.

Elsewhere in *Sur Térence*, Diderot takes issue with Montaigne on the question of literary immortality and answers him in the essayist's own terms :

> L'auteur des *Essais* a beau dire que « si la perfection du bien parler pouvoit apporter quelque gloire sortable à un grand personnage, certainement Scipion et Laelius n'eussent pas résigné l'honneur de leurs comédies, et toutes les mignardises et délices du langage latin, à un serf africain », je lui répondrai sur son ton, que le talent de s'immortaliser par les lettres n'est pas une qualité mésavenante à quelque rang que ce soit. (*Œuvres esthétiques*, p. 60.) [1]

For Diderot, the protestations of a *grand seigneur* are insincere, only a pose to be expected of one whose nobility had been rather newly acquired. In his epistolary debate with the sculptor Falconet concerning posterity, Diderot repeatedly refers to Montaigne's disdain for glory, which he finds suspect : " Et ce Michel qui pèse si bien dans sa balance toutes les fumées qui nous enivrent, si jaloux de nous apprendre ce que ses ancêtres ont été, croit-on qu'il se fût oublié, abandonné lui-même ? " [2] One almost gets the impression that the debate is between Diderot and Montaigne, with Falconet as intermediary.[3] In an earlier letter, Diderot is baffled by a passage from the essay " De la gloire ", which he paraphrases as follows :

> Montaigne, qui, oubliant une infinité de faits héroïques anciens et la protestation expresse de ceux qu'ils honorent aujourd'hui, prétend que la vertu est trop noble pour rechercher d'autre loyer que de sa propre valeur, toujours grand écrivain, mais souvent mauvais raisonneur, permet pourtant au rhéteur, au grammairien, au peintre, au statuaire, à l'artiste, de travailler pour se faire un nom. (*Corr.*, VI, 257.) [4]

---

[1] The passage within quotation marks is exact. For the rest, cf. *Essais*, Coste, I, xxxix, 254 : " C'est une espece de mocquerie et d'injure, de vouloir faire valoir un homme, par des qualitez mes-advenantes à son rang, quoy qu'elles soient autrement louables." (Pléiade, I, xl, 287.)

[2] A Falconet, 5 août 1766 (*Corr.*, VI, 257).

[3] Diderot is fond of imitating Montaigne in these letters : " Que diable voulez-vous qu'on fasse d'un homme qui passe, comme il lui plaît, du blanc au noir et du noir au blanc ? " (*Corr.*, VI, 253) ; " Vous calfeutrez de votre mieux un vaisseau criblé qui fait eau de toute part " (*ibid.*, p. 256) ; " C'est vous, mon ami, qui *sophistiquez* la nature, si vous croyez que, quand l'homme peut légitimement tirer deux moutures d'un sac, il n'y manque jamais " (*ibid.*, p. 296).

[4] Cf. *Essais*, Coste, II, xvi, 360 : " Il seroit à l'advanture excusable à un peintre ou autre artisan, ou encores à un Rhetoricien ou Grammairien, de se travailler pour acquerir nom par ses ouvrages ; mais les actions de la Vertu, elles sont trop nobles d'elles mesmes, pour rechercher autre loyer, que de leur propre valeur : et notamment pour la chercher en la vanité des jugemens humains." (Pléiade, 710.)

Diderot tends to identify artistic and intellectual creativity with acts of moral virtue, to equate the beautiful with the good. It is obviously Montaigne's position that these activities are not reliable enough as bases upon which to stake one's immortality since they depend upon the capriciousness of human vanity. Diderot pursues his paraphrase as follows :

Puis, soupçonnant que le sentiment de l'immortalité et le respect de la postérité pourraient bien servir à contenir les hommes en leur devoir et à les éveiller à la vertu, il ajoute : « *S'ils sont touchés de voir le monde bénir la mémoire de Trajan et abominer celle de Néron, s'ils sont émus d'entendre le nom de ce grand pendard, autrefois si effroyable et si redoubté, maintenant outragé et maudit librement par le premier écolier qui l'entreprend; qu'on acroisse hardiment cette opinion, et qu'on la nourrisse entre nous le plus qu'on le pourra.* » *(Ibid.)*[1]

This passage, which is a largely accurate rendition of Montaigne, would tend to support Diderot's claim that a respect for posterity is justifiable on moral grounds. However, having summoned Montaigne to his defense, Diderot immediately jumps to the offensive : " Mais, seigneur Michel, lui répondrai-je, si cette opinion est fausse, il ne faut ni la nourrir ni l'accroître, car c'est un mensonge, et le mensonge n'est jamais bon à rien " *(ibid.)*. Within his dialogue with Falconet, Diderot engages in a dialogue with Montaigne, using the *Essais* as a springboard for his own train of thought. Consistently unwilling to accommodate himself to the notion of the " useful lie ",[2] Diderot takes offense at Montaigne's pragmatism. Diderot's " honest conscience ", to use the phrase Hegel coined to describe *Moi* in the *Neveu de Rameau*, is outraged at the duplicity of aristocratic values. (Note that Montaigne refers to " les princes " while Diderot, in his paraphrase, uses " ils " to refer to " les hommes ".) The ironic " seigneur Michel " brings into relief the fact that the essayist and the Encyclopedist belong to different worlds : Montaigne, recently-arrived nobleman, anxious to affect the airs befitting his station ; Diderot, cutler's son turned *philosophe*.

But in a larger sense, it is not only a question of a different social milieu, but of a change in the ideas that dominate an age. The ideal of individualism, which characterized the Renaissance, is no longer the leading idea of eighteenth-century France. This is true despite the fact that the French Renaissance was more " moral ", more concerned with social values, and less extreme in its philosophy of individualism than its Italian forebear. In Montaigne, individualism means not the

---

[1] Cf. *Essais*, Coste, *ibid.* : " Si toutesfois cette fauce opinion sert su public à contenir les hommes en leur devoir : si le peuple en est esveillé à la vertu : si les Princes sont touchez, de voir le monde benir la memoire de Trajan, & abominer celle de Neron : si cela les esmeut, de voir le nom de ce grand pendart, autresfois si effroyable et si redoubté, maudit et outragé si librement par le premier escolier qui l'entreprend : qu'elle accroisse hardiment, & qu'on la nourrisse entre nous le plus qu'on pourra."

[2] See below, p. 46.

43

glorification of the powerful personality, nor a " Machiavellian " amoralism, but rather the cultivation of an independent inner life separate and secure from the social life. Diderot is in tune with the spirit of his time, in its evolving sense of social significance ; and, in particular, as a *philosophe*, he is committed to social criticism and reform.

In his critical edition of the *Neveu de Rameau*, Jean Fabre several times compares statements of the Nephew with passages from the *Essais*. Fabre believes that the influence of Montaigne is important, although there is but one passage in which an expression of his is used : " Perchez-vous sur l'épicycle de Mercure, et de là distribuez, si cela vous convient, et à l'imitation de Réaumur, lui la classe des mouches en couturières, arpenteuses, faucheuses, vous, l'espèce des hommes, en hommes menui-siers, charpentiers, coureurs, danseurs, chanteurs, c'est votre affaire. Je ne m'en mêle pas. Je suis dans ce monde et j'y reste." [1] Fabre remarks in his notes to this passage that " la sagesse [de Montaigne] trouve un répondant inattendu en la personne de Rameau ' le fou ' " ; that the essays " De la presumption " (II, xvii), as well as " Du pedantisme " (I, xxv) and " De l'institution des enfants " (I, xxvi), " ont été lus de très près par Rameau-Diderot " ; and concludes that " de cette attitude qui est en gros celle de Montaigne, dont la philosophie se moque de la philosophie, Rameau, avocat de la misère, devant quoi les beaux sys-tèmes paraissent autant de lâchetés ou d'évasions, dégage une revendi-cation qu'on pourrait croire révolutionnaire, si la révolte ne se dissolvait aussitôt en comédie ".[2] Working through irony and paradox, Diderot is again using Montaigne for a number of purposes. He is attacking Réaumur, the enemy of his own friend Buffon, and one who is hostile to the *Encyclopédie*. Through Réaumur, he attacks as well a certain tendency of his time to reduce the complexity of human reality to classifications and systems. But if Rameau is a disciple of Montaigne, he is a negative one. Rameau is fond of the moralists such as Theophrastus, La Bruyère and Molière, " surtout ceux qui ont mis la morale en action ", for he learns systematically from them the behavior to avoid in order to play the role of hypocrite well. What Rameau sees in Montaigne easily lends itself to what is amoral and revolutionary in Diderot's ideas. What he attempts to do is to put his interpretation of Montaigne's ethics into action. The paradox is that Rameau is using the moralists to justify his amorality, and he would have been successful had Diderot's irony not been so clearly against him. The irony is that by dint of a self-analysis more lucid and pitiless perhaps than that of Montaigne himself, Rameau has arrived at self-knowledge: he is a person of talent, not genius, who, now only too aware of what he is, tries to hide behind appearances, masks and pantomime.[3] The pity of Rameau is that the

---

[1] *Le Neveu de Rameau*, ed. Jean Fabre (Genève-Lille, 1950), p. 103.

[2] *Ibid.*, p. 236.

[3] See Otis FELLOWS, " The Theme of Genius in Diderot's *Neveu de Rameau* ", *Diderot Studies II*, ed. Otis Fellows and Norman Torrey (Syra-cuse, 1952), pp. 168-199.

appearances have become reality. There is no longer an authentic Rameau beneath the successive pantomimes.

Fabre selects another passage to comment upon, which he believes is illuminated by comparison with Montaigne. Rameau exposes his theory of " idiotismes " in order to justify the deceptions he makes use of in his profession of tutor :

Moi. — Et pourquoi employer toutes ces petites viles ruses-là ?
Lui. — Viles ! et pourquoi, s'il vous plaît ? Elles sont d'usage dans mon état. Je ne m'avilis point en faisant comme tout le monde. Ce n'est pas moi qui les ai inventées, et je serais bizarre et maladroit de ne pas m'y conformer. Vraiment, je sais bien que si vous allez appliquer à cela certains principes généraux de je ne sais quelle morale qu'ils ont tous à la bouche et qu'aucun d'eux ne pratique, il se trouvera que ce qui est blanc sera noir et que ce qui est noir sera blanc. Mais, monsieur le philosophe, il y a une conscience générale, comme il y a une grammaire générale, et puis des exceptions dans chaque langue que vous appelez, je crois, vous autres savants, des idiotismes. ... Hé bien, chaque état a ses exceptions à la conscience générale auxquelles je donnerais volontiers le nom d'idiotismes de métier. (*Neveu*, pp. 35f.) [1]

A close parallel might be made between this passage and the following one from the essay " De mesnager sa volonté " : " Un honneste homme n'est pas comptable du vice ou sottise de son mestier, et ne doibt pourtant en refuser l'exercice ; c'est l'usage de son pays, et il y a du proffict. Il faut vivre du monde et s'en prevaloir tel qu'on le trouve " (*Essais*, III, x, 1134). Although Rameau appears to have carefully followed Montaigne's precept, he has nevertheless failed to achieve that perfect separation of self and social function which Montaigne achieved in his own life. On the contrary, Rameau believes in the identification of what a man does with what he is : " Tant vaut l'homme, tant vaut le métier ; et réciproquement, à la fin, tant vaut le métier, tant vaut l'homme. On fait donc valoir le métier tant qu'on peut " *(Neveu*, p. 36). For Rameau, man in a corrupt society is the function of his occupation ; society in its economic organization reflects the anarchy of the state of nature : " Dans la nature, toutes les espèces se dévorent ; toutes les conditions se dévorent dans la société " (*ibid.*, pp. 37f.). Montaigne believed that one's social and economic function was the potential devourer of the self, if one was not careful to preserve the distinction between one's function and one's being, between one's mask and one's

---

[1] FABRE (p. 174) comments as follows : "Rameau se montre, en somme, moins radical que Montaigne qui, lui, refusait, sans autre forme de procès, toute réalité à la conscience générale." He gives the following quotation from the *Essais* to support his statement : " Il est croyable qu'il y a des lois naturelles, comme il se voit és autres creatures, mais en tout elles sont perdues, cette belle raison humaine s'ingerant partout de maistriser et de commander, brouillant et confondant le visage des choses selon sa vanité et inconstance " (*Essais*, II, xii, 654). Fabre has thus taken Montaigne's critical skepticism as his final word, and ignores his concept of nature which emerges late in Book III. See below, pp. 88-89.

essential reality: "La plus part de nos vacations sont farcesques. '*Mundus universus exercet histrionam.*' Il faut jouer deuement nostre rolle, mais comme rolle d'un personnage emprunté. Du masque et de l'apparence il n'en faut pas faire une essence réelle, ny de l'estranger le propre. ... Le Maire et Montaigne ont tousjours esté deux, d'une separation bien claire " (*Essais*, III, x, 1134). The trouble with Rameau is that he has been unable to find the mask : " Le masque ! le masque ! Je donnerais un de mes doigts pour avoir trouvé le masque " (*Neveu*, p. 52).

Rameau's use of Montaigne's philosophy is perverse. Where Montaigne sought to protect his freedom against the claims of society, Rameau seeks rather to dissolve his identity in the performance of his role as society's fool. In a sense, however, Rameau exposes the danger implicit in such a doctrine as Montaigne offers. What was valid for Montaigne is not necessarily so for anyone else. By having Rameau espouse to a limited extent Montaigne's precepts, Diderot demonstrates the perils involved when one proposes for mankind in general an ethical system derived from individual experience. He exposes also the hollowness of the *honnête homme* whose apparent morality is a mask for the rapaciousness of his ego, and who in fact practices a double morality—one for others and one for himself.

Diderot interprets such a lapse of honesty and sincerity as being very close to duplicity and falsehood. He could never condone falsehood no matter for what end. *Moi* states in the *Neveu* : "Je crois que si le mensonge peut servir un moment, il est nécessairement nuisible à la longue, et qu'au contraire, la vérité sert nécessairement à la longue, bien qu'il puisse arriver qu'elle nuise dans le moment" (p. 10).[1] Fabre comments as follows on this passage : " Montaigne, admirable à tant d'autres égards, doit être condamné pour sa théorie de ' l'illusion profitable ' " (p. 131). Here, Fabre rather overstates the case. It is hardly a question of " condemning " Montaigne, nor is it " his " theory, but rather that of Plato in the *Republic*, which Montaigne merely reports, neither condemning nor approving it. Montaigne has more sympathy for the human predicament, and is less cynical than Fabre implies : " C'est la misere de nostre condition, que souvent ce qui se presente à nostre imagination pour le plus vray, ne s'y presente pas pour le plus utile à nostre vie " (*Essais*, II, xii, 571). The opinion of *Moi*, which can be taken as Diderot's own opinion since Diderot is consistently opposed to the " mensonge profitable ", is indicative of his optimism with regard to the human condition. Montaigne is by contrast a pessimist.

Fabre relates Rameau's scorn for science to the libertine tradition stemming from Montaigne's " Apologie de Raimond Sebond ", referring

---

[1] For similar statements by Diderot elsewhere, see Letter to Falconet, Sept. 1766 (mentioned above, p. 43) ; *Réfutation d'Helvétius* (A-T, II, 446) ; *Lettre sur le commerce de la librairie* (A-T, XVIII, 66). Cf. *Essais*, II, xii, 570f.

specifically to Rameau-Diderot's use of imagery to express the disproportion between man's power and the immensity of nature : " Tenez, mon philosophe, j'ai dans la tête que la physique sera toujours une pauvre science, une goutte d'eau prise avec la pointe d'une aiguille dans le vaste océan, un grain détaché de la chaîne des Alpes. Et les raisons des phénomènes ? En vérité, il vaudroit autant ignorer que de savoir si peu et si mal " (*Neveu*, p. 32).[1] Rameau's skepticism is, however, not identical with that of Montaigne ; indeed, it is *à rebours*. Although Rameau expresses something of the doubts Diderot himself sometimes felt, he receives this stern reply from *Moi* : " Tout ce que vous venez de dire est plus spécieux que solide " *(ibid.).* Rameau's skepticism is that of the crass materialist for whom the " que sais-je ? " does not represent a continuing challenge to further inquiry.

Rameau is in many ways a grotesque caricature of Montaigne's ideas and of his portrayal of himself in the *Essais*. This " bizarre personnage " is a representative example of Montaigne's antinomical man : " C'est un composé de hauteur et de bassesse, de bon sens et de déraison. Il faut que les notions de l'honnête et du deshonnête soient bien étrangement brouillées dans sa tête. ... Rien ne dissemble plus de lui que lui-même " (p. 4). He personifies to the point of distortion the proverb espoused by both *Moi* : " Il n'y a point de grands esprits sans un grain de folie " (p. 10) and Montaigne : " Il faut avoir un peu de folie qui ne veut avoir plus de sottise " (*Essais*, III, ix, 1116). He is for Diderot an *original*, that is, what Montaigne would have termed *naïf*. The irony lies, however, in the fact that Rameau unites naïveté with its opposite—cynicism.

He is a burlesque of the skeptical essayist and his " philosophie imprémeditée et fortuite " :

Moi. — O fou, archifou, m'écriai-je, comment se fait-il que dans ta mauvaise tête il se trouve des idées si justes, pêle-mêle, avec tant d'extravagances ?

Lui. — Qui diable sait cela ? C'est le hasard qui vous les jette, et elles demeurent. Tant il y a que, quand on ne sait pas tout, on ne sait rien de bien ; on ignore où une chose va, d'où une autre vient ; où celle-ci et celle-là veulent être placées ; laquelle doit passer la première ou sera mieux la seconde. Montre-t-on bien sans la méthode ? Et la méthode, d'où naît-elle ? (*Neveu*, p. 32.)

In Rameau, Diderot objectifies and subjects to the criticism of *Moi* an aspect of his own character with which he is at times uncomfortable. To be sure, *Moi* is also under attack by *Lui*, who expresses ideas and attitudes which Diderot has in affinity with Montaigne—skepticism, disdain for method and systematic philosophy, moral antinomianism, utilitarianism—attitudes which the moralizing *Moi* cannot countenance but which Diderot himself elsewhere espouses. It is not surprising,

---

[1] Cf. *Essais*, II, xii, 494.

therefore, that Rameau should be the spokesman for many of Montaigne's ideas, seen, however, in the distorting light of satire. For the *Neveu de Rameau* is in certain important respects a satire of Diderot himself and of the ideas he holds dear. One of the butts of Diderot's satire is his own tendency to moralize. This characteristic, which he appears clearly to recognize, is objectified in *Moi* and ridiculed by *Lui*. On the other hand, a certain vein of amorality, of eroticism, present in Diderot's character, is objectified in *Lui* and seen through the self-sufficient gaze of *Moi*. *Lui* and *Moi*, then (as Daniel Mornet and others have suggested), represent an ambivalence in Diderot's own thought and character. [1] More importantly, they represent the view, which Diderot shares with Montaigne, that human nature is ambivalent.

Clearly, Rameau is a brilliantly corrupt spokesman for Montaigne's abasement of reason, and his mockery of pedantry and systematic thought. These are notions typical of Diderot, except that he is somewhat less at ease with them than the essayist. Diderot's anti-rationalism is counterpoised by a strong faith in reason ; his skepticism is a limited one and, at times, far less apparent than his confidence in *les lumières*. On the other hand, Rameau's critique of system and method is the very attitude of Diderot in his *Réfutation d'Helvétius*,[2] where he cites Montaigne when contrasting the untrammeled mind with the mind imprisoned by systematization. Similarly, Rameau's espousal of Montaigne's doctrine of self-preservation, which Rameau translates into a hedonism, is vigorously opposed by *Moi*. Diderot is both attracted to and repulsed by the self in its pure amorality. He is divided between admiration for the self that exists only in relation to and for the benefit of others, and nostalgia for the full and supreme satisfaction of the unsocialized ego. This dichotomy, however, is opposed by the paradox implicit in the *Neveu:* Rameau, the amoral hedonist, is devoid of a self-sufficient ego, while *Moi*, the philosopher, the voice of morality, is, perhaps, the sole being free from having to dance " la vile pantomime ". Diderot attempts to reconcile the contradictory claims of society and the individual, the conflict between the ideal of the philosopher's retreat from society and the opposite ideal of his full participation and fulfillment in it. Ultimately, Montaigne's solution is Diderot's as well. The lesson of " De mesnager sa volonté ", to keep separate one's public and private lives, is clearly the wisdom upon which Diderot came to organize his life's work : to keep " une arrière boutique toute sienne " quite apart from the *Encyclopédie* and the other works published during his lifetime.

In the *Entretien d'un père avec ses enfants* (1771-73 and later), Diderot presents arguments for and against disobedience to the law if

---

[1] Daniel MORNET, " La Véritable Signification du *Neveu de Rameau* ", *Revue des Deux Mondes* (15 août 1927), 881-908. On the question of man's ambivalence, see below, pp. 102f., 106f.

[2] See below, pp. 53.f.

one's judgment directs a contrary action. The dialogue is a discussion of a series of " cas de conscience ". Diderot believes here that instinctively we tend to act justly, but that our innate sense of justice is often perverted by our artificial notions of right and wrong :

Est-ce que l'homme n'est pas antérieur à l'homme de loi ? Est-ce que la raison de l'espèce humaine n'est pas tout autrement sacrée que la raison d'un législateur ? Nous nous appelons civilisés, et nous sommes pires que des sauvages. Il semble qu'il nous faille encore tournoyer pendant des siècles, d'extravagances en extravagances et d'erreurs en erreurs, pour arriver où la première étincelle de jugement, l'instinct seul, nous eût menés tout droit. (Œuvres phil., p. 436.)

The reply of Diderot's father, " le bon coutelier de Langres ", is traditionalist, conservative and respectful of civil law : " Mon fils, mon fils, c'est un bon oreiller, que celui de la raison ; mais je trouve que ma tête repose plus doucement encore sur celui de la religion et des lois " (ibid.). We note that Diderot père's reply is couched in Montaigne's image of the " doux et mol chevet " which appears in the early pages of the essay " De l'experience ".

It seems significant that it is precisely in the beginning of this essay that Montaigne discusses the relation between the law and human actions. For Montaigne, laws do not have universal validity, for they are human inventions and, as such, can make no claim to be absolute. Laws, no matter how numerous, will never correspond to the variety of human actions. " Il y a peu de relation de nos actions, qui sont en perpetuelle mutation, avec les loix fixes et immobiles " (Essais, III, xiii, 1196). Natural laws are superior to man-made laws : " Nature les donne tousjours plus heureuses que ne sont celles que nous nous donnons. Tesmoing la peinture de l'aage doré des poëtes, et l'estat où nous voyons vivre les nations qui n'en ont point d'autres " (ibid.). In the fashion of these naïve societies, in which the first passer-by on the mountain-side is chosen to decide the justice of a cause, why not choose a wise man to pronounce on such matters in our civilized societies : " Quel danger y auroit-il que les plus sages vuidassent ainsi les nostres, selon les occurrences et à l'œil, sans obligation d'exemple et de consequence ? " (Ibid.)

Is it not likely that Diderot had read these lines and had formed a similar opinion ? In the Entretien, he seems to echo Montaigne's ideas : " La nature a fait les bonnes lois de toute éternité ; c'est une force légitime qui en assure l'exécution ; et cette force, qui peut tout contre le méchant, ne peut rien contre l'homme de bien. Je suis cet homme de bien ; et dans ces circonstances et beaucoup d'autres que je vous détaillerais, je la cite au tribunal de mon cœur, de ma raison, de ma conscience, au tribunal de l'équité naturelle " (Œuvres phil., p. 430). Diderot believes that there is a moral elite in tune with natural equity, more competent than the law to deal with ethical questions. But such ideas are not meant to be bruited about : " Je ne les prêcherai pas ; il y a des vérités qui ne sont pas faites pour les fous ; mais je les garderai pour moi. — Pour toi qui es un sage ? — Assurément " (ibid.). There is

undoubtedly a touch of irony and paradox in these lines. (We should recall the subtitle of the dialogue : " Du danger de se mettre au-dessus des lois ".) This is also true of the closing lines of the dialogue :

— Mon père, c'est qu'à la rigueur il n'y a point de lois pour le sage...
— Parlez plus bas...
— Toutes étant sujettes à des exceptions, c'est à lui qu'il appartient de juger des cas où il faut s'y soumettre ou s'en affranchir.
— Je ne serais pas trop fâché, me répondit-il, qu'il y eût dans la ville un ou deux citoyens comme toi ; mais je n'y habiterais pas, s'ils pensaient tous de même. (*Œuvres phil.*, p. 443.)

Diderot is thus aware of the potential dangers involved in advocating such moral autonomy and presents this idea in the framework of a charming vignette of provincial life, centered about an evocative portrait of his beloved father, who personifies all the best in bourgeois morality. On the other hand, Diderot cherishes the ideal of the autonomous philosopher-king of Platonic tradition who is free from bondage to the shadows of the cave and basks in the pure light of natural Goodness. But this is only an ideal in Diderot's " arrière boutique ". He is well aware that society depends upon obedience to law ; without it, there is only anarchy. A passage from the *Supplément au voyage de Bougainville* is the corrective for the sentiments expressed in the *Entretien d'un père* : " Nous parlerons contre les lois insensées jusqu'à ce qu'on les réforme ; et, en attendant, nous nous y soumettrons. Celui qui, de son autorité privée, enfreint une loi mauvaise, autorise tout autre à enfreindre les bonnes. Il y a moins d'inconvénients à être fou avec des fous, qu'à être sage tout seul " (*Œuvres phil.*, p. 515).

The *Entretien* is a typically Diderotean mixture of realism and invention, its source being an actual conversation that must have taken place in the Diderot home in Langres during Diderot's visit there in 1754. He worked on it at different periods between 1771 until his death, expanding it with additional material. Diderot *père*'s Montaignean imagery may very well be a more or less close paraphrase of his actual words. However, it makes little difference whether we ascribe to Diderot or to his father this paraphrase of Montaigne. What is important and clear from the context is that Diderot *père* is using Montaigne's expression to phrase a thought quite the reverse of the original.

Let us turn briefly to the context in " De l'experience " : " Le plus simplement se commettre à nature, c'est s'y commettre le plus sagement. O que c'est un doux et mol chevet, et sain, que l'ignorance et l'incuriosité, à reposer une teste bien faicte " (*Essais*, III, xiii, 1205). This is the conclusion to a development of the idea that Montaigne sets little store by laws and the inferences of experience that depend upon supposed resemblances between disparate events. Laws are not reliable indices to knowledge because they are based on analogy. Now, no single event can be precisely analogous to any other. Therefore, the experience of others can never be as reliable as our own experience. When Montaigne speaks of " ignorance et incuriosité ", he does not mean that he relies on the

judgments of others, on the ready-made precepts of religion and laws. He means that he relies on his own instinctive judgment and personal experience rather than seek the authority of others, whether that authority be the law or the sophistry of the philosophers. For no human institution is sacrosanct:

> Les loix se maintiennent en credit, non par ce qu'elles sont justes, mais par ce qu'elles sont loix. C'est le fondement mystique de leur authorité ; elles n'en ont poinct d'autre. Qui bien leur sert. Elles sont souvent faictes par des sots, plus souvent par des gens qui, en haine d'equalité, ont faute d'equité, mais tousjours par des hommes, autheurs vains et irresolus.
>
> Il n'est rien si lourdement et largement fautier que les loix, ny si ordinairement. Quiconque leur obeyt parce qu'elles sont justes, ne leur obeyt pas justement par où il doibt. (*Ibid.*, p. 1203.) [1]

Thus we see that although Diderot *père* uses Montaigne in such a way that he appears to be paraphrasing him, he is in actuality not doing so at all. Diderot *père* is afraid to trust his natural impulse. Diderot *fils* is the truer interpreter of Montaigne. He, too, doubts the sanctity of laws and seeks autonomy for the sage. But neither Montaigne nor Diderot advocates revolution or blatant civil disobedience. Montaigne judges himself by his own standards: " J'ay mes loix et ma court pour juger de moy, et m'y adresse plus qu'ailleurs " (*Essais*, III, ii, 903), but in public matters Montaigne's private court is of no consequence: " la raison privée n'a qu'une jurisdiction privée " (I, xxiii, 151). Where Montaigne and Diderot differ is in degree and in emphasis. Diderot would replace the authority of the Church by the authority of private conscience. The dialogue reflects Diderot's taste for casuistry, perhaps stemming from his early Jesuit training, although his rebellion against the Church is complete and uncompromising. What the *philosophe* seeks is freedom from the control of the Church and the priesthood in matters of conscience. The *philosophe* is his own " directeur de conscience ".

In *Jacques le fataliste* (1773-75), Diderot adapts at will a passage from Montaigne's essay " Sur des vers de Virgile " in defense of the novel's mild licentiousness. He follows Montaigne in censuring the reader for his hypocrisy and for blushing at the mention of the sexual act. Let us compare side by side the passage in the original with Diderot's version:

Diderot	Montaigne
[See below.]	Qu'a faict l'action genitale aux hommes, si naturelle, si necessaire, & si juste, pour n'en oser parler sans vergogne, & pour l'exclurre des propos serieux et reglez ?

---

[1] It is worth noting that Montaigne's relativism has another eighteenth-century descendant in Montesquieu's *Esprit des Lois*, which Diderot had doubtless pondered well.

Vous prononcez hardiment tuer, voler, trahir, et l'autre vous ne l'oseriez qu'entre les dents !

Est-ce que moins vous exhalez de ces prétendues impuretés en paroles, plus il vous en reste dans la pensée ?

Et que vous a fait l'action génitale, si naturelle, si nécessaire et si juste, pour en exclure le signe de vos entretiens, et pour imaginer que votre bouche, vos yeux et vos oreilles en seraient souillés ?

Il est bon que les expressions les moins usitées, les moins écrites, les mieux tues soient les mieux sues et les plus généralement connues ;

aussi cela est ;

aussi le mot *futuo* n'est-il pas moins familier que le mot pain ; nul âge ne l'ignore, nul idiome n'en est privé :

il a mille synonymes dans toutes les langues,

il s'imprime en chacune sans être exprimé, sans voix, sans figure, et le sexe qui le fait le plus, a usage de le taire le plus. (A-T, VI, 222 ; *Œuvres romanesques*, p. 715.)

Nous prononçons hardiment, *tuer, desrober, trahir:* & cela, nous n'oserions qu'entre les dents.

Est-ce à dire, que moins nous en exhalons en parole, d'autant nous avons loy d'en grossir la pensée ?

[See above.]

Car il est bon, que les mots qui sont le moins en usage, moins escrits, & mieux teus, sont les mieux sceus, & plus generalement cognus.

Nul aage, nulles meurs l'ignorent non plus que le pain.

Ils s'impriment en chascun, sans estre exprimez & sans voix et sans figure. Et le sexe qui le fait le plus, a charge de le taire le plus. (*Essais,* Coste, III, v, 70f. ; Pléiade, 947.)

It is obvious that Diderot was extremely familiar with this passage ; indeed, he must have known it for a long time. In the *Bijoux indiscrets*, he had expressed in his own terms the very same idea contained in the above passage.[1] But in *Jacques le fataliste* he no longer wishes to disguise his source, and prefers to quote Montaigne directly (or to appear to do so). Diderot has made Montaigne's text an integral part of his own, necessitating certain changes such as that from *nous* to *vous*. We note again that Diderot does not simply quote Montaigne ; he amplifies Montaigne's thought, comments on it, carries it forward, making it serve a specific purpose. It is Diderot's intention here to use Montaigne in his defense of obscenity, and to take the reader unawares by revealing the irreverent voice of the revered essayist : " ' Fi, le cynique ! Fi, l'impudent ! Fi, le sophiste !...' Courage, insultez bien un auteur estimable que vous avez sans cesse entre les mains, et dont je ne suis

---

[1] Mangogul chides Mirzoza for her *pudeur:* " Je voudrais bien que vous me dissiez à quoi sert cette hypocrisie qui vous est commune à toutes, sages ou libertines. Sont-ce les choses qui vous effarouchent ? Non ; car vous les savez. Sont-ce les mots ? en vérité, cela n'en vaut pas la peine. S'il est ridicule de rougir de l'action, ne l'est-il pas infiniment davantage de rougir de l'expression ? " (Ch. xviii.)

ici que le traducteur. La licence de son style m'est presque un garant de la pureté de ses mœurs ; c'est Montaigne " (A-T, VI, 223 ; Œuvres rom., p. 715).[1] However, it is not quite Montaigne, for the essayist does not mention the word " futuo " here. Let us recall the several meanings of the word " traducteur ". Diderot is simultaneously betraying and " handing down " a tradition. One of the original features of Jacques is precisely Diderot's candid and conscious imitation of traditional (and contemporary) models, which he weaves into the texture of his novel.

Montaigne himself suspected that his book would become " le bréviaire des honnêtes gens ". He says on the same page where the passage used by Diderot occurs : " Je m'ennuye que mes Essais servent les Dames de meuble commun seulement, & de meuble de sale : ce Chapitre me fera du cabinet. J'ayme leur commerce un peu privé " (Essais, Coste, III, v, 70 ; Pléiade, 947). Then follows the passage in question, in which Montaigne speaks privately to the reader of those actions we perform but of which we dare not speak. For Montaigne, such a false morality is an obstacle to moral freedom and ultimately to self-knowledge ; for those who hide their actions from others generally hide them from themselves. Thus Montaigne's justification for his licence in this essay is that frankness in such matters is part of moral hygiene and requisite to self-improvement.

Similarly, Diderot's purpose is evidently moralistic. Certainly the author of the Bijoux indiscrets need not invoke Montaigne to justify licentiousness. In Jacques, Diderot returns to the realism of Rabelais. It is not the lascivious grin of Boucher's cupids, which Diderot so detested, that lurks beneath the racy tales in Jacques, but the bemused smile of the compassionate moralist, striving to represent the truth of human reality. This critique of hypocrisy, however, is also a declaration of innocence. Diderot dissociates himself from the reader, proclaiming his own moral superiority : " Lecteur, à vous parler franchement, je trouve que le plus méchant de nous deux, ce n'est pas moi " (A-T, VI, 222 ; Œuvres rom., p. 714). The passage from Montaigne's Essais, which Diderot uses in Jacques, may be viewed as one of the sources of Diderot's conception of the novel—the reflecting mirror held up to human nature. Thus, Diderot's defense of Montaigne is an indirect defense of himself and of his novel : " Je m'amuse à écrire sous des noms empruntés les sottises que vous faites " (ibid.).

Although Diderot never compared his style directly with that of Montaigne, he revealed much about himself when he compared Helvétius with Montaigne in the Réfutation du livre d'Helvétius intitulé l'Homme (1773-74) : " Quel livre que celui d'Helvétius, s'il eût été écrit au temps et dans la langue de Montaigne ! Il serait autant au-dessus des Essais

---

[1] Cf. Salon de 1767 (A-T, XI, 56) where Diderot speaks of a woman " qui fait tous les matins son oraison dans Montaigne, et qui a appris de lui, bien ou mal à propos, à voir plus de malhonnêteté dans les choses que dans les mots ".

que les *Essais* sont au-dessus de tous les moralistes qui ont paru depuis "
(A-T, II, 290). He speculates on the possibility of Montaigne's influence
on Helvétius :

Je ne sais quel cas Helvétius faisait de Montaigne et si la lecture lui en
était bien familière, mais il y a beaucoup de rapport entre leur manière de
voir et de dire. Montaigne est cynique, Helvétius l'est aussi ; ils ont l'un
et l'autre les pédants en horreur ; la science des mœurs est pour tous deux la
science par excellence ; ils accordent beaucoup aux circonstances et aux
hasards ; ils ont de l'imagination, beaucoup de familiarité dans le style, de la
hardiesse et de la singularité dans l'expression, des métaphores qui leur
sont propres. *(Ibid.)* [1]

What is revealed in this passage is, of course, Diderot's familiarity with
Montaigne's work, which he admires for its bold unconventionality. The
affinities between Montaigne and Helvétius (and the Encyclopedist)
are limited, however, by the differences between the times in which they
lived : " Helvétius au temps de Montaigne en aurait eu à peu près le
style, et Montaigne au temps d'Helvétius aurait à peu près écrit comme
lui ; c'est-à-dire qu'il eût eu moins d'énergie et plus de correction, moins
d'originalité et plus de méthode " *(ibid.)*. The antinomy of originality
and method, which Diderot finds a factor marking the difference between
the Renaissance and the eighteenth century, is his own concern as well.
The advance of scientific experimentation convinces him of the need
for rigorous method ; yet although Helvétius " est plus lié, plus suivi
que Montaigne ", Diderot is unwilling to sacrifice " les circonstances et
les hasards " *(ibid.,* p. 394).

Herbert Dieckmann saw this conflict very clearly in the opening
pages of Diderot's last major work, the *Essai sur les règnes de Claude
et de Néron* (1778), in which Montaigne's influence is so evident.[2] The
essay begins much in the essayist's manner :

Je ne compose point, je ne suis point auteur ; je lis ou je converse, j'interroge ou je réponds. Si l'on n'entend que moi, on me reprochera d'être
décousu, peut-être même obscur, surtout aux endroits où j'examine les
ouvrages de Sénèque ; et l'on me lira je ne dis pas avec autant de plaisir,
comme on lit les *Maximes* de La Rochefoucauld, et un chapitre de

---

[1] This is the second time we have occasion to note Diderot's statement
of Montaigne's supposed cynicism (cf. passage quoted above, p. 31).
Diderot seems to be troubled by the apparent contradiction between Montaigne's sage aloofness, his obedience to the law and, at the same time, his
self-appointed role as skeptical critic of human foibles. Cf. the following
undated passage : " Je voudrais bien savoir pourquoi ces faiseurs de
maximes, à commencer par Montaigne, La Rochefoucauld, Nicole, La
Bruyère, Trublet, et finissant par ce dernier, M. de Bignicourt, ont tous été
pénétrés du plus profond mépris pour l'espèce humaine. Montaigne nous
croit incapables de rien savoir et de rien connaître " (A-T, IV, 90).

[2] Dieckmann remarks : " Diderot est partagé entre... l'idéal de la suite
logique des idées, de l'objectivité de la pensée, d'une présentation systématique, et... d'une forte résistance contre cette exigence " *(Cinq Leçons sur
Diderot* [Genève-Paris, 1959], p. 79).

La Bruyère : mais si l'on jette alternativement les yeux sur la page de Sénèque et sur la mienne, on remarquera dans celle-ci plus d'ordre, plus de clarté, selon qu'on se mettra plus fidèlement à ma place, qu'on aura plus ou moins d'analogie avec le philosophe et avec moi ; et l'on ne tardera pas à s'apercevoir que c'est autant mon âme que je peins, que celle des différents personnages qui s'offrent à mon récit. (A-T, III, 10.)

As Dieckmann observes, Montaigne is not named directly, but we recognize him easily in the turns of phrase and concepts Diderot uses,[1] (i.e., " je ne compose point..., je lis ou je converse..., c'est autant mon âme que je peins ", etc.). The borrowing of Montaigne's manner for his own and the repeated appearances of Montaigne in the course of the essay, would indicate that Montaigne is very much at its heart. It is as if Diderot, towards the end of his career, at last recognized the importance of Montaigne's influence on his work and set out deliberately to write an essay *à la Montaigne* which remains nevertheless very much *à la Diderot.*

Diderot is self-conscious about the practice of borrowing from authors of the past. He takes Montaigne as his model of honesty in this respect :

De combien de grandes et belles pensées, d'idées ingénieuses, et même bizarres, on dépouillerait quelques-uns de nos plus célèbres écrivains, si l'on restituait à Plutarque, à Sénèque, à Machiavel, et à Montaigne, ce qu'ils en ont pris sans les citer ! J'aime la franchise de ce dernier : « Mon livre, dit-il (*Essais*, liv. II, chap. xxxii) est maçonné des dépouilles des deux autres. » Je permets d'emprunter, mais non de voler, moins encore d'injurier celui qu'on a volé. (A-T, III, 196ff.)

Diderot may have had Rousseau in mind in this passage. Indeed, Naigeon, convinced of this, appended a long note to the phrase " nos plus célèbres écrivains ", which was for a long time imputed to Diderot. A violently invidious comparison of Montaigne and Rousseau, it is unthinkable that Diderot could have written it. The tone is undeniably Naigeon's.[2] In contrast, Diderot's wistful recollection of his early closeness to Jean-Jacques, now recently deceased, is a moving evoca-

[1] DIECKMANN, *Cinq leçons*, p. 79.
[2] Cf. Naigeon's parallel between Diderot and Montaigne quoted above, pp. 17f. and his comparison of Montaigne and Rousseau : « En effet, [Rousseau] n'est ni un penseur profond, ni un logicien exact et sévère, ni un moraliste aussi instructif, aussi original, aussi agréable à lire que Montaigne, ni même un ami, très-sincère et très-zélé de la vérité : c'est un écrivain très-éloquent, dont le style vif, élégant, rapide et plein d'énergie, entraîne presque toujours sans persuader ; c'est un sophiste adroit, quelquefois même très-subtil, qui se met fort peu en peine de se contredire, et à qui le choix des opinions est en général à peu près indifférent, pourvu que celle qu'il embrasse, vraie ou fausse, lui offre un champ assez vaste pour faire briller tous ses talents. ... Tant que les langues latine et française subsisteront, Sénèque et Montaigne seront lus, médités et admirés des bons esprits : et toute l'éloquence de M. Rousseau, qui, en s'appropriant si souvent leurs pensées, s'est, pour ainsi dire, associé à leur gloire, et a brillé parmi nous d'un éclat emprunté, ne les fera jamais oublier » (A-T, III, 196ff.).

tion (inspired directly by Montaigne's famous lines on La Boétie) of the deep friendship of two young men : "L'amour est l'ivresse de l'homme adulte : l'amitié est la passion de la jeunesse ; c'est alors que j'étais lui, qu'il était moi" (A-T, III, 204).[1]

Diderot espouses Montaigne's poor opinion of the historian Dio Cassius and quotes the paragraph from the essay " Defence de Seneque et de Plutarque " in which Montaigne defends Seneca's honor against the testimony of Dio. Diderot remarks : " Ce que l'auteur des *Essais* dit de Dion est indistinctement applicable à tous les censeurs de Sénèque." [2] Diderot agrees with Montaigne in preferring the manner of Seneca to that of Cicero.[3] In reply to an objection that " si Montaigne a dit qu'il ne trouvait que du vent dans Cicéron, c'est une gasconnade ridicule du philosophe de la Garonne ", Diderot retorts :

> Une gasconnade ridicule ! Il me semble qu'on aurait pu s'exprimer plus décemment sur un aussi grand penseur, sur un aussi grand écrivain, sur un auteur original qui a passé pour le bréviaire des honnêtes gens, qui n'est pas encore tombé de leurs mains, et qui pourrait bien y rester à jamais. Jusqu'à ce que la suffisance soit devenue la mesure du mérite, il faudrait se garder d'en prendre le ton. (A-T, III, 234.)

To the objection that " Montaigne est suspect ", Diderot replies : " Et pourquoi ? Montaigne, qui parlait la langue des Anciens comme la sienne, et dont les citations sans nombre montrent combien la lecture lui en était familière, s'entendait en style et en bonne logique " *(ibid.,* p. 235). Answering the charge that " on n'a jamais cité Montaigne en fait de goût ", Diderot leaps to his defense as a stylist : " Montaigne est riche en expressions, il est énergique, il est philosophe, il est grand peintre et grand coloriste. Il déploie en cent endroits tout ce que l'éloquence a de force ; il est tout ce qu'il lui plaît d'être. Il a tout le goût que l'on pouvait avoir de son temps, et qui convenait à son sujet " *(ibid.).* This is Diderot's most energetic praise of Montaigne's style, a style characterized by its force and its freedom, of which Diderot gives an example :

> C'est lui qui a dit de la mort : « Je me plonge stupidement et tête baissée dans cette profondeur muette qui m'engloutit et m'étouffe en un moment, plein d'insipidité et d'indolence. La mort, qui n'est qu'un quart d'heure de passion sans conséquence et sans nuisance, ne mérite pas des préceptes particuliers. » Cela n'est pas trop religieux, mais cela est beau. Il y a dans son inimitable ouvrage mille endroits de la même force. *(Ibid.)*

---

[1] Cf. *Essais,* I, xxviii, 224 : " En l'amitié dequoy je parle, [les ames] se meslent et confondent l'une en l'autre, d'un melange si universel, qu'elles effacent et ne retrouvent plus la couture qui les a jointes. Si on me presse de dire pourquoy je l'aymois, je sens que cela ne se peut exprimer, qu'en respondant : Par ce que c'estoit luy ; par ce que c'estoit moy."

[2] A-T, III, 120.

[3] *Ibid.,* p. 233.

The first sentence of Diderot's quotation (" Je me plonge... indolence ") is from " De la vanité " (*Essais*, III, ix, 1087) ; the second is from " De la phisionomie " (*Essais*, III, xii, 1180). Again we observe that Diderot has brought together two separate *loci* in the *Essais*, and that there are significant inexactitudes in the first part of the quotation, though not in the second. The text of the Coste edition reads as follows : " Je me plonge la teste baissée, stupidement dans la mort, sans la considerer et recognoistre, comme dans une profondeur muette & obscure, qui m'engloutit d'un saut, & m'estouffe en un instant, d'un puissant sommeil, plein d'insipidité & indolence " (III, ix, 214).[1] A number of observations can be made. Diderot tightens the passage considerably by leaving out the word " obscure " and the phrases " dans la mort ", " sans la considerer et recognoistre ", " d'un saut ", " d'un puissant sommeil ". The phrase " plein d'insipidité " no longer applies to " sommeil " but to either " un moment " or " me ". He compresses Montaigne's simile into a metaphor and substitutes the demonstrative adjective for the indefinite article. Of course we do not know if Diderot made these changes consciously or whether they are the transformations of memory. He may well have revised the passage in the act of transcribing it in a notebook,[2] under the heading " Mort ", together with the passage from " De la phisionomie ". The fact that the two quotations occur roughly one hundred pages apart in the original, would lend support to this view. Consciously or unconsciously, Diderot has intensified Montaigne's depiction of death as a momentary reduction to nothingness, heightening what the eighteenth century chose to regard as his atheistic tendencies.[3]

Diderot goes on to recommend other passages of the *Essais* in which Montaigne displays vigor of language and sureness of taste and literary judgment :

Il faut y lire le morceau sur sa manière de lutter contre les Anciens.

Parmi le grand nombre de jugements divers qu'il prononce au chapitre des livres, il n'y en a pas un où l'on ne reconnaisse un tact sûr et délicat.

Ne dédaignons ni son analyse de quelques beaux vers de Lucrèce, ni ce qu'il ajoute sur la véritable éloquence et sur les langues. (A-T, III, 236.)[4]

---

[1] The Bordeaux Copy makes the following emendation : " ... qui m'engloutit d'un saut, et *accable* en un instant..."

[2] See above, p. 39.

[3] Diderot seems not to have shared Montaigne's early obsession with death. In one of the rare passages in his writings where he does speak of death, it is as a soothing, lulling, sinking into sleep : " ... c'est que la vie n'est, pour certaines personnes, qu'un long jour de fatigue, et la mort qu'un long sommeil, et le cercueil qu'un lit de repos, et la terre qu'un oreiller où il est doux à la fin d'aller mettre sa tête pour ne la plus relever " (*Corr.*, IV, 165).

[4] Of the three portions of the *Essais* to which Diderot makes reference, the first seems to be to " De l'institution des enfants " (I, xxvi, 179). The others are, of course, to " Des livres " (II, x) and " Sur des vers de Virgile " (III, v).

Diderot allows himself to be carried away by his enthusiasm for Montaigne and continues to praise the essayist's taste :

Un critique aura bien du goût lorsqu'il sentira celui de Montaigne ; il est condamné à n'en point avoir, si la richesse, la chaleur et la vie du passage suivant lui échappent.
— Mais les lettres de Sénèque ?...
— J'y reviendrai quand je pourrai ; partout où je me trouve bien, j'y reste, et ce que je dirais ne vaudra pas ce que Montaigne va dire. *(Ibid.)*

Diderot then proceeds to quote verbatim a long passage from the essay " Des boyteux " and ends with the comment : " Je donnerais volontiers la meilleure de mes pages pour celle-là." [1] We shall not join Louis Ducros and say that " le lecteur ne peut qu'être de l'avis de Diderot ".[2]

We note Diderot's extravagant praise for Montaigne's style and his own self-effacing modesty. It will be remembered that Diderot often made use of this and other passages from " Des boyteux " in his earlier works. Here, however, he does not paraphrase the passage as he did in the *Essai sur le mérite et la vertu*, but instead is scrupulously accurate in his quotation. The passage was long one of his favorites, but now, at the end of his life, its artistic qualities especially evoke his admiration.

Having thus come full circle, we must now attempt to draw some conclusions from the foregoing view of Diderot's Montaigne. The chronological procedure has disclosed Diderot's lifelong attachment to the *Essais*, and the continuity of their presence in his work. On the other hand, despite his frequent praise of the essayist and his many borrowings from him, it is not quite true, as Gillot claimed, that Diderot " admirait Montaigne sans réserve ".[3] He often differed with Montaigne's opinions and, even when appearing to be in complete agreement with him, he is found, upon closer scrutiny, to be using Montaigne as a springboard for his own thought. This is, after all, the action of one original mind upon another ; it is synthesis, not wholesale appropriation.

We have also been able to observe an evolution in Diderot's special interest in the *Essais*. At first, Montaigne is the young Diderot's intellectual guide (in the *Pensées philosophiques*) and the standard-bearer of skepticism (in the *Promenade du sceptique*). Diderot sees him chiefly as a critic of dogmatism and religious fanaticism. But gradually, as Diderot himself moves away from skepticism towards scientific speculation and the positivism of the *Encyclopédie*, his interest shifts from what one might call the intellectual Montaigne to the moralist, and ultimately

---

[1] The passage quoted is from *Essais*, Coste, III, xi, 277f. ; Pléiade, 1152f. It begins with the line " J'ay veu la naissance de plusieurs miracles de mon temps..." Diderot here interpolates parenthetically " (et moi aussi) " and continues the quotation through " une presse où les fols surpassent de tant les sages en nombre ".

[2] *Les Encyclopédistes* (Paris, 1900), p. 20.

[3] H. GILLOT, *Denis Diderot: L'Homme, ses idées philosophiques, esthétiques, et littéraires* (Paris, 1937), p. xiv.

to the literary artist. Montaigne is replaced as an intellectual guide by Bacon and Bayle, but retains his authority in matters of style.[1] After 1765, Diderot becomes more and more sensitive to the aesthetic, humanistic *Weltanschauung* that unfolds and matures in the *Essais*.

In the main, we have considered in this chapter Diderot's explicit references to Montaigne. In those to follow, we intend to go deeper into the implicit affinities between Montaigne and Diderot with respect to questions of philosophic outlook, ethics, and literary form.

---

[1] *Claude et Néron* (A-T, III, 234, 236).

II. THE SKEPTIC'S WAY

Quid ergo sectabor iter?

DESCARTES

Le premier pas

The question of Diderot's skepticism has been taken up briefly in a recent article by Richard Popkin.[1] According to Popkin, the *philosophes*, unlike the Pyrrhonists, were in general confident in the capacity of man to arrive at a rational interpretation of the world, and were little troubled, as was Hume, by an abyss of doubt threatening to open beneath their feet. In his appraisal of the extent of Diderot's skepticism, Popkin quotes the closing paragraphs of the article " Pyrrhonienne " in the *Encyclopédie* as Diderot's definitive and, as it were, sole statement on skepticism :

Pour nous, nous conclurons que, tout étant lié dans la nature, il n'y a rien, à proprement parler, dont l'homme ait une connaissance parfaite, absolue, complète, pas même des axiomes les plus évidents, parce qu'il faudrait qu'il eût la connaissance de tout.

Tout étant lié, s'il ne connaît pas tout, il faudra nécessairement que, de discussions en discussions, il arrive à quelque chose d'inconnu ; donc, en remontant de ce point inconnu, on sera fondé à conclure contre lui, ou l'ignorance, ou l'obscurité, ou l'incertitude du point qui précède, et de celui qui précède celui-ci ; et ainsi jusqu'au principe le plus évident.

Il y a donc une sorte de sobriété dans l'usage de la raison, à laquelle il faut s'assujettir, ou se résoudre à flotter dans l'incertitude ; un moment où sa lumière, qui avait toujours été en croissant, commence à s'affaiblir, et où il faut s'arrêter dans toutes discussions. (A-T, XVI, 491.)

Popkin's conclusion that Diderot's skepticism is of a limited nature seems valid enough, but on the basis of this single quotation, it is

---

[1] Richard H. POPKIN, " Scepticism in the Enlightenment ", in *Studies on Voltaire and the Eighteenth Century*, XXVI, ed. Theodore Besterman (Geneva, 1963), 1321-1345.

perhaps an over-simplification to say that Diderot exemplifies the " great gulf... between the *philosophes* and the Pyrrhonists, ancient and modern ".[1] It is especially dangerous to consider the *Encyclopédie* articles as the expression of Diderot's definitive opinion on any subject. One must look into his other writings as well, keeping in mind the evolutive nature of his thought.

We shall examine first the nature of Diderot's skepticism in the series of early works, from the *Pensées philosophiques* to the *Lettre sur les aveugles*, which have been described as forming a coherent progression from deism to atheism.[2] The brief span from 1746 to 1749 might, however, more properly be called Diderot's skeptical period, for the products of these years are generally works of exploration, in which Diderot hesitates and seems unable to commit himself to a single position, although he does follow a path in the direction of materialist atheism. The unifying principle in these works is their skeptical attitude which seems finally to result in Diderot's rejection of Christian dogma from his cosmological scheme. During this period of his intellectual development, Diderot would seem, at least on the surface, to be freeing himself from finalism, which in turn enables him to replace the creativity of Deity by that of Nature.

According to Robert Niklaus, the *Pensées philosophiques* " sont pour une bonne part une sorte de conversation entre un athée, un super-stitieux et un déiste où les arguments du chrétien se retournent contre lui, où l'athée ne trouve pas son compte et où le déiste seul a l'avantage, parce qu'il s'appuie sur la nature et la passion bien comprise ".[3] Of particular interest are the cosmological arguments of the deist and the atheist concerning the existence of God. The deist refutes the atheist by appealing to the evidence of experimental physics : God exists because order and design in nature reveal a Supreme Intelligence. Replying that the universe does not indicate the existence of a supreme rational principle, the atheist presents the Lucretian argument that, given an infinite number of atoms and an infinite number of possible combinations, one should rather be surprised at a hypothetical duration of chaos than at the actual birth of the universe. These two arguments confront one another, but Diderot does not yet appear to choose between them ; they will in fact continue to oppose each other in the *Promenade du sceptique* and the *Lettre sur les aveugles*. Rather than debate the merits of these arguments, Diderot gives the deist a certain *moral* advantage over the atheist and the skeptic :

Le déiste assure l'existence d'un Dieu, l'immortalité de l'âme et ses suites : le sceptique n'est point décidé sur ces articles : l'athée les nie. Le

---

[1] *Op. cit.*, p. 1336.

[2] See Aram VARTANIAN, " From Deist to A theist, Diderot's Philosoph-ical Orientation 1746-1749 ", in *Diderot Studies I*, ed. Otis Fellows and Norman Torrey (Syracuse, 1949), 46-63.

[3] Robert NIKLAUS, ed. *Pensées philosophiques* (Genève-Paris, 1957), p. xx.

sceptique a donc pour être vertueux un motif de plus que l'athée, et quelque raison de moins que le déiste. Sans la crainte du législateur, la pente du tempérament, et la connaissance des avantages actuels de la vertu, la probité de l'athée manquerait de fondement, et celle du sceptique serait fondée sur un *peut-être*. (*Pensée* xxiii, *Œuvres phil.*, p. 23f.)

However, as Vernière remarks : " Diderot s'appuie sur Montaigne et oppose déjà au déiste une figure nouvelle, celle du sceptique ",[1] whose position severely limits the supposed victory of the deist. In fact, an impressive portion of the work (*Pensées* xxiv-xl) is devoted to an exposition of the skeptic attitude. By its length and its place in the *Pensées*, the skeptical position is of prime importance.

Diderot considers as true skeptics that minority of independent thinkers who doubt only after having carefully examined all the arguments for and against :

Le scepticisme ne convient pas à tout le monde. Il suppose un examen profond et désintéressé. Celui qui doute parce qu'il ne connaît pas les raisons de crédibilité, n'est qu'un ignorant. Le vrai sceptique a compté et pesé les raisons. Mais ce n'est pas une petite affaire que de peser des raisonnements. Qui de nous en connaît exactement la valeur ? qu'on apporte cent preuves de la même vérité, aucune ne manquera de partisans. Chaque esprit a son télescope. (*Pensée* xxiv, *ibid.*, p. 24.)

The difficulty arises both from the complex nature of truth and its relation to the observer. " Si nous sommes divisés sur la valeur intrin-sèque, comment nous accorderons-nous sur le poids relatif ? Dites-moi, combien faut-il de preuves morales pour contrebalancer une conclu-sion métaphysique ? " *(Ibid.)* If all questions have almost equally valid reasons for and against, whence comes our dogmatic decisiveness ? Here Diderot's attitude is precisely that of Montaigne in " Des boyteux " (*Essais*, III, xi), from which he quotes to illustrate his contention that the skeptical mind can appreciate evidence of verisimilitude but is revolted by claims of infallibility.[2]

Certain temperaments, of course, cannot easily accept the neutrality of the skeptic :

Les esprits bouillants, les imaginations ardentes ne s'accommodent pas de l'indolence du sceptique. Ils aiment mieux hasarder un choix que de n'en faire aucun ; se tromper que de vivre incertains : soit qu'ils se méfient de leurs bras, soit qu'ils craignent la profondeur des eaux, on les voit toujours suspendus à des branches dont ils sentent toute la faiblesse, et auxquelles ils aiment mieux demeurer accrochés que de s'abandonner au torrent. (*Pensée* xxviii, p. 26.)

Such individuals cannot understand how one may unite tranquillity of mind with indecision : " ' Le moyen de vivre heureux sans savoir qui

---

[1] Paul VERNIÈRE, ed. *Œuvres philosophiques*, p. 6.
[2] See above, p. 29.

l'on est, d'où l'on vient, où l'on va, pourquoi l'on est venu ! ' " (*Ibid.*, p. 27.) The skeptic coldly replies : " Je me pique d'ignorer tout cela, sans en être plus malheureux. Ce n'est point ma faute si j'ai trouvé ma raison muette quand je l'ai questionnée sur mon état. Toute ma vie j'ignorerai sans chagrin ce qu'il m'est impossible de savoir " *(ibid.)*.[1] In *Pensée* xxix, no longer quoting an interlocutor but speaking directly, Diderot formulates his own principle of skeptical inquiry : " On doit exiger de moi que je cherche la vérité mais non que je la trouve." [2] There is a nuance of difference between this statement and that of the imaginary skeptic. It lacks all trace of that indolence which, according to Diderot, characterizes the skeptic. Perhaps he realizes that he too is one of those " esprits bouillants " given to exaltation, who allow themselves to be carried away by their ardent imaginations, and who prefer to choose rather than to remain in doubt. This will be borne out later in the " Pyrrhonienne " article and in the *Rêve de d'Alembert*.

Nevertheless, Diderot considers himself a skeptic and not a Pyrrhonist. In *Pensée* xxx, he distinguishes between the two : " Qu'est-ce qu'un sceptique ? C'est un philosophe qui a douté de tout ce qu'il croit et qui croit ce qu'un usage légitime de sa raison et de ses sens lui a démontré vrai. Voulez-vous quelque chose de plus précis ? Rendez sincère le pyrrhonien, et vous aurez le sceptique " (p. 27f.).[3] Fundamentally confident in the power of reason, Diderot does not separate philosophy from morality. He seems to confuse epistemological optimism with sincerity. Diderot does not appear to accept the possibility (as did Hume) that by dint of sincerity and intellectual honesty carried to their limits, reason may reach conclusions which deny its very foundations.

Skepticism is for him positive. It is the necessary foundation for true belief : " Ce qu'on n'a jamais mis en question n'a point été prouvé. Ce qu'on n'a point examiné sans prévention n'a jamais été bien examiné. Le scepticisme est donc le premier pas vers la vérité. Il doit être général, car il en est la pierre de touche " (*Pensée* xxxi, p. 28). Its critical spirit is the touchstone of all truth, wherever it is found. It may even prove to be, not the enemy of religion, but its ally :

Quand les dévots se déchaînent contre le scepticisme, il me semble qu'ils entendent mal leur intérêt, ou qu'ils se contredisent. S'il est certain qu'un culte vrai pour être embrassé, et qu'un faux culte pour être abandonné, n'ont besoin que d'être bien connus, il serait à souhaiter qu'un doute universel se repandît sur la surface de la terre, et que tous les peuples

---

[1] Perhaps Diderot's prototypes for this exchange are Montaigne and Pascal, to whom Diderot seems to be replying on Montaigne's behalf. According to NIKLAUS (*op. cit.*, p. viii), the *Pensées philosophiques* is Diderot's answer to the *Pensées*.

[2] Cf. *Essais*, II, xii, 556 : " J'ouvre les choses plus que je ne les descouvre."

[3] This distinction is perhaps also valid for Montaigne, who at times seems to consider himself a skeptic, but not a Pyrrhonist. Cf. *Essais*, II, xii, 630, 643, 651.

voulussent bien mettre en question la vérité de leurs religions. (*Pensée* xxxvi, p. 29.)

As a point of balance, skepticism avoids the extremes of credulity and incredulity, fanatical belief and atheism (*Pensées* xxxii, xxxiii) ; but, to be valid, it must be total :

Un semi-scepticisme est la marque d'un esprit faible : il décèle un raisonneur pusillanime qui se laisse effrayer par les conséquences ; un superstitieux qui croit honorer son Dieu par les entraves où il met sa raison ; une espèce d'incrédule qui craint de se démasquer à lui-même ; car si la vérité n'a rien à perdre à l'examen, comme en est convaincu le semi-sceptique, que pense-t-il au fond de son âme de ces notions privilégiées qu'il appréhende de sonder, et qui sont placées dans un recoin de sa cervelle comme dans un sanctuaire dont il n'ose approcher ? (*Pensée* xxxiv, p. 28f.) [1]

Diderot's skepticism in the *Pensées philosophiques* is thus not at all a profound metaphysical doubt of the possibility of knowledge. Rather, he remains convinced of the rational demonstrability of truth.

This is in marked contrast to Montaigne's outlook in the " Apologie de Raimond Sebond ". Montaigne's position in this work is mainly negative. He abases human reason and denies its validity to make judgments on the divine sphere. This is perhaps why Diderot does not quote from the " Apologie " at all, but rather from the closing chapters of the *Essais*, " Des boyteux " (III, xi) and " De l'experience " (III, xiii), where Montaigne's skepticism is more positive. If we turn to " Des boyteux " we realize that Diderot had read this essay carefully,[2] and that Montaigne's presence in the *Pensées philosophiques* lies deeper than the explicit references to him.

Diderot's critique of contemporary " miracles ", for example, seems inspired by Montaigne's passage on the same subject : " Il me semble qu'on est pardonnable de mescroire une merveille, autant au moins qu'on peut en destourner et elider la verification par voie non merveilleuse. Et suis l'advis de Sainct Augustin, qu'il vaut mieux pancher vers le doute que vers l'asseurance és choses de difficile preuve et dangereuse creance " (*Essais*, III, xi, 1158). And further : " en plusieurs choses... surpassant nostre connoissance, je suis d'advis que nous soustenons [suspendions] nostre jugement aussi bien à rejetter qu'à recevoir " (*ibid.*, p. 1155). Montaigne analyzes the genesis of superstition. He recognizes that we are easily fooled by appearances : " Outre la flexibilité de nostre invention à forger des raisons à toute sorte de songes, nostre imagination se trouve pareillement facile à recevoir des impressions de la fauceté par bien frivoles apparences " (*ibid.*, p. 1160).

---

[1] Such a semi-skepticism as Diderot describes might with some justification be applied to Montaigne's attitude towards religion. I doubt, however, that Diderot had Montaigne in mind. For Diderot, and his century in general, the essayist passed for an unbeliever.

[2] Niklaus points this out in his edition of the *Pensées philosophiques*, p. 20 footnote.

Diderot, carrying to a further degree Montaigne's disbelief in the supernatural, would want the truth of religion to be itself rationally demonstrable :

Une seule démonstration me frappe plus que cinquante faits. ... Veux-tu que je devienne ton prosélyte ; laisse tous ces prestiges, et raisonnons. Je suis plus sûr de mon jugement que de mes yeux. Si la religion que tu m'annonce est vraie, sa vérité peut être mise en évidence et se démontrer par des raisons invincibles. Trouve-les ces raisons. Pourquoi me harceler par des prodiges, quand tu n'as besoin pour me terrasser que d'un syllogisme. (*Pensée* 1, p. 41.)

Diderot maintains a stanch rationalism, rejecting the fideist aspect of Montaigne's skepticism. He is more aggressively polemical than Montaigne, for he attacks directly the authority of the Church. While Montaigne was skeptical of what man can know about God, the *philosophe* is skeptical of religion itself. Indeed, what Diderot's skepticism accomplishes is the clearing away of religious modes of thought. His supposed deism passes imperceptibly into natural religion and thence to naturalism. Diderot will become increasingly aware of the rights of intuition, insight and experience, moving beyond what some may take to be his rather naïve faith in the power of the syllogism. In this respect, far from leaving Montaigne behind, he will draw closer to him.

We stated earlier that the two major arguments presented by the deist and the atheist in the *Pensées philosophiques* are not subjected to any dialectical examination in that work. Diderot apparently was attached in some degree to each one and was as yet unable, or unwilling, to give suitable counter-arguments to either, leaving it to the reader to make up his own mind. In the *Promenade du sceptique* (1747), a third contender, the Spinozist, is opposed to the deist and the atheist.

The most important section of this work is the " Allée des Maronniers ", the Skeptics' Lane. It is here, under Montaigne's banner, that the debates between Athéos (the atheist) and Cléobule (the deist), and between Cléobule and the Spinozist take place. The deist's argument is essentially the same one that had been presented in the *Pensées philosophiques*. But this time it is answered by Athéos, who exposes the anthropocentric presumption of deism. He denies Cléobule's assertion that the existence of God may be inferred from the organization of matter, which in itself proves nothing but that matter is organized. Diderot supplies no convincing refutation of Athéos' objections to deism ; nor does Athéos present any new argument in favor of atheism. If Diderot is unwilling to commit himself to atheism at this point, it is because he has as yet found no suitable substitute for God in his world-picture. Thus, although he perceives the objections to deism, he is not prepared to forsake the concept of Deity.

The concluding argument of Oribaze, the Spinozist, should not necessarily be taken as the expression of Diderot's Spinozism.[1] Rather,

---

[1] In 1949, Vartanian expressed the opinion that " Diderot's inclination towards Spinozism should not be taken in any sense as a sympathy with

it serves to give deism the coup de grâce. The deist had been termed an enthusiast by Athéos, who, however, was not able to defend his own position. Oribaze now confounds Cléobule with a systematic, syllogistic proof of pantheist monism. One such chain of reasoning, however, is hardly sufficient to prove an entire philosophic system. It should therefore not be taken at face value; it is an obvious attempt to imitate the Spinozist style of demonstration.[1] Indeed, immediately following the exposition of this argument, a cloud passes in front of the sun, blotting it out, plunging the landscape in darkness. While we do not wish to insist on the concept of " pathetic fallacy ", perhaps Diderot's answer to the deist and to the pantheist as well is the darkness and silence of the void.

In the *Promenade*, then, Diderot does not fully embrace any one of the philosophic positions represented by his imaginary interlocutors. Here again, as in the *Pensées philosophiques*, Diderot's real position is not to be seen in an apparent victory of one interlocutor over the others, but in his skeptical hesitation in choosing from among them. He has left Christianity behind, has all but abandoned deism and is toying with atheism and pantheism, but remains as yet uncommitted. We would be inclined to agree with Niklaus that Diderot, " qui possède son Montaigne, termine la Promenade en faveur du Sceptique, et son spinozisme marque seulement un pas dans le sens du naturalisme ".[2]

The *Lettre sur les aveugles* (1749) may be considered as representing the culmination of Diderot's exploratory period. Here, with the reader's indulgence, we shall recall the " que sais-je ? " with which Diderot concludes this work :

De ce que nos sens ne sont pas en contradiction sur les formes, s'ensuit-il qu'elles nous soient mieux connues ? Qui nous a dit que nous n'avons point affaire à de faux témoins ? Nous jugeons pourtant. Hélas ! madame, quand on a mis les connaissances humaines dans la balance de Montaigne, on n'est pas éloigné de prendre sa devise. Car, que savons-nous ? ce que c'est que la matière ? nullement ; ce que c'est que l'esprit et la pensée ? encore moins ; ce que c'est que le mouvement, l'espace et la durée ? point du tout. ... Nous ne savons donc presque rien. (*Œuvres phil.*, p. 146.)

In his doubt concerning the reliability of the senses to provide us with knowledge of reality, and in his dialectical examination of sensa-

---

that thought in essence " (" From Deist to Atheist ", p. 55). By contrast, Arthur Wilson, in 1957, writes that Diderot " comes to rest " in the *Promenade* at a " half-way station " (Pantheism) between deism and atheism *(Diderot: The Testing Years*, p. 63). I disagree with the latter view.

[1] Cf. Paul VERNIÈRE (*Spinoza et la pensée française...*, p. 571), who takes as evidence of Diderot's " engagement personnel " what may only be his irony. That Diderot repeated this argument in almost identical form in his famous letter to Voltaire of June 11, 1749, is not sufficient evidence that it represents his own belief in the *Promenade*. Certainly Diderot was careful not to offend the Patriarch of Ferney, who could be expected to accommodate himself more readily to Spinozism than to atheism.

[2] Robert NIKLAUS, ed. *Lettre sur les aveugles* (Genève, 1951), p. xviii.

tionalism, empiricism and innate ideas, Diderot is the disciple of the author of the " Apologie de Raimond Sebond ". Once again, however, one should not overlook the tiny word " presque ". Diderot's use of Montaigne's motto is less an expression of total skepticism than an evidence of Diderot's exasperation at being unable to answer the questions he raises. The suspended judgment of the skeptic does not satisfy his thirst for certainties, even if they be provisional ones destined to be contradicted. As J. R. Loy remarks : " Diderot's *devise* was not precisely Montaigne's ; not ' que sais-je ? ' ... but rather ' que [de choses] me reste-t-il encore à savoir ! ' " [1]

It is clear that Diderot's skepticism is already of a different stamp than that of Montaigne, for he refuses to accept the essayist's " doux et mol chevet " with respect to knowledge of externals. Twenty years later, in the *Entretien entre d'Alembert et Diderot*, he will doubt that the skeptic's suspension of judgment is psychologically possible. This question is related in his mind to the problem of the freedom of in-difference :

Diderot. — Croyez-vous qu'il y ait une seule question discutée sur laquelle un homme reste avec une égale et rigoureuse mesure de raison pour et contre ?
D'Alembert. — Non, ce serait l'âne de Buridan.
Diderot. — En ce cas, il n'y a donc point de sceptique, puisqu'à l'exception des questions de mathématiques, qui ne comportent pas la moindre incertitude, il y a du pour et du contre dans toutes les autres. La balance n'est donc jamais égale, et il est impossible qu'elle ne penche pas du côté où nous croyons le plus de vraisemblance.
D'Alembert. — Mais je vois le matin la vraisemblance à ma droite, et l'après-midi elle est à ma gauche.
Diderot. — C'est-à-dire que vous êtes dogmatique pour, le matin, et dogmatique contre, l'après-midi.
D'Alembert. — Et le soir, quand je me rappelle cette inconstance si rapide de mes jugements, je ne crois rien, ni du matin, ni de l'après-midi.
Diderot. — C'est-à-dire que vous ne vous rappelez plus la prépondérance des deux opinions entre lesquelles vous avez oscillé ; que cette prépondérance vous paraît trop légère pour asseoir un sentiment fixe, et que vous prenez le parti de ne plus vous occuper de sujets aussi problématiques, d'en abandonner la discussion aux autres, et de n'en pas disputer davantage.
D'Alembert. — Cela se peut.
Diderot. — Mais si quelqu'un vous tirait à l'écart, et vous questionnant d'amitié, vous demandait, en conscience, des deux partis quel est celui où vous trouvez le moins de difficultés, de bonne foi seriez-vous embarrassé de répondre, et réaliseriez-vous l'âne de Buridan ?
D'Alembert. — Je crois que non. (*Œuvres phil.*, p. 282f.)

There is undoubtedly in this exchange a strong element of irony directed at d'Alembert, in preparation for the dream which follows.

---

[1] J. Robert Loy, " Nature, Reason, Enlightenment ", in *Studies on Voltaire and the Eighteenth Century*, XXVI, ed. Theodore Besterman (Geneva, 1963), 1104. The bracketed phrase is Loy's.

The mental portrait here presented is one of inconstancy of judgment and oscillation between contradictory extremes. True belief is defined only as habitual disposition :

> Tenez, mon ami, si vous y pensez bien, vous trouverez qu'en tout, notre véritable sentiment n'est pas celui dans lequel nous n'avons jamais vacillé, mais celui auquel nous sommes le plus habituellement revenus. *(Ibid.)*

Diderot is, of course, speaking from experience ; he has found skepticism, in this sense of the term, to be fundamentally at odds with his nature.

Even his critique of skepticism, however, has a parallel in Montaigne's *Essais*. In " Comme nostre esprit s'empesche soy-mesmes ", Montaigne is amused by the " plaisante imagination de concevoir un esprit balancé justement entre deux pareilles envyes " (II, xiv, 689). Considering the given terms of the problem, " qui nous logeroit entre le bouteille et le jambon, avec egal appetit de boire et de menger, il n'y auroit sans doute remede que de mourir de soif et de fain " *(ibid.,* p. 690). In other words, it is the scholastic problem of Buridan's ass. But Montaigne rejects the answer of the Stoics, that the impulse to choose is external, accidental and fortuitous : " Il se pourroit dire, ce me semble, plustost, que aucune chose ne se presente à nous où il n'y ait quelque difference, pour legiere qu'elle soit ; et que, ou à la veue ou à l'atouchement, il y a tousjours quelque plus qui nous attire, quoy que ce soit imperceptiblement " *(ibid.).* For Montaigne, as for Diderot, the scale is never exactly balanced. His answer to the problem is the same. That is to say, both reject the problem as given because it sets up conditions which are incompatible with the complexity of reality, conditions which are artificial because they are imposed by reason and do not meet the test of experience.

We have said that Diderot's skepticism is essentially positive ; it leads him further out of himself and into the world. In general, Montaigne's skepticism is far more pervasive ; yet it too has its limits, for the " que sais-je ? " is not a negation nor an affirmation, but rather a query. It is a warning against the mind's presumption ; against prejudice, precipitation and the dogmatism of system ; against all attempts to reduce the complexity of truth to simplistic, all-embracing propositions. It testifies to Montaigne's inherently open and inquiring mind. For him, too, skepticism is a dialectically necessary step in the development of his thought—from the denial and negation of life to its acceptance and affirmation. To consider the particular form that skepticism takes in the " Apologie " as Montaigne's definitive intellectual position is to neglect the more profound insights that emerge in the later essays of Book III. His skepticism in the " Apologie ", like that of Diderot in his early works, is, in a sense, a first step towards truth.

The world in flux

Recently, scholars have begun to have reservations about Villey's term " skeptical crisis " in the evolution of Montaigne's *Essais*. Skepti-

cism in Montaigne may be viewed less as a crisis than as a constant factor in his intellectual temper. Donald Frame, for example, has characterized Montaigne's skepticism as going far back into the man : he is skeptical in the etymological sense of being capable of viewing all sides of a question before making an intellectual commitment; skeptical in that the diversity, the unlikeness of things, impresses him more than the similarities; skeptical in his conviction that the human mind can arrive at no absolutes by dint of our contingent nature and the impermanence of all terrestrial existence.[1]

The conclusion of the " Apologie " evokes a world in perpetual flux. Subject to the same instability as external reality, the mind is incapable of reaching beyond itself, either in the physical or in the metaphysical world. Albert Thibaudet reduces Montaigne's so-called Pyrrhonism essentially to this awareness of movement and change : " Le pyrrhonisme, chez Montaigne comme chez ses prédécesseurs grecs, n'est autre qu'un mobilisme, un accent mis sur le changement, une intuition du monde comme d'une chose qui change et qui dure, ou plutôt d'un changement et d'une durée qui ne sont pas ' chose '." [2] This " mobilisme " may be what Georges May had in mind when he spoke of the " sentiment de complexité que [Diderot] a hérité de Montaigne ".[3] Henri Peyre, in a bold stroke, sees this sense of mobility as the filiation connecting Heraclitus, Montaigne, Diderot and Romanticism : " One of the most momentous discoveries of mankind, first anticipated by Heraclitus and driven to its fullest consequences by Diderot and the German romantics, may be credited in its modern formulation to Montaigne : the rejection of being in favor of becoming, of *l'être* in order to delineate what changes, *le passage.*" [4] Of course, such a statement has validity only as a broad view of the constants in human thought. Yet it suggests a specific link between Montaigne's method of self-portrayal and Diderot's intuitions of organic nature.

The closing pages of the " Apologie " and the opening paragraphs of " Du repentir " (III, ii) are the classic statements of Montaigne's " Heraklitisches Weltbild ".[5] *Branler, branle, branloire, mutation, varieté, discordance, dissemblance, ondoyant, divers* — these are key words in the *Essais,* appearing throughout the book with unfailing frequency. Movement is almost an obsession with Montaigne. It is the essential characteristic of his subjective landscape. All is floating, vague, uncertain, in continual vicissitude. Man, a creature of constant change, can have no knowledge of the world or of himself because of the flux of both subject and object :

[1] Donald M. FRAME, *Montaigne's Discovery of Man* (New York, 1955), p. 8.

[2] Albert THIBAUDET, " Montaigne au Portugal ", *Candide* (April 6, 1933). Quoted in Floyd GRAY, *Le Style de Montaigne* (Paris, 1958), p. 196.

[3] Georges MAY, *Quatre Visages de Denis Diderot* (Paris, 1951), p. 151.

[4] Henri PEYRE, *Literature and Sincerity* (New Haven, 1963), p. 38.

[5] Hugo FRIEDRICH, *Montaigne* (Berne, 1949), p. 173.

Finalement, il n'y a aucune constante existence, ny de nostre estre, ny de celuy des objects. Et nous, et nostre jugement, et toutes choses mortelles, vont coulant et roulant sans cesse. Ainsi il ne se peut establir rien de certain de l'un à l'autre, et le jugeant et le jugé estans en continuelle mutation et branle.

Nous n'avons aucune communication à l'estre, par ce que toute humaine nature est toujours au milieu entre le naistre et le mourir, ne baillant de soy qu'une obscure apparence et ombre, et une incertaine et debile opinion. (*Essais*, II, xii, 679f.)

The cosmic vision that Montaigne evokes in the " Apologie " is of nature, on the one hand, in continual " mutation et branle " ; and of God, on the other, unchanging, immobile and eternal. God alone is exempt from the perpetual oscillation between extremes, the continual passage between life and death. He is the stable counterpoise in the moving, mutable universe ; but there can be no communication with him, except perhaps through grace. The consequences of such a world-view are first of all negative. Montaigne renounces the attempt to understand the complexity of nature. An ingenious commingling of contrary qualities, any seeming similarities can only be misleading :

La consequence que nous voulons tirer de la ressemblance des evenemens est mal seure, d'autant qu'ils sont tousjours dissemblables ; il n'est aucune qualité si universelle en cette image des choses que la diversité et varieté. ... La ressemblance ne faict pas tant un comme la difference faict autre. Nature s'est obligée à ne rien faire autre, qui ne fust dissemblable. (*Essais*, III, xiii, 1195.)

Thus, in Montaigne's view, nature tends towards the discrete and the discontinuous. He is skeptical of the validity of general laws, abstractions, or analogies by means of which reality may be reduced to simpler parts and ultimately to unity.

This acute perception of the flux of nature arouses in some thinkers the equally acute sense of their own immutability. The mind exists then as the single powerful principle of unity and stability in a world that is never the same. The mind constitutes order in the midst of chaos, resists the torrent that seeks to drag it along towards the abyss. Such a mind creates vast systems of thought, embracing the diversity of events until it becomes larger than the universe, because it comprehends the universe and includes it within itself.

Montaigne's mind was not of such a cast. He preferred to see diversity rather than similarity, and to accept an incomprehensible universe rather than one reduced to his own scale. He did not erect a system of thought that would explain the inexplicable multiplicity of experience. On the contrary, he was acutely aware of the flux within himself.

Paradoxically, it is precisely in this failure to construct a rational, systematic synthesis that Montaigne's great achievement lies. What Montaigne perceives as his negative characteristics—his inconsistency, his inconstancy, his contradictoriness—later become the object of his study and are transformed into positive, and eminently human,

qualities. Montaigne comes to view man as God's imperfect creation: a creature who *is* not, but who embodies almost limitless possibility. Montaigne gradually becomes aware of his changed attitude towards himself and his book. It is fully apparent in the opening paragraph of "Du repentir" (III, ii), that celebrated passage in which Montaigne's apprehension of the flux of matter and that of his inner being are inseparable and seem intertwined in the very structure of the sentences:

Les autres forment l'homme; je le recite et en represente un particulier bien mal formé, et lequel, si j'avoy à façonner de nouveau, je ferois vraiment bien autre qu'il n'est. Mes-huy c'est fait. Or les traits de ma peinture ne forvoyent point, quoy qu'ils se changent et diversifient. Le monde n'est qu'une branloire perenne. Toutes choses y branlent sans cesse: la terre, les rochers du Caucase, les pyramides d'Ægypte, et du branle public et du leur. La constance mesme n'est autre chose qu'un branle plus languissant. Je ne puis assurer mon object. Il va trouble et chancelant, d'une yvresse naturelle. Je le prens en ce point, comme il est, en l'instant que je m'amuse à luy. Je ne peints pas l'estre. Je peints le passage: non un passage d'aage en autre, ou, comme dict le peuple, de sept en sept ans, mais de jour en jour, de minute en minute. (P. 899.)

Montaigne's universe is in continual flux, for underlying all things, even those that appear most solid and unshakable, is a secret shifting motion that prevents all that exists from belonging to that which truly *is*. How much more unstable therefore is a human being! What characterizes nature is change and diversity to the point of contradiction, because Montaigne's universe exists in time and thus cannot be said to *be* ("je ne peints pas l'estre"), but only to be in process of *becoming* ("je peints le passage").

The world is expressed as phenomena in temporal succession which in their unaccountable disorder constitute the very truth of reality. Nature and human nature are analogous in that they are both subject to the temporal process of change. For Montaigne, the "essence" of existence is change. When he claims to be depicting "passage", he means that the subject of his book is not being, but process, of which the *Essais* are the record. Thus Montaigne cannot speak of Man *sub specie æternitatis* ("les autres forment l'homme"); he can but recount his careful observations of himself ("je le recite").

But such a recounting, such a record of change, is in itself an attempt to give form to the formless, to give permanence to the ephemeral, to endow that which consists only in passage with the quality of being. At the same time that Montaigne is fascinated by the dynamics of becoming, he is equally at pains to seize hold of his Protean self, to calm its agitation, to achieve a state of harmony. It would be inaccurate to say that Montaigne rejects being, to take him at his word when he states: "Je ne peints pas l'estre. Je peints le passage." Rather, what Montaigne depicts is the paradox of being and becoming. True being for the human being is not to be conceived in the abstract; that is the condition of Deity. The human condition consists in the perpetual

activity of thought upon the raw material of existence. The paradox is that time becomes for Montaigne the source of being : being consists in becoming. The self can only be fully realized as consisting of a multiplicity of potential selves immanent in the passage of each successive moment.[1]

The *Essais* become the reconstitution of the totality of the self in its incessant vicissitudes. Montaigne's intuition of mobility convinces him of the futility of human knowledge, but it eventually leads him to self-knowledge and to communication with being through self-reflection.

Now, Diderot's awareness of complexity and mobility leads him to quite opposite conclusions. His early skepticism gives way to conviction and adherence to vitalist materialism. The latter is not unrelated in its general philosophical orientation to the Heraclitean tradition carried forward by Montaigne. We now propose to examine Diderot's " mobilisme " in parallel with that of Montaigne.

The *Lettre sur les aveugles*, in addition to being the final work of Diderot's skeptical period, is also the true continuation of what was merely latent in *Pensée* xxi of the *Pensées philosophiques*, and which comes to full fruition in the *Rêve de d'Alembert*. It is thus a transitional work bridging the gap between Diderot's preliminary skepticism and his adoption of a set of positive principles. The blind Saunderson presents a fuller development of the Lucretian argument of *Pensée* xxi and at last fully refutes the deistic argument from design. He is free from the prejudices of those who see and thus is a better qualified spokesman for the atheistic point of view. His lyric imagination evokes images of worlds bypassed and yet to come, in a universe composed of capricious and mobile matter :

Combien de mondes estropiés, manqués, se sont dissipés, se reforment et se dissipent peut-être à chaque instant dans des espaces éloignés, où je ne touche point, et où vous ne voyez pas, mais où le mouvement continue et continuera de combiner des amas de matière, jusqu'à ce qu'ils aient obtenu quelque arrangement dans lequel ils puissent persévérer ? O philosophes ! transportez-vous donc avec moi sur les confins de cet univers, au-delà du point où je touche, et où vous voyez des êtres organisés ; promenez-vous sur ce nouvel océan, et cherchez à travers ses agitations irrégulières quelques vestiges de cet être intelligent dont vous admirez ici la sagesse ! (*Œuvres phil.*, p. 123.)

Saunderson, the *illuminé*, in a moment of quasi-religious ecstasy, has an insight into the order of the universe, which is the rebuttal to the Christian as well as to the deist and the Spinozist. He takes us into outer space, to the edges of a cosmos far beyond the limits of our poor sense organs. He places man in a world of which he is no longer the center, a world which has not been designed for him by a benevolent Providence. The order the deist observes is illusory ; the Spinozist's absolutes are artificial abstractions. Eternity is an illusion of the moment. To comprehend the order of the world, one must abandon

---

[1] See Georges POULET, *Etudes sur le temps humain* (Paris, 1950), pp. 1-15.

one's imagination to the incessant mobility of matter, follow it in its groping, its trial-and-error, its monstrous failures as well as its successes.

What is true in space is true on earth itself. There is no need to imagine other worlds when we can observe the same dynamism of matter all around us, if we but observe with an unprejudiced eye :

Mais à quoi bon vous tirer de votre élément ? Qu'est-ce que ce monde, monsieur Holmes ? Un composé sujet à des révolutions, qui toutes indiquent une tendance continuelle à la destruction ; une succession rapide d'êtres qui s'entresuivent, se poussent et disparaissent ; une symétrie passagère ; un ordre momentané. Je vous reprochais tout à l'heure d'estimer la perfection des choses par votre capacité ; et je pourrais vous accuser ici d'en mesurer la durée sur celle de vos jours. Vous jugez de l'existence successive du monde, comme la mouche éphémère de la vôtre. Le monde est éternel pour vous, comme vous êtes éternel pour l'être qui ne vit qu'un instant. Encore l'insecte est-il plus raisonnable que vous. Quelle suite prodigieuse de générations d'éphémères atteste votre éternité ! quelle tradition immense ! Cependant nous passerons tous, sans qu'on puisse assigner ni l'étendue réelle que nous occupons, ni le temps précis que nous aurons duré. Le temps, la matière et l'espace ne sont peut-être qu'un point. *(Ibid.)*

No stable order may be imposed on a universe in continual flux. Our very conceptions of time, space and matter are perhaps nothing more than the ephemeral aspects of the instant. Indeed, " le repos absolu est un concept abstrait qui n'existe point en nature ".[1] Diderot sees the world in constant process of being destroyed and remade :

J'arrête mes yeux sur l'amas général des corps ; je vois tout en action et en réaction ; tout se détruisant sous une forme ; tout se recomposant sous une autre ; des sublimations, des dissolutions, des combinaisons de toutes les espèces, phénomènes incompatibles avec l'homogénéité de la matière ; d'où je conclus qu'elle est hétérogène ; qu'il existe une infinité d'éléments divers dans la nature ; que chacun de ces éléments, par sa diversité, a sa force particulière, innée, immuable, éternelle, indestructible ; et que ces forces intimes au corps ont leurs actions hors du corps : d'où naît le mouvement ou plutôt la fermentation générale dans l'univers.[2]

This " fermentation générale " extends throughout the universe ; it involves the interlacing of all levels of matter, organic and inanimate.

The dreaming d'Alembert, in spite of his incoherence, sketches Diderot's version of the Heraclitean flux, in which we recognize also the concept of the " chain of being " :

Tous les êtres circulent les uns dans les autres, par conséquent toutes les espèces... tout est en un flux perpétuel. ... Tout animal est plus ou moins homme ; tout minéral est plus ou moins plante ; toute plante est plus ou moins animal. Il n'y a rien de précis en nature. ... Toute chose est plus ou

---

[1] *Eléments de physiologie*, A-T, IX, 154. For Montaigne as well, absolute rest is a meaningless concept : " La constance mesme n'est autre chose qu'un branle plus languissant " (*Essais*, III, ii, 899).

[2] *Principes philosophiques sur la matière et le mouvement*, in *Œuvres philosophiques*, p. 398.

moins une chose quelconque, plus ou moins terre, plus ou moins eau, plus ou moins air, plus ou moins feu ; plus ou moins d'un règne ou d'un autre ... donc rien n'est de l'essence d'un être particulier. ... Non, sans doute, puisqu'il n'y a aucune qualité dont aucun être ne soit participant. (*Œuvres phil.*, pp. 311f.)

The principle of continuity, one of the leading ideas of the Enlightenment, is an important concept to which Diderot returns again and again.[1] Contrary to Montaigne, the keywords in Diderot's writings are not those which denote difference and diversity. Whether it be with respect to natural philosophy, ethics or aesthetics, Diderot speaks constantly of *rapports, enchaînement, le tout.* The obstacle in the way of knowledge of the universe is not that everything is *ondoyant et divers*, but that everything is so interrelated, " qu'il semble que pour parler pertinemment d'une aiguille, il faudrait posséder la science universelle " (A-T, IV, 22). Although Diderot instinctively abandons skeptical doubt and is confident regarding the capacity of human reason to acquire knowledge of the world, there is a residual skepticism underlying his rationalism. It takes the form of a sense of complexity, which does not rest upon the perception of difference but upon continuity : " Pour nous, nous conclurons que tout étant lié dans la nature, il n'y a rien, à proprement parler, dont l'homme ait une connaissance parfaite, absolue, complète, pas même des axiomes les plus évidents, parce qu'il faudrait qu'il eût la connaissance de tout " (A-T, XVI, 491).

Although Montaigne insists on the discontinuity between the nature of man and the nature of God, and although he seems by temperament more sensitive to difference than to resemblance, by the third book of the *Essais* Montaigne comes more and more to recognize similarity where earlier he had seen only difference. In " De l'experience " he sees resemblance and diversity as two aspects of the same underlying unity : " Comme nul evenement et nulle forme ressemble entierement à une autre, aussi ne differe nulle de l'autre entierement. Ingenieux meslange de nature " (*Essais*, III, xiii, 1200).

Diderot's vitalist materialism in the *Rêve* has much in common with the ideas of Heraclitus, with which Montaigne was imbued. There are no absolute opposites ; everything intermingles, flows into everything else. Antinomies do not remain in static, diametric opposition, but coexist in harmony : " Men do not know how what is at variance agrees with itself. It is an attunement of opposite tensions, like that of the bow and the lyre." [2] The outlines separating one thing from another are blurred, all sharpness of difference falling away in the flux of the

---

[1] See A. O. LOVEJOY, *The Great Chain of Being* (Cambridge, Mass., 1936). Cf. Ernst Cassirer for whom " continuity means unity in multiplicity, being in becoming, constancy in change. It signifies a connection which becomes manifest only in change and amid the unceasing mutation of qualities—a connection, therefore, which requires diversity just as fundamentally as unity " (*Philosophy of the Enlightenment* [Boston, 1955], p. 30).

[2] HERACLITUS, fragment 45, text reproduced in John Burnet, *Early Greek Philosophy*, 4th ed. (1930).

whole. Montaigne recognizes the antithetical nature of truth: " Il n'y a raison qui n'en aye une contraire, dict le plus sage party des philosophes " (*Essais*, II, xv, 690). Diderot inherits this aspect of the essayist's skepticism: " S'il n'est point de questions qui n'en aient pour et contre, et presque toujours à égale mesure, pourquoi tranchons-nous si vite? "[1] Hence the inherent inadequacy of logical schematizations. For reality does not answer to the preconceptions of the mind. The systematic mind runs the risk of falsifying the truth of reality, which can only consist of a total truth and not a partial, dogmatic truth abstracted from the rest of things. Every system is by nature such an abstraction, for it is selective, necessarily choosing certain aspects of reality and neglecting or ignoring others.

It is here, in their opposition to systematic logic, that Montaigne and Diderot join each other. Montaigne's critique of knowledge and Diderot's distrust of systematic thought both stem from their intuition of change. For both Montaigne and Diderot, any rigid adherence to system, to single-minded formulation of truth, must be equated with dogmatism. The only means of approaching the truth of reality is by maintaining a flexibility of mind and of thought which corresponds to the fleeting, changing character of nature. The only kind of thought which can hope to comprehend the infinite diversity of the universe, its constant mutation and flux, is a thought which itself changes, adapts, evolves, and unfolds in time. The criteria of truth forbid static formulations. Truth reflects the dynamism, the organic quality of nature.

De l'Interprétation de la nature (1754) has been termed " le Discours de la méthode du XVIIIe siècle ".[2] However, such a formula may be somewhat misleading. Diderot's skepticism is a methodological doubt closer to that of Montaigne and Bayle than to Cartesianism.[3] Will G. Moore has suggested the influence of Montaigne's essay " De l'experience " upon Diderot's empiricism.[4] This is perhaps fanciful, although

---

[1] *Pensées phil.*, *Œuvres phil.*, p. 24. We discuss below, pp. 127-131, Montaigne's and Diderot's use of dialogue.

[2] Jean Luc, *Diderot* (Paris, 1938), p. 107. Quoted in Vernière edition of *Œuvres philosophiques*, p. 167.

[3] Cf. Norman Torrey's comment on a censored portion of the " Pyrrhonienne " article: " This passage describes a methodical doubt quite different in conception and purpose from that of Descartes. Both Bayle and Diderot would have ascribed it to their acknowledged master in skepticism, Montaigne " (Douglas H. Gordon and Norman L. Torrey, *The Censoring of Diderot's Encyclopédie and the Re-Established Text* [New York, 1947], p. 51). The censored passage (referring to Bayle) is the following: " pour pallier son pyrrhonisme, lorsqu'il l'établissait, c'était toujours sous prétexte de ramener la révélation qu'il savait bien sapper, quand l'occasion s'en présentait. Il faisait alternativement l'apologie de la raison contre l'autorité, et de l'autorité contre la raison, bien sûr que les hommes ne se départiraient pas de leur apanage et de leur liberté, en faveur d'un joug qui les importunait et qu'ils ne demandaient pas mieux que de secouer. Il savait trop pour tout croire, ou pour douter de tout."

[4] " Montaigne's Notion of Experience ", in *The French Mind: Studies in honour of Gustave Rudler* (Oxford, 1952), pp. 34-52.

the possibility of Diderot's having absorbed the wisdom of this essay is by no means unimaginable. Vartanian has presented a convincing case for the direct influence of Cartesian and Newtonian-Baconian thought in the *Interprétation de la nature,* and suggests that the scientific naturalism of Diderot and his circle resulted from the synthesis of the " Cartesian-Newtonian polarity ".[1]

We do not propose to demonstrate the direct influence of Montaigne upon Diderot on the specific question of scientific method. Such an attempt would represent an obvious *contre-sens.* Montaigne renounces the possibility of man's understanding nature. For him, experience is not experimentalism. Experience is something felt or perceived in an immediate and lively way, with the force of personal acquaintance or participation ; it is a knowledge of things acquired through long use and practice ; it is knowledge not of nature, but of the nature of living. What does concern us is the fact that, despite Montaigne's lack of interest in the investigation of nature, Diderot views Montaigne's method in the *Essais* as fundamentally experimental and applicable to the study of nature as well as to self-study.

In the foreword to *De l'Interprétation de la nature,* Diderot follows Montaigne in his warning " Aux jeunes gens qui se disposent à l'étude de la philosophie naturelle " :

Jeune homme, prends et lis. Si tu peux aller jusqu'à la fin de cet ouvrage, tu ne sera pas incapable d'en entendre un meilleur. Comme je me suis moins proposé de t'instruire que de t'exercer, il n'importe peu que tu adoptes mes idées ou que tu les rejettes, pourvu qu'elles emploient toute ton attention. Un plus habile t'apprendra à connaître les forces de la nature ; il me suffira de t'avoir fait essayer les tiennes. Adieu. (*Œuvres phil.*, p. 175.)

These lines breathe the spirit of the *Essais* in the tone of intimacy with which Diderot addresses the reader (" prends et lis "), and the Montaignean verbs " exercer " and " essayer ", as opposed to " instruire " and " apprendre ", remind one of Montaigne's pedagogical ideas, his insistence not on the acquisition of so-called truths but on the proper exercise and formation of judgment. There is a disarming air of modesty, of the tentative and provisional, of the unpremeditated, the fortuitous and the unsystematic, which recalls Montaigne. Indeed, following an oblique reference to the essayist, Diderot avows his own ignorance and underlines the importance of such avowals in scientific investigation :

Une grande leçon qu'on a souvent occasion de donner, c'est l'aveu de son insuffisance. Ne vaut-il pas mieux se concilier la confiance des autres, par la sincérité d'un *je n'en sais rien,* que de balbutier des mots, et se faire pitié à soi-même, en s'efforçant de tout expliquer? Celui qui confesse librement qu'il ne sait pas ce qu'il ignore, me dispose à croire ce dont il entreprend de me rendre raison. (*Ibid.*, p. 186.) [2]

---

[1] Aram VARTANIAN, *Diderot and Descartes* (Princeton, 1953), *passim.*

[2] Cf. *Essais*, I, 1, 339 : " Je ne voy le tout de rien : Ne font pas, ceux qui promettent de nous le faire veoir."

Diderot follows Montaigne in warning the interpreter of nature against being caught up in the seductiveness of his own systems: " *Laidem habeto, dummodo te Lais non habeat.* C'est un conseil que je donnerais encore à ceux qui ont l'esprit assez étendu pour imaginer des systèmes, et qui sont assez opulents pour les vérifier par l'expérience : ayez un système, j'y consens ; mais ne vous en laissez pas dominer " (*ibid.*, p. 195).

But the main difficulty confronting the interpreter of nature is the fact that nature embodies processes of change. The perception of an underlying order in the universe is vitiated by the very nature of reality. " Nature " is defined as " le résultat général actuel, ou les résultats généraux successifs de la combinaison des éléments " (*ibid.*, p. 239). The introduction of temporal succession in his definition of nature creates a number of problems of which Diderot is aware in attempting to develop a philosophy of science. First of all, without unity and continuity in nature there can be no knowledge, for knowledge requires the perception of unity in multiplicity : " Si les phénomènes ne sont pas enchaînés les uns aux autres, il n'y a point de philosophie " (*ibid.*, p. 240). Secondly, how is it possible to have knowledge of that which changes and passes? " Les phénomènes seraient tous enchaînés, que l'état de chacun d'eux pourrait être sans permanence " *(ibid.).* But such *enchaînement* is not static ; it must be thought of as " temporalized ". Finally, if nature is a process of continual destruction and renewal, how can we presume to observe it from our ephemeral, prejudiced point in time? " Mais si l'état des êtres est dans une vicissitude perpétuelle ; si la nature est encore à l'ouvrage, malgré la chaîne qui lie les phénomènes, il n'y a point de philosophie. Toute notre science naturelle devient aussi transitoire que les mots. Ce que nous prenons pour l'histoire de la nature n'est que l'histoire très incomplète d'un instant " *(ibid.).*

Diderot is aware of the implicit contradiction between a materialist determinism and a doctrine of organic evolution which implies a finalism.[1] Although he has moved beyond skepticism, there persists a doubt as to the validity of our attempts to describe nature : " Après avoir médité profondément sur certains phénomènes, un doute qu'on vous pardonnerait peut-être, ô sceptiques, ce n'est pas que le monde ait été créé, mais qu'il soit tel qu'il a été et qu'il sera " (*ibid.*, p. 241). This is essentially Montaigne's doubt in man's capacity to communicate with Being, the spuriousness of all man's attempts to view the world *sub specie æternitatis.* Like Montaigne, Diderot guards against such a point of view ; for him, the world is remade with each passing moment : " C'est que tout tient dans la nature, et que celui qui suppose un nouveau phénomène ou ramène un instant passé, recrée un nouveau monde " (*Entretien entre d'Alembert et Diderot, Œuvres phil.*, p. 269). Never was Diderot more clearly conscious, as was Montaigne, of the relativity of

---

[1] VERNIÈRE, ed. *Œuvres phil.*, p. 240 fn.

truth and the immense disproportion between the magnitude of the world and that of the human understanding:

L'entendement a ses préjugés; le sens, son incertitude; la mémoire, ses limites; l'imagination, ses lueurs; les instruments, leur imperfection. Les phénomènes sont infinis; les causes, cachées; les formes, peut-être transitoires. Nous n'avons contre tant d'obstacles que nous trouvons en nous, et que la nature nous oppose au dehors, qu'une expérience lente, qu'une réflexion bornée. Voilà les léviers avec lesquels la philosophie s'est proposé de remuer le monde. (*Interprétation, ibid.*, p. 192.)

Working with such imperfect instruments, the interpreter of nature does not erect a *système de la nature* or compose a *traité*, abstract constructions to which the observations of reality are made to conform. Diderot chooses an unsystematic presentation in *De l'Interprétation de la nature;* it is not methodical but almost haphazard: "C'est de la nature que je vais écrire. Je laisserai les pensées se succéder sous ma plume, dans l'ordre même selon lequel les objets se sont offerts à ma réflexion; parce qu'elles n'en représenteront que mieux les mouvements et la marche de mon esprit" (*ibid.*, p. 177). The mind as interpreter of nature must permit itself to participate in the processes of matter in movement, must itself as a phenomenon interact with other phenomena. It is a reciprocal movement of subject and object.

But such an effort to comprehend nature requires an abandonment to the irrationality of the universe. By leaving oneself open to chance, one avoids becoming the prisoner of one's preconceptions, one exchanges the arbitrariness of chance for that of one's private constructions. The interpreter of nature is one who possesses precisely this quality of being free from prejudice. It is a quality of mind, an "esprit de divination" by means of which "on *subodore*, pour ainsi dire, des procédés inconnus, des expériences nouvelles, des résultats ignorés" (*ibid.*, p. 197), a facility for perceiving subtle oppositions and analogies and the ability both to isolate these perceptions and to consider them in combination. The interplay of perception and memory, of experience and reason, is, in the mind of the interpreter of nature, "une histoire fidèle de toutes les extravagances apparentes qui lui ont passé par la tête. Je dis *extravagances*; car quel autre nom donner à cet enchaînement de conjectures fondées sur des oppositions ou des ressemblances si éloignées, si imperceptibles, que les rêves d'un malade ne paraissent ni plus bizarres, ni plus décousus?" (*Ibid.*)

Now, if we turn to the "Pyrrhonienne" article, we find an analysis of the associative processes of the mind of which the *Essais* are the "image fidèle", an analysis which recalls the very same terms of the above passage from "*De l'Interprétation de la nature*":

[Montaigne] n'est ni plus lié, ni plus décousu en écrivant qu'en pensant ou en rêvant; or il est impossible que l'homme qui pense ou qui rêve soit tout à fait décousu. Il faudrait qu'un effet pût cesser sans cause, et qu'un autre effet pût commencer subitement et de lui-même. Il y a une liaison

nécessaire entre les deux pensées les plus disparates ; cette liaison est, ou dans la sensation, ou dans les mots, ou dans la mémoire, ou au dedans, ou au dehors de l'homme. C'est une règle à laquelle les fous même sont assujettis dans leur plus grand désordre de raison. Si nous avions l'histoire complète de tout ce qui se passe en eux, nous verrions que tout y tient, ainsi que dans l'homme le plus sage et le plus sensé. (A-T, XVI, 485.)

Montaigne's method in the *Essais* is an example of the intimation of reality that forms part of the experimental method described in *De l'Interprétation de la nature*. Certainly, Montaigne cannot be credited with an interest in science or in the investigation of nature. Diderot was well aware of this. Nevertheless, he looked upon Montaigne's method of self-investigation as valid also for the inquiry into the external world. While there appears to be no particular connection between Diderot's interest in Montaigne and his period of scientific inquiry, there is a profound connection with respect to methodology. For Diderot does not now interpret Montaigne's skepticism in the sense of suspension of judgment. Rather, for him, Montaigne's method is a conscious participation in the nature of things, and is thus no longer a critical method—a weapon against dogmatism—but a means of interpreting reality. It is here that we must pause to observe that Montaigne's method is capable of bridging the gap between science and art ; the interpretation of reality is the aim of both these fields of human activity. We shall bear this in mind when we come to consider Diderot's application of Montaigne's example in literary creation.

Critique of language

Realizing that all philosophical thought must be conceived and expressed ultimately in linguistic form, Montaigne and Diderot early turned their attention to the problem of language.

Montaigne did not undertake a systematic critique of language, although his isolated remarks on the subject are strewn throughout the *Essais*.[1] His sensitivity to complexity, diversity, and change makes him wary of the tendency of language to confuse unlike things, to blur their particularity, and thus to falsify our knowledge of the world and of ourselves.

The fundamental thought underlying Montaigne's critique of language is that there is no absolute correspondence between reality and language : " Il y a le nom et la chose : le nom, ce n'est pas une partie de la chose ny de la substance, c'est une piece estrangere joincte à la chose, et hors d'elle " (*Essais*, II, xvi, 697). This quotation, which opens the essay " De la gloire ", is a paraphrase of a passage from Chapter 191 of Sebond's *Theologia Naturalis*, but with an important little difference. Sebond had written (in Montaigne's translation) :

---

[1] See FRIEDRICH, *Montaigne*, pp. 195-204, for a treatment of Montaigne's critique of language.

" C'est le nom qui représente et signifie toute sa chose." [1] Montaigne, in his paraphrase of the passage, omits the word " toute " and writes " qui remarque et signifie *la* chose ". That is, there is no unity, no consubstantiality of name and object (" le nom, c'est une voix... une piece estrangere ").

In its context in the essay, Montaigne's nominalism has particular relevance to his conception of reputation and fame. He is at pains to show that there is no necessary connection between a man's reputation, the name that the outside world bestows upon him, and his virtue, which is something only he himself can know : " Les estrangers ne voyent que les evenements et apparences externes. ... Voilà comment tous ces jugemens qui se font des apparences externes, sont merveilleusement incertains et douteux ; et n'est aucun si asseuré tesmoing comme chacun à soy-mesme " (*Essais*, II, xvi, 706).

Names do not correspond to the diversity of reality : " Quelque diversité d'herbes qu'il y ait, tout s'enveloppe sous le nom de salade " (I, xlvi, 312) ; nor do given names correspond to human diversity : " Et ce Pierre ou Guillaume, qu'est-ce qu'une voix pour tous potages ? ... Ce sont traicts de plume communs à mill'hommes. Combien y a il, en toutes les races, de personnes de mesme nom et surnom ? ... Qui empesche mon palefrenier de s'appeler Pompée le grand ? " (*Ibid.*, p. 316.) Beneath the lightness of tone and the homely imagery lies a more serious intent : the manifold complexity of individual existence cannot be summed up in a word or in a name, nor conceptualized in universal propositions. " Je n'ay point de nom qui soit assez mien " (II, xvi, 707).

Apart from the sense Montaigne has that word and object are not bound by any essential necessity, his criticism of language is grounded also in his awareness of the ambiguity of linguistic expression. The uncertainty of human knowledge is increased by the imprecision of language, which leads to misunderstanding, contradictory interpretation and the quarreling of sects. In a famous passage in the " Apologie de Raimond Sebond ", Montaigne wishes to show how language, the medium by means of which human reason must express itself, is a faulty tool of understanding. Words have so many possible meanings that all our discussions center around attempts to arrive at exact definitions : " Nostre parler a ses foiblesses et ses defauts, comme tout le reste. La plus part des occasions des troubles du monde sont Grammairiennes. ... Combien de querelles et combien importantes a produit au monde le doubte du sens de cette syllabe, HOC ! " (*Essais*, II, xii, 589.) The trouble with language is that it is not sufficiently analytic ; it leads to eternal glosses and interpretations of interpretations. It is this very defect of language which, for Diderot, is also its great resource as a medium of communication. If language were ideally analytic, there could be no communication, for reasons which we shall shortly see.[2]

---

[1] MONTAIGNE, *Œuvres complètes*, ed. A. Armaingaud (Paris, 1924-1941), IX, 343.

[2] See below, p. 83.

For Montaigne, on the contrary, the lack of precision in language does not aid in the process of communication but renders it more difficult. Nevertheless, it sometimes enriches it : " Un suffisant lecteur descouvre souvent és escrits d'autruy des perfections autres que celles que l'autheur y a mises et apperçeües, et y preste des sens et des visages plus riches " (*Essais*, I, xxiv, 157).

It is Montaigne's view that the function of language is to make distinctions. Rationality breaks down the undifferentiated whole of reality and renders it comprehensible, reducing it to the level of the human understanding. It is for this reason that Montaigne objects in the " Apologie " to the method of Sebond. It is blasphemy to reduce the concept of God to the level of human understanding, to which the nature of God is forever inaccessible :

> Il m'a tousjours semblé qu'à un homme Chrestien cette sorte de parler est pleine d'indiscretion et d'irreverance : Dieu ne peut faire cecy ou cela. Je ne trouve pas bon d'enfermer ainsi la puissance divine soubs les loix de nostre parolle. Et l'apparance qui s'offre à nous en ces propositions, il la faudroit representer plus reveramment et plus religieusement. (*Essais*, II, xii, 588f.)

It is clearly absurd to define God in linguistic terms, when language is inadequate to express without equivocation the truth of even a simple syllogism :

> Prenons la clause que la logique mesmes nous presentera pour la plus claire. Si vous dictes : Il faict beau temps, et que vous dissiez verité, il fait donc beau temps. Voylà pas une forme de parler certaine ? Encore nous trompera elle. Qu'il soit ainsi, suyvons l'exemple. Si vous dictes : Je ments, et que vous dissiez vray, vous mentez donc. L'art, la raison, la force de la conclusion de cette cy sont pareilles à l'autre ; toutes fois nous voylà embourbez. (*Ibid.*, p. 589.)

The logic of language cannot accommodate the truth of contradictions. Truth and falsehood are thus obscured by the forms of language, purely grammatical concepts which have no necessary correspondence with reality.

The *philosophes* were more directly concerned with the problems of language than was Montaigne, who was chiefly at pains to free himself from the verbal forms of Scholasticism. Analogous to the sixteenth century's reaction against the Schoolmen, was the Enlightenment's philosophical investigation of language, and the objections raised by the *philosophes* to the Cartesian point of view represented by the heritage of the *Grammaire générale et raisonnée de Port-Royal*.[1] Diderot, in particular, was early interested in evolving a theory of language which would fit into his naturalist and vitalist vision of reality. As in the case of Montaigne, Diderot did not expose his ideas on language in a systematic treatise ; his interest in it is implicit in many other areas which absorbed

---

[1] Cf. VENTURI, *Jeunesse de Diderot*, p. 243.

his attention. He first touches on this question in the *Lettre sur les aveugles*, but it is rather the *Lettre sur les sourds et muets* which deals most directly with language.

In the *Lettre sur les sourds et muets*, Diderot develops the idea that language serves two fundamentally opposed functions which are expressed in two linguistic orders : " l'ordre naturel " and " l'ordre d'institution ou scientifique ". The latter is analytic and corresponds to the character of discursive, logical thought ; the former is synthetic and is the language of artistic expression. In a crucial passage, Diderot attempts to define the spirit that animates poetry, for which the categories of rhetoric and the criteria of discursive logic do not account :

Qu'est-ce que cet esprit ? J'en ai quelquefois senti la présence ; mais tout ce que j'en sais, c'est que c'est lui qui fait que les choses sont dites et représentées tout à la fois ; que dans le même temps que l'entendement les saisit, l'âme en est émue, l'imagination les voit et l'oreille les entend, et que le discours n'est plus seulement un enchaînement de termes mais que c'est encore un tissu d'hiéroglyphes entassés les uns sur les autres qui la peignent. Je pourrais dire en ce sens, que toute poésie est emblématique. (A-T, I, 374.)

The truly poetic style reproduces the unity existing in the soul before the analytic intelligence has had a chance to alter it.

Discursive language, since it is analytic, necessarily breaks down the unity of inner experience : " L'état de l'âme, dans un instant indivisible, fut représenté par une foule de termes que la précision du langage exigea, et qui distribuèrent une impression totale en parties " (*ibid.*, p. 369). Analysis destroys the organic wholeness of lived experience and reduces the myriad complexity of the instant to a succession of events : "... et parce que ces termes se prononçaient successivement et ne s'entendaient qu'à mesure qu'ils se prononçaient, on fut porté à croire que les affections de l'âme qu'ils représentaient, avaient la même succession. Mais il n'en est rien " (*ibid.*). Language does not render the order of psychic events because of the mind's mobility : " Notre âme est un tableau mouvant, d'après lequel nous peignons sans cesse : nous employons bien du temps à le rendre avec fidélité ; mais il existe en entier, et tout à la fois : l'esprit ne va pas à pas comptés comme l'expression " (*ibid.*). The poet alone, by means of the " hiéroglyphe " and the " emblême ", recreates the simultaneous unity of experience. Poetic expression views the world from the vantage point of the indivisible instant in which all is present all at once. It is an intimation of eternity, a timelessness without duration or succession, contained in each indivisible instant of the soul's life.

But poetic expression is exceptional, as is genius. Apart from these " idiotismes ", linguistic expression is by nature fragmentary. Language renders reality in discrete parcels. It is not rich and nuanced enough to correspond to the diversity of phenomena : " Il n'y a dans la même pensée rendue dans les mêmes expressions, dans les deux mêmes vers faits sur un même sujet, qu'une identité de phénomène apparente ; et

c'est la pauvreté de la langue qui a occasionné cette apparence d'identité " (A-T, XI, 135). Two men writing the same two lines of verse or expressing a thought in identical terms would have expressed themselves in an entirely different way had language been rich enough to respond to the variety of their sensations. Since no man perfectly resembles another, " Nous n'entendons jamais précisément, nous ne sommes jamais précisément entendus ; il y a du plus ou du moins en tout : notre discours est toujours en deçà ou au-delà de la sensation " (*Rêve de d'Alembert, Œuvres phil.*, p. 370). In spite of the levelling effect of language, which reduces diversity to apparent identity, the paucity of vocabulary is itself responsible for misunderstanding. Language often leads men into conflict because words are forced to serve as common coin for a diversity of functions : " Les mots réveillent des idées, des images si diverses selon les têtes, qu'il produisent quelquefois deux effets opposés, ou de mettre les hommes en contradiction, quand ils sont d'accord, ou de les montrer d'accord quand ils sont en contradiction. Viennent-ils à s'expliquer, ils ne s'entendent plus." [1]

Curiously, another fragment from the *fonds Vandeul* speaks of the poverty of language and the lack of communication among minds, but here the faults of language are referred to as fortunate flaws : " Combien les hommes sont peu d'accord ? Combien ils s'accorderaient moins encore si la langue suffisait à toute la variété de leurs sensations ; mais heureusement elle est pauvre ; et en sentant tout diversement, ils parlent à peu près de même." [2] Improving the analytic qualities of language would thus result in even greater semantic problems, for we would not comprehend the speech of another man if we had not ourselves experienced the sensations he was expressing. Our imperfect means of communication lead us to believe that we understand one another. Otherwise we might each one of us be an isolated center of sensation capable of articulating to ourselves the state of our inner being but incapable of making ourselves understood by anyone else.

Diderot's view of the intellectual process of abstraction is expressed in the *Lettre sur les aveugles:* " L'abstraction ne consiste qu'à séparer par la pensée les qualités sensibles des corps, ou les unes des autres, ou du corps même qui leur sert de base " (*Œuvres phil.*, p. 98). Abstraction is the process whereby particulars are reduced to universals. Our daily conversation consists of nothing but abstract expressions " qui désignent des idées, des vues plus ou moins générales de l'esprit, et des expressions représentatives qui désignent des êtres physiques " (*Salon de 1767*, A-T, XI, 132f.). Diderot quickly sketches the passage from the concrete to the abstract in the history of the individual ; it parallels the passage from infancy to adulthood :

Nous avons été enfants, il y a malheureusement longtemps. ... Dans l'enfance on nous prononçait des mots ; ces mots se fixaient dans notre

---

[1] Fragment entitled " Langue " (included in Dieckmann, *Inventaire du fonds Vandeul* [Genève-Lille, 1951], p. 214).

[2] *Ibid.*, p. 199.

mémoire, et le sens dans notre entendement, ou par une idée, ou par une image ; et cette idée ou image était accompagnée d'aversion, de haine, de plaisir, de terreur, de désir, d'indignation, de mépris ; pendant un assez grand nombre d'années, à chaque mot prononcé, l'idée ou l'image nous revenait avec la sensation qui lui était propre ; mais à la longue nous en avons usé avec les mots, comme avec les pièces de monnaie. ... Un discours prononcé n'est plus qu'une longue suite de sons et de sensations primitivement excitées. Le cœur et les oreilles sont en jeu, l'esprit n'y est plus ; c'est à l'effet successif de ces sensations, à leur violence, à leur somme, que nous nous entendons et jugeons. Sans cette abréviation nous ne pourrions converser ; il nous faudrait une journée pour dire et apprécier une phrase un peu longue. Et que fait le philosophe qui pèse, s'arrête, analyse, décompose ? il revient par le soupçon, le doute, à l'état de l'enfance. (A-T, XI, 133.)

Language itself thus undergoes the same civilizing process through which the individual passes. Words lose the emotive force they once possessed in childhood. The process of analytic thought is a return, as it were, to infancy. The philosopher's doubt is, in this sense, not a super-refined intellectualism, but paradoxically, a primitivism, a return to origins—in this case to the origins of language and its direct connection with thought, sensation and emotion. It is a mistrust of the linguistic shorthand which, over the years, has taken the place of the primary longhand of infancy. It is in this sense of "loss" that Diderot's linguistic theorizing is primitivist. He speaks of a separation, a disjunction that has taken place, a primal unity lost but which may be regained.

In contrast to Montaigne, who insists on the discontinuity between word and thing, Diderot believes in their essential identity, if we could but get back to it. In the *Rêve de d'Alembert*, for example, Diderot-Bordeu is called upon by d'Alembert to explain "les abstractions". He replies :

Il n'y en a point ; il n'y a que des réticences habituelles, des ellipses qui rendent les propositions plus générales et le langage plus rapide et plus commode. Ce sont les signes du langage qui ont donné naissance aux sciences abstraites. ... On n'a nulle idée d'un mot abstrait. ... Toute abstraction n'est qu'un signe vide d'idée. Toute science abstraite n'est qu'une combinaison de signes. On a exclu l'idée en séparant le signe de l'objet physique et ce n'est qu'en rattachant le signe à l'objet physique que la science redevient une science d'idées ; de là le besoin, si fréquent dans la conversation, dans les ouvrages, d'en venir à des exemples. Lorsque, après une longue combinaison de signes, vous demandez un exemple, vous n'exigez autre chose de celui qui parle, sinon de donner du corps, de la forme, de la réalité, de l'idée au bruit successif de ses accents, en y appliquant des sensations éprouvées. (*Œuvres phil.*, p. 369.)

Abstractions have no existence apart from physical reality. They are merely tools of linguistic convenience. Above all, Diderot calls for a return to things-in-themselves, to what is experienced. He seeks to incorporate the phenomenon of language into his materialist world-view by insisting on its concreteness ; for language is not a creation of the abstract intellect but originates in and survives by its intimate

association with physical reality, with sensation, emotion, action. Language belongs not to the realm of spirit as opposed to the realm of matter, but is itself the product of material organization. Thought and intellect are not divorced from life and physical experience. The word is a palpable entity enclosing within itself whole complexes of thought, emotion and experience.

As we have seen in the course of this chapter, the skepticism of Montaigne and that of Diderot rests mainly on their awareness of the contradictions between a kinetic, changing reality and our static formulations. Language is unable to keep abreast of a world in flux, nor can it admit to the coexistence of contraries. Considered on the purely philosophical plane, the problem of language appears to Montaigne and Diderot insoluble. But where the philosopher fails, the literary artist may find a way.

III. NATURE AND NATURAL MAN

> Si j'estois du mestier, je naturaliserois l'art autant
> comme ils artialisent la nature.
>
> MONTAIGNE (Essais, III, v, 978)

The complex history of the word " nature " poses many obstacles
to the student of ideas. One has only to refer to the work of Lovejoy
and Boas [1] to realize that it is practically impossible to separate the
meanings which have been given to this word, not only by different
authors writing at different periods, but by the same author in various
contexts. Montaigne's use of the term still perplexes readers of the
Essais.[2] Even a cursory examination of the *Essais* shows that Montaigne
uses the term for a wide variety of purposes according to the context.
What has not been clear is the evolution of the concept within that of
the *Essais* as a whole.

In the early essays, where Montaigne is mainly concerned with
assuming the moral stance of the stoical humanists and where death is
the prime fact of life, the word nature is clearly associated with death
and the dissolution of the body.[3] In the essay " Que philosopher c'est
apprendre à mourir ", for example, nature assists the stoical humanist

---

[1] A. O. LOVEJOY and G. BOAS, *Primitivism and Related Ideas in Antiquity* (Baltimore, 1935).

[2] Neal Dow's short book, *The Concept and Term " Nature " in Montaigne's Essays* (Philadelphia, 1940), is not the last word on the subject.

[3] In the relative dating of the *Essais*, I follow the chronology established
by Pierre VILLEY (*Les Sources et l'évolution des Essais de Montaigne* [Paris,
1908]). Apart from the specific modifications the meanings of the word
" nature " undergo throughout the *Essais*, the term as Montaigne inherited
it from the Ancients still retains its larger pagan resonance. Cf. Villey
ibid., II, 379 : " Lorsqu'il parle de nature il a dans l'esprit une idée très
complexe, un peu flottante, qui enveloppe dans ses vastes plis un profond
mystère et tout le monde qui nous entoure. Il y a bien là quelque chose
de l'immense force créatrice chantée par Lucrèce."

in his scorn for life and preparation for death : " Nature mesme nous preste la main, et nous donne courage. Si c'est une mort courte et violente, nous n'avons pas loisir de la craindre ; si elle est autre, je m'apperçois qu'à mesure que je m'engage dans la maladie, j'entre naturellement en quelque desdein de la vie " (*Essais*, I, xx, 114). In the major essays of Book I, particularly chapters xiv, xx, and xxxix, Montaigne's negative, death-oriented, and defensive attitude colors in like manner his view of nature. Like the stoics upon whom he attempts to model himself, Montaigne places reason and will in a position superior to nature. His prime concern is to achieve mastery over pain.

In the early essays of Book II, Montaigne begins to criticize the position of stoical humanism, which involves as well a change in his view of nature. He rejects stoicism principally because it is anti-natural : " Et l'opinion qui desdaigne nostre vie, elle est ridicule. Car en fin c'est notre estre, c'est nostre tout. Les choses qui ont un estre plus noble et plus riche, peuvent accuser le nostre ; mais c'est contre nature que nous nous mesprisons et mettons nous mesmes à nonchaloir " (*Essais*, II, iii, 389). It is not yet clear exactly what Montaigne means by " nature " but he has already moved a good distance beyond his earlier view. It is a question of death against life, and life has begun to take the ascendancy.

In the " Apologie de Raimond Sebond " the concept of " nature " assumes much larger proportions than heretofore. One of Montaigne's intentions in this long essay is to place man in close relation to the animal world and to all of nature : " J'ay dit tout cecy pour maintenir cette ressemblance qu'il y a aux choses humaines, et pour nous ramener et joindre au nombre. Nous ne sommes ny au dessus, ny au dessoubs du reste. ... Il y a quelque difference, il y a des ordres et des degrez ; mais c'est soubs le visage d'une mesme nature " (*Essais*, II, xii, 506). The many examples of animal intelligence, taken mainly from Plutarch, serve to show that animal instinct and human reason differ not qualitatively but quantitatively. This paradox, in turn, serves Montaigne's larger purpose of humbling man's reason : it is a kind of instinct just as the instincts that guide the nest-building birds and the spinners of webs are a kind of intelligence. Montaigne has a sense of the unity of nature and of its infinite variety and gradation. Nature, all-inclusive, yet remains separate from God. The natural is thus in contradistinction to the supernatural. Montaigne may be exaggerating in the " Apologie " for rhetorical purposes when he insists so strongly on the negative aspects of nature as opposed to the divine. Witness the following striking passage in which nature connotes weakness, sickness, presumption, and degradation :

La presomption est nostre maladie naturelle et originelle. La plus calamiteuse et fraile de toutes les creatures, c'est l'homme, et quant et quant la plus orgueilleuse. Elle se sent et se void logée icy, parmi la bourbe et le fient du monde, attachée et clouée à la pire, plus morte et croupie partie de l'univers, au dernier estage du logis et le plus esloigné de la voute celeste. (*Essais*, II, xii, 497.)

It is not until such essays as " De l'institution des enfants " (I, xxvi) and " Des cannibales " (I, xxxi) that Montaigne's attitudes towards nature become more positive. Nature is that which is primary : the original, the unacquired, the unlearned. Thus he now opposes " jugement naturel " to book learning,[1] the advantages of primitive and savage nature to art and civilized society,[2] sexual realism to hypocrisy and artificial social conventions.[3]

By the time we reach the late essays of Book III, Montaigne will have moved even beyond these dichotomies to a sense of the wholeness of man and of nature. In some cases, Montaigne's final statements are direct contradictions of earlier positions. Reason is no longer opposed to appetite : " Nature a maternellement observé cela, que les actions qu'elle nous a enjoinctes pour nostre besoing nous fussent aussi voluptueuses, et nous y convie non seulement par la raison mais aussi par l'appétit : c'est injuste de corrompre ses regles " (*Essais*, III, xiii, 1246). Natural impulse is no longer opposed to habit and custom : " Appellons encore nature l'usage et condition de chacun de nous. ... L'accoustumance est une seconde nature, et non moins puissante " (*Essais*, III, x, 1132). Thus, " following nature " does not simply mean passive abandonment to impulse, but implies something much more active. It is the fruit of Montaigne's method of self-study and self-regard, which requires exertion of will and constant watchfulness over oneself. He who knows how to follow nature is " celuy qui a l'heur de sçavoir s'employer naïvement et ordonnément, c'est-à-dire naturellement " (*Essais*, III, xiii, 1204). The alliance of the two adverbs " naïvement et ordonnément " emphasizes this alliance of impulse and will, or artlessness and reason. Thus, nature is no longer opposed to reason or to art.

We noted that in the " Apologie " Montaigne had set up a dichotomy between human reason and divine reason, and between nature and God. Now, in the last essays and in his additions after 1588, Montaigne has a tendency to use the terms " nature " and " God " in close proximity as if they were synonymous. In an identical context he uses the two words interchangeably : " Pour moy donc, j'ayme la vie et la cultive telle qu'il a pleu à Dieu nous l'octroier. ... J'accepte de bon cœur, et recognoissant, ce que nature a faict pour moy, et m'en agrée et m'en loue. On faict tort à ce grand et tout puissant donneur de refuser son don, l'annuler et desfigurer " (*Essais*, III, xiii, 1253). Two pages later : " Il n'y a piece indigne de nostre soin en ce present que Dieu nous a faict " (p. 1255). Thus, while I think one would be mistaken to speak of Montaigne's " pantheism ", there is no doubt that his use of the two terms indicates that the two concepts tend to become closely related in his mind. Where Montaigne had previously seen discreteness, diver-

---

[1] " De l'institution des enfants " follows hard upon Montaigne's attack on pedantry (" Du pedantisme ", I, xxv).

[2] " Des cannibales ", I, xxxi.

[3] " Sur des vers de Virgile ", III, v.

sity, and change in nature, he now sees unity : " C'est une mesme nature qui roule son cours. Qui en auroit suffisamment jugé le present estat, en pourroit seurement conclurre et tout l'advenir et tout le passé " (*Essais*, II, xii, 515). Nature, the creation of God, shares in His attributes ; thus the laws of nature, which depend ultimately upon the infinite wisdom of God, are beyond man's comprehension : " Les philosophes, avec grand raison, nous renvoyent aux regles de Nature ; mais elles n'ont que faire de si sublime cognoissance : ils les falsifient et nous presentent son visage peint trop haut en couleur et trop sophistiqué, d'où naissent tant de divers pourtraits d'un subject si uniforme " (*Essais*, III, xiii, 1204).

The inadequacy of human reason prevents man from perceiving the relationships amongst all things. Even a physical anomaly has its place in the natural order :

Ce que nous appellons monstres, ne le sont pas à Dieu, qui voit en l'immensité de son ouvrage l'infinité des formes qu'il y a comprinses ; et est à croire que cette figure qui nous estonne, se rapporte et tient à quelque autre figure de mesme genre inconnu à l'homme. De sa toute sagesse il ne part rien que bon et commun et reglé ; mais nous n'en voyons pas l'assortiment et la relation. (*Essais*, II, xxx, 798.)

Human laws are variable and prejudiced. Nothing that is may be said to be against nature, but only against what we are used to : " Nous appelons contre nature ce qui advient contre la coustume : rien n'est que selon elle, quel qu'il soit. Que cette raison universelle et naturelle chasse de nous l'erreur et l'estonnement que la nouvelleté nous apporte " (*ibid.*, p. 799).

What appears evident from the foregoing review is that Montaigne's notions of " nature " and its various antitheses have passed beyond such intellectualized polarizations to a deeply felt apprehension of a synthesis : " En ceste université, je me laisse ignoramment et negligemment manier à la loy generale du monde. Je la sçauray assez quand je la sentiray " (*Essais*, III, xiii, 1204). Montaigne finally arrives at a serene insight into the universal harmony which has been achieved through the full realization of the self.

Now, as we have seen in the previous chapter, Diderot and his century part company with the essayist for they consider " nature " a legitimate object of scientific inquiry. For Diderot, " nature " is first of all the sum total of the observable phenomena of the physical world, which is not static, immutable, eternal, but which undergoes change in time. Yet in spite of his belief in the unity of nature and his faith in science, there remains a vestige of Montaignean doubt with respect to man's capacity in comparison to the magnitude of the universe. Late in life he writes :

Quelle machine que l'univers ! Quand tous les faits seront-ils connus ? Entre les faits, les plus importants ou les plus féconds ne se déroberont-ils pas à jamais à notre connaissance par la faiblesse de nos organes et l'imperfection de nos instruments ? La limite du monde est-elle à la portée de nos

télescopes ? Si nous possédions le recueil complet des phénomènes, il n'y aurait plus qu'une cause ou supposition. Alors on saurait peut-être si le mouvement est essentiel à la matière, et si la matière est créée ou incréée ; ... si sa diversité ne répugne pas plus à la raison que sa simplicité : car ce n'est peut-être que par notre ignorance que son unité ou homogénéité nous paraît si difficile à concilier avec la variété des phénomènes. (*Claude et Néron*, A-T, III, 360.)

Apart from the natural sciences, the word " nature " is used in the eighteenth century to denote one of the terms of a number of dichotomies : " nature " means the non-rational as opposed to reason and art ; the non-moral as opposed to the values of civilized society ; spontaneous impulse in contrast to reflection ; and sexual freedom as opposed to sexual constraint. It is evident that the Enlightenment could find in the *Essais* arms for the revolution it undertook to bring about when it questioned whether it was possible for natural man to lead a moral life.[1] Diderot, as one of the representative minds of his time, is, of course, concerned with the conflicts between nature and morality. Two ideas present themselves to his mind : the all-inclusiveness of nature and the rejection of prejudice. In the *Suite de l'Entretien*, the third dialogue of the *Rêve de d'Alembert*, we find a passage expressing these ideas in much the same way Montaigne expressed them. Dr. Bordeu holds a brief for the performance of certain " unnatural " sexual practices such as homosexuality and masturbation, as well as self-imposed abstinence, and justifies them all as being natural and included within the natural order : " Tout ce qui est ne peut être ni contre nature ni hors de nature, je n'en excepte pas même la chasteté et la continence volontaires qui seraient les premiers des crimes contre nature, si l'on pouvait pécher contre nature " (*Œuvres phil.*, p. 380).

Like Montaigne, Diderot seems to be searching for a synthesis of contraries, for a way of resolving the conflicts which split a man into two warring halves—the natural and the social. It is to this question that we shall now turn.

Critics have remarked a parallel between Montaigne's essay " Des cannibales " and Diderot's *Supplément au voyage de Bougainville*. Although there is no doubt that Diderot was familiar with Montaigne's essay, it is difficult to do more than conjecture about the latter's influence on Diderot's dialogue. However this may be, both works have a place in the history of what Lovejoy and Boas call " cultural primitivism ", which according to their definition is " the discontent of the civilized with civilization, or with some conspicuous and characteristic feature of it. It is the belief of men living in a relatively highly evolved and complex cultural condition that a life far simpler and less sophisticated in some or in all respects is a more desirable life ".[2]

Primitivism so defined differs from chronological primitivism, which assumes a belief that the former age was superior to the present and thus

---

[1] Lester G. Crocker, *An Age of Crisis* (Baltimore, 1959), p. xx.
[2] *Op. cit.*, p. 7.

that any real progress must be viewed as a return to nature, or to a golden age, which existed in the past. Cultural primitivism views the golden age as possible and existing here and now, in savage or under-developed societies.

Both the *Supplément* and "Des cannibales" place their ideal primitive societies in newly discovered regions which were the object of travelers' reports. That is, the ideal society depicted in both works exists here and now. In this respect, the *Supplément* and Montaigne's essay differ from Rousseau's *Discourses*. The latter are attempts at historical analysis, by means of which Rousseau sought to understand in a systematic manner the genesis of cultural institutions. Such a return to origins through abstraction is not the procedure followed by Montaigne and Diderot. They do not analyze civilized society, stripping it one by one of its cultural accretions—property, marriage, laws, religion, ethical practices, and the like. They are content rather to describe what exists than to presume to reduce the complexity of cultural development by means of abstract analysis to a hypothetical portrait of " natural man ".

It is necessary to inquire to what extent Montaigne and Diderot may be termed primitivists according to Lovejoy's and Boas's definition. Let us first consider the essayist.

" Des cannibales " opens with a reference to the Greeks' manner of describing all foreign nations as " barbarous ". It is dangerous to allow the customs of one's own country to become prejudices which interfere with the proper exercise of judgment : " Il se faut garder de s'atacher aux opinions vulgaires, et les faut juger par la voye de la raison, non par la voix commune " (*Essais*, I, xxxi, 239). This is a major theme of the essay, a theme which is echoed several times. After a digression on the possibility that the newly discovered lands in the New World may be the lost isle of Atlantis, Montaigne turns to the subject of floods and the movements of the earth. He observes this movement in his own environment and speculates that, if the earth moved at the same rate as the Dordogne in its shifting course, " la figure du monde seroit renversée " (p. 241). This digression is, of course, more than remotely related to the theme of the essay. It is the idea of instability in human events, of movements backward and forward, of sudden and violent changes and slow inexorable ones. Events, places, and persons are never exactly the same and do not follow a steady, straïght-line movement.

Montaigne's live witness, the man who spent ten or twelve years in the New World, is an example of the primitive naïveté which is praised in the essay : " Cet homme que j'avoy, estoit homme simple et grossier, qui est une condition propre à rendre veritable tesmoignage " (p. 242). Subtle, sophisticated people are not reliable witnesses ; for, although they notice more, they cloud the objectivity of their report by their own interpretations : " Ils ne vous representent jamais les choses pures, ils les inclinents et masquent selon le visage qu'ils leur ont veu " *(ibid.)*. Simplicity versus finesse is one of the antitheses in the essay. It is also one of the ambiguities of the essay ; for although Montaigne claims

he has been content with the information obtained from his naïve witness and has not had recourse to explorers' accounts, scholarship has shown that Montaigne borrowed an extended passage from Girolamo Benzoni's *Histoire nouvelle du nouveau monde* (French translation of Urbain Chauveton, 1579) and that he had probably read Jean de Léry's *Histoire d'un voyage fait en la terre du Brésil* (1578) and perhaps André Thévet's *Singularitez de la France antarctique* (1558).[1] Thus, Montaigne's firsthand information fused with some details from his readings, the whole having filtered through his own subtle mind. The essay itself, then, while presenting the antithesis of the natural and the artificial, effects a synthesis of the two.

Montaigne is not merely playing another variation on a bucolic theme inherited from Antiquity; he has read the reports of travellers and talked with an eye-witness; he is fascinated by the ways of a primitive people in actual existence. They represent a degree of perfection not attained by Plato in his intellectually conceived Republic; they surpass in purity and simplicity all the poetic pictures of the golden age; they have no commerce, no literature, no mathematics, no government, no property, no family distinctions, no clothing, no agriculture, no labors of any kind. These savages, in their state of innocence, are unaware of the sins of civilized man : falsehood, treason, greed, envy. All that is demanded of them is bravery in war and kindness to their wives. Of course, Montaigne is horrified at their cannibalism which he neither condemns nor condones. Their morality is simple and their vengeance terrible.

But it is here that Montaigne raises his voice in indignation against the evils of Europe and against the corrupting influence of Europeans on the savages, whose practices were at least free from the taint of vice. The barbarism of the cannibals is obvious, but the barbarism of civilized Europeans cloaks itself under the guise of piety. The atrocities committed in France among Catholics and Protestants evokes anguished accents of pain and horror far different from the tone of ironic detachment with which Montaigne describes the customs of the savages :

> Je ne suis pas marry que nous remerquons l'horreur barbaresque qu'il y a en une telle action, mais ouy bien dequoy, jugeans bien de leurs fautes, nous soyons si aveuglez aux nostres. Je pense qu'il y a plus de barbarie à manger un homme vivant qu'à le manger mort, à deschirer, par tourmens et par geenes, un corps encore plein de sentiment, le faire rostir par le menu, le faire mordre et meurtrir aux chiens et aux pourceaux (comme nous l'avons, non seulement leu, mais veu de fresche memoire, non entre des ennemis anciens, mais entre des voisins et concitoyens, et, qui pis est, sous pretexte de pieté et de religion), que de le rostir et manger apres qu'il est trespassé. (*Essais*, I, xxxi, 247f.)

This passage is central in the essay and is of a vehemence of tone unmatched elsewhere in the chapter. Its rhetoric is carefully calculated

---

[1] See Gilbert CHINARD, *L'Exotisme américain dans la littérature française du seizième siècle* (Paris, 1911), pp. 193-218.

to impress the reader with the barbarousness of Christians who outdo the cannibals in cruelty and inhumanity, not merely to their enemies but to their own brethren : " Nous les pouvons donq bien appeller barbares, eu esgard aux regles de la raison, mais non pas eu esgard à nous, qui les surpassons en toute sorte de barbarie " (p. 248). The borderlines between the civilized and the primitive are blurred so that it is questionable which is aberrant. The essay presents a paradox which, when it is not moving Montaigne to indignant rage or to poetry (as in the lines imitated by Shakespeare in the *Tempest*), is surely a source of amusement to him. We the civilized are savages with respect to the cannibals, who at least act according to nature and not to laws of their own fabrication : " Sans mentir, au pris de nous, voilà des hommes bien sauvages ; car, ou il faut qu'ils le soyent bien à bon escient, ou que nous le soyons : il y a une merveilleuse distance entre leur forme et la nostre " (p. 251). We the civilized have stifled and destroyed the purity of nature. It is this destruction that ought properly to be called savage. The fruits that nature has produced, which we call wild, possess true strength and vigor ; while those we cultivate should rather be called wild, for they merely serve the pleasure of our corrupt palates. In all, nature is superior to art : " Ce n'est pas raison que l'art gaigne le point d'honneur sur nostre grande et puissante mere nature " (p. 243).

For all that, however, Montaigne is not preaching the return to nature nor extolling the virtues of cannibalism. He is, through the medium of the savage, taking an opportunity to criticize indirectly certain abuses of his own society which the eighteenth-century *philosophes* were also to criticize : acquisitiveness, luxury, poverty, bigotry. The last page of the essay contains Montaigne's report of the eye-witness account of three savages who paid a visit to Rouen and were asked what they had found most admirable. Their reply is an implicit critique of monarchy, aristocracy, and the unequal distribution of wealth, and suggests violent revolution as a remedy to the inequities of European society :

Ils dirent qu'ils trouvoient en premier lieu fort estrange que tant de grands hommes, portans barbe, forts et armez, qui estoient autour du Roy (il est vray-semblable que ils parloient des Suisses de sa garde), se soubs-missent à obeyr à un enfant, et qu'on ne choississoit plus tost quelqu'un d'entr'eux pour commander ; secondement (ils ont une façon de leur langage telle, qu'ils nomment les hommes moitié les uns des autres) qu'ils avoyent aperceu qu'il y avoit parmy nous des hommes pleins et gorgez de toutes sortes de commoditez, et que leurs moitiez estoient mendians à leurs portes, decharnez de faim et de pauvreté ; et trouvoient estrange comme ces moitiez icy necessiteuses pouvoient souffrir une telle injustice, qu'ils ne prinsent les autres à la gorge, ou missent le feu à leurs maisons. (P. 253.)

Certainly Montaigne is not filled with the reforming zeal of the *philosophes*, but his criticism is clear and pointed. The ironic final sentence of the essay, " Tout cela ne va pas trop mal : mais quoy, ils ne portent

point de haut de chausses " is the direct ancestor of Montesquieu's
" Comment peut-on être Persan? "

The rather over-simplified antithesis drawn in the essay " Des
cannibales " between the savage and the corrupt European, is modified
in the essay " Des coches " (III, vi) of which the real subjects are the
extravagances of princes and the cruelty of the Spaniards in the New
World. In this essay, Montaigne does not speak of the superiority of
nature to art and of the primitive to the civilized. Had the peoples of
Mexico and Peru fallen under the Greek or Roman heel, such a noble
conquest would have resulted in a synthesis of art and nature.[1] But
instead, they were brutalized by their Spanish conquerors who took
advantage of their ignorance and simplicity and led them to pattern
themselves after European depravity. Here, [Montaigne's rhetoric
rises to a ringing condemnation : " Tant de villes rasées, tant de nations
exterminées, tant de millions de peuples passez au fil de l'espée, et la
plus riche et belle partie du monde bouleversée pour la negotiation des
perles et du poivre " *(ibid.)*. Montaigne's complaint is not against
civilization *per se*, but against the corrupting influence of wealth and
luxury which perverts nature. He is aware of the vices and abuses of
European political and economic organization. The vision of the
virtuous cannibal (a paradox in itself) is not an ideal of lost innocence, of
humanity in its perfection. His supposed primitivism is not really
primitivism at all, for he does not call for a return to a pre-civilized form
of social organization.

Let us now turn to the question of Diderot's primitivism.[2] The
philosophe had imagined a " beau paradoxe " : " Je suis convaincu qu'il
ne peut y avoir de vrai bonheur pour l'espèce humaine que dans un état
social où il n'y aurait ni roi, ni magistrat, ni prêtre, ni lois, ni tien, ni
mien, ni propriété mobilière, ni propriété foncière, ni vices, ni vertus ; et
cet état social est diablement idéal " (A-T, VI, 439). This devilishly
ideal society is a fine paradox for a number of reasons. The perfect
society is anarchy, ideal anarchy ; and, as such, is nonexistent and
impossible of realization. But this anarchic dream is by no means
Diderot's last word on the subject, nor does it really represent his
considered opinion. It is related to Diderot's profound need to reconcile
the conflicts between ethical man and natural man. What Diderot
really means by his " beau paradoxe " is that there can be no real

---

[1] *Essais*, III, vi, 1020.

[2] Diderot's attitudes towards primitivism have been discussed in an
unpublished dissertation (Wynona Moore Lipman, " Attitudes of Diderot
Toward Primitivism ", Columbia University, 1953). Mrs. Lipman gives the
broadest possible interpretation to primitivism, taking it to include Diderot's
interest in cosmology and cosmogony. Thus, for Mrs. Lipman, an atomistic
world-view of matter in flux is a logical extension of primitivism. We shall,
for our part, restrict the meaning of the term to its use by Lovejoy and Boas.
Mrs. Lipman's conclusion is that Diderot was neither a primitivist nor an
anti-primitivist, but that he sought a synthesis of these two positions. If
such indeed be the case, then, *mutatis mutandis*, Montaigne's attitude
towards primitivism is much the same.

happiness for natural man in a society which by its institutions and structure sets up ethical norms which are at odds with the impulses of natural man. Natural man knows nothing of society and its rules, of right and wrong, of yours and mine.

In the *Neveu de Rameau*, the cynicism of the Nephew is outdone by the clairvoyant realism of *Moi* on this question of the claims of natural man versus those of ethical man. *Lui* believes that if he left his son to himself without inculcating in him any moral ideas, " il voudrait être richement vêtu, splendidement nourri, chéri des hommes, aimé des femmes, et rassembler sur lui tous les bonheurs de la vie " (ed. Fabre, p. 95). Borrowing from Hobbes,[1] *Moi* shows that *Lui*'s cynicism is itself a pallid product of social and ethical conditioning : " Si le petit sauvage était abandonné à lui-même ; qu'il conservât toute son imbé-cillité et qu'il réunît au peu de raison de l'enfant au berceau la violence des passions de l'homme de trente ans, il tordrait le cou à son père et coucherait avec sa mère " *(ibid.).* If the child were left to his natural impulses, the result would be the destruction of the family group. This is the state of nature, the pure anarchy of instinct and pre-rationality which renders social organization impossible.

Diderot often conceives of the state of nature in terms of sexual freedom, and of civilized society in terms of the constraints it places on sexuality. It is this dichotomy which is discussed in the *Supplément au Voyage de Bougainville.* The subtitle of the work specifically states its theme : *Dialogue entre A et B sur l'inconvénient d'attacher des idées morales à certaines actions physiques qui n'en comportent pas.* The theme is thus the problem of maintaining the freedom of sexual expression existing in the state of nature, and achieving the unity of natural and ethical man by detaching moral notions from the physical act which in itself is innocent. The right of religion to dictate moral standards is the principal butt of Diderot's criticism, since these rules of morality are arbitrary and claim to be absolute, yet have no basis in nature.

Tahiti is an ideal society in which the claims of nature and ethics do not contradict one another. Its inhabitants, unperverted by artificial laws and needs, follow the pure instinct of nature ; there is no private property, and incest as a moral concept does not exist. In Part II of the *Supplément*, " Les Adieux du Vieillard ", the virtues of the Tahitians are extolled at the expense of Europeans : " Laisse-nous nos mœurs ; elles sont plus sages et plus honnêtes que les tiennes ; ... Tout ce qui nous est nécessaire et bon, nous le possédons. Sommes-nous dignes de mépris, parce que nous n'avons pas su nous faire des besoins super-flus ? " (*Œuvres phil.*, p. 468.) Montaigne praised his cannibals in much the same manner : " Ils n'ont que faire d'agrandir leurs limites. Ils sont encore en cet heureux point, de ne desirer qu'au tant que leurs necessitez naturelles leur ordonnent : tout ce qui est au-delà, est superflu pour eux "

---

[1] See FABRE, ed. *Neveu de Rameau*, p. 230 ; also, Leland THIELEMANN, " Diderot and Hobbes ", *Diderot Studies II*, ed. Otis Fellows and Norman Torrey (Syracuse, 1952), p. 235.

(*Essais*, I, xxxi, 248). Diderot agrees with Montaigne that art should not win the point of honor over puissant Mother Nature. The Tahitians have found that point of equilibrium which constitutes happiness; they have found the limits to their desires and toils, the balance between nature and art, and between the savage and the civilized; they have stopped short in their development and have avoided the corruption of nature which is the product of sophistication. Diderot formulated this belief in his refutation of Helvétius : " Je crois qu'il y a... un terme dans la civilisation, un terme plus conforme à la félicité de l'homme en général et bien moins éloigné de la condition sauvage qu'on ne l'imagine ; mais comment y revenir quand on s'en est écarté, comment y rester quand on y serait ? " (A-T, II, 431.) Thus, the seeds of the Tahitians' decline are implicit in their happy state, while civilized societies have become so complicated that reform is practically impossible.

This notion of limits to man's industry fits definitely into the primitivist thesis and illustrates that side of Diderot's thought which is conservative and pessimistic. It is in tune with Montaigne's cautious skepticism with regard to progress and change. There is nevertheless in both Montaigne and Diderot a destroyer : skeptical and critical of received ideas and institutions and fond of proposing astonishing paradoxes ; and a preserver : conservative and resistant to breaking with tradition. This double-sidedness is apparent in the *Supplément*. The revolutionary morality of the Tahitians is not seriously proposed as suitable for highly developed societies.

There are two myths in the *Supplément*. One is the famous parable of the two men in the cave : " Voulez-vous savoir l'histoire abrégée de presque toute notre misère ? La voici. Il existait un homme naturel : on a introduit au dedans de cet homme un homme artificiel ; et il s'est élevé dans la caverne une guerre continuelle qui dure toute la vie " (*Œuvres phil.*, p. 511). The primitivist thesis, which advocates the return to the state of nature, would eliminate artificial man, thus bringing an end to the conflict. But such a state, " triste et sauvage ",[1] while it may be conceived abstractly, exists perhaps nowhere on earth, not even in Tahiti. Half-fictional, half-real, Tahiti is not the state of nature ; it is not a state of primitive innocence. Tahiti, as Diderot presents it, is an evolved society organized towards definite ends, with moral laws geared to those ends. The Tahitians are dedicated to the multiplication of their kind, but it is not the pure instinct of nature that commands them. They have elevated instinct to the rank of moral imperative : " Quel sentiment plus honnête et plus grand pourrais-tu mettre à la place de celui que nous leur avons inspiré, et qui les anime ? Ils pensent que le moment d'enrichir la nation et la famille d'un nouveau citoyen est venu, et ils s'en glorifient " (*Œuvres phil.*, p. 470). Such an institutionalization of the sexual act for the glorification of the state threatens to be even more tyrannical and inimical to individual freedom than European, Christian morality. The Tahitians too are bound by the

---

[1] *Œuvres phil.*, p. 508.

conventions of their society which, though different from accepted European standards, are nonetheless human institutions.

The sexual mores of Tahiti are depicted as the antithesis of Christian practice; but the fable of Tahiti, while it is presented in an atmosphere of strict factual accuracy, is a vision seen through European eyes. Interlocutor A finds beneath the savage eloquence of the venerable old man " des idées et des tournures européennes " [1] and the speech of Orou " un peu modelé à l'européenne ".[2] The supposed explanation for this is that Orou knew Spanish and served as interpreter. This concern for verisimilitude in a fictional context occurs constantly in Diderot's works. In the *Supplément*, the real Tahiti, Bougainville's Tahiti—which itself is an interpretation—and Diderot's Tahiti, combine to form a mythical Tahiti, floating loosely somewhere between the enchanted isles of literary tradition and the documented reports of travellers. Tahiti is both fact in the objective world, and a projection of the European mind in critical reflection upon itself. Diderot is not nostalgic for the state of nature. His point of view is not romantic, but ironic and skeptical: ironic because of his ambivalence with regard to reality and invention; skeptical because of his critical attitude towards both the primitive and the civilized.

The *Supplément* is constructed entirely of dialogues: between A and B, nameless voices whose lack of precise identification places the work in abstract context; between Orou and the Aumônier, the natural and the artificial man, precise embodiments of the warring men in the cavern. Its structure is emblematic of its meaning. The two inter-locutors A and B represent the ambivalence of Diderot's own attitude towards primitivism. B is more or less of a primitivist, although he declines to commit himself to a preference for the state of nature over civilization. But he cannot be taken as standing exclusively for Diderot's own view, since A, the more skeptical of the two, presents arguments that Diderot will use two years later against Rousseau in the *Réfutation d'Helvétius*.[3] In the latter work, Diderot's position is more clearly anti-primitivist than in the *Supplément*, although he still refuses to commit himself exclusively to either view. He is a primitivist to the extent that he believes that the state of nature is necessarily a state of innocence and of peace, while society is a state of war and of crime.[4] But the state of nature is not therefore preferable to society; to be so, one would have to show that there is less happiness in society. Diderot does not reject the value of civilization even though it entails vice and the sins of over-refinement: " Oui, monsieur Rousseau, j'aime mieux le vice raffiné sous un habit de soie que la stupidité féroce sous une peau de bête. J'aime mieux la volupté entre les lambris dorés et sur la mollesse des coussins d'un palais, que la misère pâle, sale et hideuse étendue sur

---

[1] *Œuvres phil.*, p. 472.

[2] *Ibid.*, p. 503.

[3] *Ibid.*, p. 513, note 2.

[4] A-T, II, 287.

la terre humide et malsaine et récelée avec la frayeur dans le fond d'un antre sauvage " (*ibid.*, p. 411).

The ideal that Diderot cherishes is less the anarchy of the state of nature than a mean between the state of nature and sophistication. For Diderot, primitivism in an extreme form cannot be taken seriously. Rousseau's doctrine, for example, sins because of its exaggerations: " Si Rousseau, au lieu de nous prêcher le retour dans la forêt, s'était occupé à imaginer une espèce de société moitié policée et moitié sauvage, on aurait eu, je crois, bien de la peine à lui répondre " (*ibid.*, p. 431). It is patently absurd to advocate a return to nature. Such a proposal is both impracticable and undesirable. It must be stressed that Diderot eschews utopian idealism. His Tahiti is an amalgam of the real and the imaginary.[1] It does not fit into the category of the earthly paradise as a purely literary phenomenon, a product of intellectual analysis. Rather, Diderot prefers to bridge the gap between experience and imagination, here not for an aesthetic purpose, but for a philosophical and critical one. The ideal society emerges as a paradoxical one, " moitié policée et moitié sauvage ", half-real and half-artificial. It is only in such a society that the paradoxical nature of man, half-natural, half-artificial, can find its truest and freest expression.

Now the structure of the *Supplément* is important to the understanding of the work. The dialogue form, Diderot's preferred means of expression, is the literary medium that translates the anarchical quality of human experience. In the *Supplément*, specifically, it represents a transmutation of theme into form. The problem of the warring men in the cave, to which no solution is given, is resolved by the structure of the work. The dialogue between Orou and the Aumônier is a dialogue between natural man and artificial man. That is, these dialogues represent the resolution of the dichotomy not through subjugation of either one of the disputants by the other, but by the transformation of the battle into dialogue. The solution of the Aumônier, " moine en France, sauvage dans Tahiti ", is to recognize the claims of the natural man within himself, to keep Tahiti alive in a corner of his being, without renouncing the precious advantages of civilized society. It is to remain in Paris and to abandon oneself from time to time to the dream of Tahiti. It is not, however, license for anarchy ; it is a method for preserving the integrity of one's nature, for guaranteeing the liberty of the individual against all onslaughts. If the dialogue between the civilized man and the natural man is maintained—that is, between our social and moral self and our " savage " amoral self—the total, unified self resulting therefrom is protected from the ravages of both. This means that we shall neither civilize man completely nor abandon him to his instincts ; neither return to nature nor blindly submit to laws without criticizing them. But we shall, in a civilized society, submit

---

[1] Indeed, literary creation for Diderot consists in such syntheses of the real and the invented, as in the *Neveu, La Religieuse*, the *contes, Jacques le fataliste*, to name only the outstanding fictional works.

to them : " Nous parlerons contre les lois insensées jusqu'à ce qu'on les réforme ; et, en attendant, nous nous y soumettrons. Celui qui, de son autorité privée, enfreint une loi mauvaise, autorise tout autre à enfreindre les bonnes " (*Œuvres phil.*, p. 515). The standard by which we shall judge the value of laws is the law of nature which we bear within ourselves, that untamed voice which cries out for its rights and whose plea is guiltless : " Disons-nous à nous-mêmes, crions incessamment qu'on a attaché la honte, le châtiment et l'ignominie à des actions innocentes en elles-mêmes ; mais ne les commettons pas, parce que la honte, le châtiment et l'ignominie sont les plus grands de tous les maux " *(ibid.).* Politically speaking, Diderot is here no revolutionary, and in this regard he rejoins Montaigne. His doctrine is that the amelioration of society's evils should take place in a natural, that is, evolutionary way— imitating nature's long, gradual processes. For the time being, " il y a moins d'inconvénients à être fou avec des fous, qu'à être sage tout seul " *(ibid).*

In sum, neither Montaigne nor Diderot proposes a return to a primitive state of nature, nor does either suffer from a nostalgia for such a supposed golden age. The primitivist theme serves a more serious purpose in our two authors. It is used as a vehicle for direct criticism of existing institutions and practices. In both, primitivism is considered chiefly in the form of the antithesis between nature and culture, represented by the contrast between a newly discovered contemporary primitive society and European civilization. Both Montaigne and Diderot broaden the theme to include the humanitarian perspective of the contact between the two : the corrupting effects of the latter upon the former, the crimes of the European conqueror, the outrages committed at the expense of the innocent savage. Both proclaim the goodness of nature and its superiority over art, but neither one calls for a return to nature or the destruction of society. Each makes use of the theme in order to criticize the evils of civilization in the modest hope of having contributed, in the long run, something to their eradication.

For both Montaigne and Diderot, education is the cornerstone of moral philosophy and the means of effectuating in practice a balance between natural and civilized man. Jean Thomas has rightly pointed out that Diderot's *Plan d'une université* bears to the rest of his work a relationship analogous to the position of " De l'institution des enfants " in the *Essais*.[1] There is, of course, a fundamental difference in orientation. Diderot's program of studies resembles more the rigorous encyclopedic education of Gargantua than the lyrical permissiveness of Montaigne's upbringing. Montaigne's pedagogy—aristocratic, individual, non-specialized—leads to the development of self-sufficiency and independent judgment. It is designed to form an " honnête

---

[1] *L'Humanisme de Diderot*, p. 77. The *Essais*, of course, are to be included in the list of works from which ethical teachings are to be derived : " Et puis feuilleter la nuée des moralistes tels que Montaigne, Nicole et d'autres qui ont ressassé nos devoirs particuliers, pour en tirer ce qu'ils ont dit de plus sensé " (*Plan d'une université*, A-T, III, 492).

homme ". Diderot's system of free public education, however, serves the ends of a changed world. It produces not the cultivated gentleman, but the modern citizen trained to perform a useful function in society and tutored in public morality : " Instruire une nation, c'est la civiliser. ... L'instruction adoucit les caractères, éclaire sur les devoirs, subtilise les vices, les étouffe ou les voile, inspire l'amour de l'ordre, de la justice et des vertus, et accelère la naissance du bon goût dans toutes les choses de la vie " (A-T, III, 429).

Were it not for the fact that Diderot is aware of the needs of a modern nation, his ideas on education would resemble those of Montaigne very closely. Public education is a necessity and must be vastly improved, but it is not to be preferred, by those who can afford it, to private tutoring : " Changer, du commencement jusqu'à la fin, la méthode de l'enseignement public. Ensuite ? Ensuite, quand on est riche, élever son enfant chez soi " (*Réfutation d'Helvétius*, A-T, II, 451). Diderot's statements on the education of children often echo Montaigne's remarks in " De l'institution des enfants ". For example, he writes to Sophie Volland : " *Pas trop élever* est une maxime qui convient surtout aux garçons. Il faut un peu les abandonner à l'énergie de nature. J'aime qu'ils soient violents, étourdis, capricieux. Une tête ébouriffée me plaît plus qu'une tête bien peignée. Laissons-leur prendre une physionomie qui leur appartienne " (*Corr.*, V, 65). And in the *Plan d'une université :* " Il vaut mieux savoir peu et bien, même ignorer, que de savoir mal ; la fausse science fait les entêtés et les confiants ; l'ignorance absolue dicte la circonspection et inspire la docilité " (A-T, III, 526f.).

Diderot remains fundamentally in agreement with Montaigne that education must be in accord with natural talents and its goal should be to develop moral awareness. Despite their differences, which are principally those of historical moment, education for both the essayist and the Encyclopedist remains the crucial link in the dialectic of the self and society.

100

IV. THE HUMAN CENTER

> Il n'est rien si dissociable et sociable que l'homme :
> l'un par son vice, l'autre par sa nature.
>
> MONTAIGNE (*Essais*, I, xxxix, 275)

The study and portrayal of the self

Let us recall the consequences of Montaigne's skeptical phase in the " Apologie ". His disaparagement of human reason rests upon a critique of the senses. Since we can have no immediate communication with reality but must depend upon the intermediary of the sense organs, all individual judgments are of such great diversity that it would be unwise to rely upon them. This negative aspect of Montaigne's skepticism leads to his conservatism and his submission of private judgment, in matters of public concern, to law and custom.

His critique of the senses also has a positive consequence. If we can have no certainty of objective truth, by the same token the only thing we might have surer knowledge of is our subjective consciousness. Thus, it is after the period of the " Apologie " that Montaigne begins seriously to study and portray himself in the *Essais*.

From his reading in the *Essais*, Diderot must have found abundant confirmation of the complexity he observed in his own mind and character. Human inconstancy is a recurring *leitmotiv* in the *Essais*.

The essay " De l'inconstance de nos actions " (II, i) is the *locus classicus* of Montaigne's portrayal of the inner flux which is our natural condition and which mirrors that of the phenomenal world. This essay is Montaigne's answer to those moralists who would explain and interpret human actions and reduce them to conformity with absolute principles :

Veu la naturelle instabilité de nos meurs et opinions, il m'a semblé souvent que les bons autheurs mesmes ont tort de s'opiniastrer à former de nous une constante et solide contexture. Ils choisissent un air universel,

et suyvant cette image, vont rengeant et interpretant toutes les actions d'un personnage, et, s'ils ne les peuvent assez tordre, les vont renvoyant à la dissimulation. (*Essais*, II, i, 368.)

There is nothing more inimical to man than consistency, nor more natural than inconsistency.[1] Man is not free; he is carried away by the winds of circumstance. He is inconstant, unable to control his own desires or his own actions. He is continually taken by surprise. He is, as it were, a marionnette, a plaything of chance and exterior circumstance :

Nostre facon ordinaire, c'est d'aller apres les inclinations de nostre apetit, à gauche, à dextre, contremont, contre-bas, selon que le vent des occasions nous emporte. Nous ne pensons ce que nous voulons, qu'à l'instant que nous le voulons, et changeons comme cet animal qui prend la couleur du lieu où on le couche. Ce que nous avons à cett'heure proposé, nous le changeons tantost, et tantost encore retournons sur nos pas : ce n'est que branle et inconstance,
    Ducimur ut nervis alienis mobile lignum.
(*Essais*, II, i, 368f.)

No pattern establishes itself in our actions ; thus, there is no justification for defining a man in terms of some of his actions to the neglect of others. Every moment in existence implies the possibility of difference : " Nous sommes tous de lopins, et d'une contexture si informe et diverse, que chaque piece, chaque momant faict son jeu. Et se trouve autant de difference de nous à nous mesmes, que de nous à autruy " (p. 374).
    The contradictoriness of human nature is so extreme that Montaigne contemplates the doubleness of character which can lead an individual to behave as if he were not one but two : " Cette variation et contradiction qui se void en nous, si souple, a faict qu'aucuns nous songent deux ames, d'autres deux puissances qui nous accompagnent et agitent, chacune à sa mode, vers le bien l'une, l'autre vers le mal, une si brusque diversité ne se pouvant bien assortir à un subjet simple " (p. 371). This moral complexity has an intellectual counterpart. In another essay, Montaigne writes : " Mais nous sommes, je ne sçay comment, doubles en nous mesmes, qui faict que ce que nous croyons, nous ne le croyons pas, et nous ne pouvons deffaire de ce que nous condamnons " (*Essais*, II, xvi, 699).
    If, in observing others, Montaigne finds nothing but inconstancy, his perceptions of himself change not only with the " winds of circumstance " but also with the fluctuations of the observer. This is the difficulty of introspection :

Non seulement le vent des accidens me remue selon son inclination, mais en outre je me remue et trouble moy mesme par l'instabilité de ma posture ; et qui y regarde primement, ne se trouve guere deux fois en mesme estat. Je donne à mon ame tantost un visage, tantost un autre, selon le

---

[1] Montaigne will discover, however, the paradox that knowledge of our inconsistency can give rise to consistency. Cf. below, p. 107.

costé où je la couche. Si je parle diversement de moy, c'est que je me regarde diversement. Toutes les contrarietez s'y trouvent selon quelque tour et en quelque façon. Honteux, insolent ; chaste, luxurieux ; bavard, taciturne ; laborieux, delicat ; ingenieux, hebeté ; chagrin, debonaire ; menteur, veritable ; sçavant, ignorant, et liberal et avare, et prodigue, tout cela, je le vois en moy aucunement, selon que je me vire ; et quiconque s'estudie bien attentifvement trouve en soy, voire et en son jugement mesme, cette volubilité et discordance. Je n'ay rien à dire de moy, entierement, simplement, et solidement, sans confusion et sans meslange, ny en un mot. (*Essais*, II, i, 371.) [1]

Because man is movement, change, variety, " il faut suivre longuement et curieusement sa trace " (p. 373), observing him " en destail et distinctement piece à piece " (p. 368). Montaigne is always prepared to revise his view of himself : " Je ne vise icy qu'à decouvrir moy mesmes, qui seray par adventure autre demain, si nouveau apprentissage me change " (*Essais*, I, xxvi, 180).

Thus, Montaigne's Heraclitean world-view extends to the realm of human experience. Man himself is ambivalent, an amalgam of contraries flowing one into another. The essay " Nous ne goustons rien de pur " (II, xx) treats of this " mixtion humaine ". Pleasure and pain, good and evil, virtue and vice, laughter and tears, justice and injustice, cannot be abstracted and isolated : " Des plaisirs et biens que nous avons, il n'en est aucun exempt de quelque meslange de mal et d'incommodité. ... Nostre extreme volupté a quelque air de gemissement et de plainte. ... Les loix mesmes de la justice ne peuvent subsister sans quelque meslange d'injustice " (*Essais*, II, xx, 758ff.). The complexities of human experience, resisting compartmentalized thought, do not correspond to linguistic conventions. The ambiguity of moral qualities is rooted ultimately in our biologic nature : " Nature nous descouvre cette confusion : les peintres tiennent que les mouvemens et plis du visage qui servent au pleurer, servent aussi au rire. De vray, avant que l'un ou l'autre soyent achevez d'exprimer, regardez à la conduicte de la peinture : vous estes en doubte vers lequel c'est qu'on va. Et l'extremité du rire se mesle aux larmes " (*ibid.*, pp. 759f.). This means that vice and virtue are meaningless as abstract concepts. They have signification only in reference to concrete facts—the individual, the situation, the action, the consequences—which are of infinite diversity and variety. Nor can they be separated from one another : " Quand je me confesse à moy religieusement, je trouve que la meilleure bonté que j'aye, a de la teinture vicieuse " (*ibid.*, p. 760) ; " et il y a des vices qui ont je ne sçay quoy de genereux, s'il le faut ainsi dire. Il y en a où la science se mesle, le diligence, la vaillance, la prudence, l'adresse et la finesse " (*Essais*, II, ii, 375). It is from the study of particulars, the actions of others,

---

[1] Diderot also recognizes in himself a mercurial temperament. See his critique of Michel Van Loo's portrait of him which he feels does not do justice to his variety of expression and emotion (A-T, XI, 21). However, he feels that it is possible, by dint of effort, to overcome his restless " tête de Langrois " (*Corr.*, II, 207).

and finally of himself, that Montaigne learns to distinguish and refine the essences from the confused whole of human experience.

Montaigne's naturalism in essays v, ix, xii, and xiii of Book III consists precisely in his opposition to traditional dualism and his urgent reminder that man is a material being. Montaigne is essentially a realist. He recognizes that psychological experience is indissolubly bound up with the physical basis of human existence, that the human being is a psychophysical unity. But Montaigne's embrace of Nature is not synonymous with aestheticism or with an indulgence in bodily pleasure. The chapters of Book III, which are in a sense Montaigne's dialogue with himself, seek to effect a harmony between natural man in all his complexity, and man as he relates to society. The counterpoint to the " Nature chapters " are the " moral chapters " (i, ii, vi, x) in which Montaigne places greater stress on ethical principle. The claims of physical man are egocentric, self-oriented ; those of moral man are opposed to the self, lead out of the self towards society. The two are essentially inimical and, in the abstract, mutually exclusive. But for Montaigne, living is not an abstract problem to which reason can provide the answers, but a continuing series of practical problems in which only experience can be of aid. Ethics consists precisely in the continual shifting of man's center of gravity between what one owes to the inner self and what one owes to others.

For Montaigne, then, the problem of ethics consists primarily in defining the self and in achieving an inner order as well as a harmony between the self and the world. The essay " Sur des vers de Virgile " (III, v) insists on the honest recognition of the facts of human sexuality. Selfish and capricious, it is incompatible with a social institution such as marriage, which exists not for the sake of the individual but for that of the race (ibid., p. 950). Montaigne's morality is not hedonistic, however, for he realizes that social institutions are useful.

On the other hand, utility is not Montaigne's greatest good. The essay " De l'utile et de l'honneste " (III, i) treats this traditional moral dichotomy. Montaigne's opinion is one of high-minded principle : private utility does not justify the compromise of one's integrity, for which the only justification may possibly be the public good.

" De la vanité " (III, ix), in its turns and windings, represents the wavering movements of man's nature ; but its conclusion is Montaigne's exordium to follow the " commandement paradoxe " of the Delphic oracle, paradoxical because it is contrary to man's nature to study himself. Nature directs man's gaze outward. Montaigne's principle of following nature, expressed in " De l'experience " (III, xiii), is thus complex. Following nature does not mean abandoning oneself to one's body ; nor is it a capitulation of the will. On the contrary, the point of departure of ethics is self-study (" Du repentir ", III, ii) and its goal is freedom, the liberation of the self from the conflicting demands of both the physical self and the social self.

The essay " De mesnager sa volonté " (III, x) is the clearest statement of Montaigne's views on the individual's " engagement " in public

affairs and of the distinction he makes between the inner and outer man. The essay is in part a defense of Montaigne's relatively uneventful first term in office as Mayor of Bordeaux, and his practice of never giving completely of himself in order to retain his freedom. But aside from being an *apologia pro domo*, its moral lesson is to keep clear the separation between one's essential being as a man and one's function in society. " Le maire et Montaigne ont toujours esté deux, d'une separation bien claire " (*Essais*, III, x, 1134).

Montaigne's own reply to this essay is in " De la phisionomie " (III, xii). Here Montaigne has found the metaphor to express his definition of the self and of personality, which is the basis of his moral philosophy. He takes Socrates as the example of human perfection. By force of reason, Socrates overcame his exterior ugliness and rendered his soul beautiful. But Socrates is an exception to what Montaigne takes as nature's general rule : " la conformité et relation du corps à l'esprit " (*ibid.*, p. 1187). Montaigne feels himself to be quite the reverse of Socrates ; he has not corrected his natural disposition by force of reason. In contrast to the mask of appearance against which he earlier warned in " De mesnager sa volonté ", and to Socrates, who is too rare an example of virtue to serve as model, Montaigne proposes the example of his own life.

At the conclusion of the essay, Montaigne relates two personal experiences to illustrate the harmony between his physiognomy and his character. In both cases, Montaigne's outward appearance was responsible for his deliverance from his enemies. There is thus perfect accord between his appearance and his essence ; he wears no masks, simply that of his natural " complexion ". His awareness of his natural disposition enables him to achieve a unity of self. Self-awareness, however, is not self-consciousness. Montaigne's method of self-study leads him to the firm possession of personality which results in the conformity of the inner and outer man. The experiences described in " De la physionomie " provide an objective confirmation of Montaigne's estimate of himself. The inner knowledge to which introspection had led him is also apparent to those who meet him for the first time. The strength and freedom which Montaigne had nurtured within himself were thus capable of being projected externally and of imposing themselves on his would-be captors. The supreme test of Montaigne's subjectivity is this confirmation by the most objective of observers, one's enemies. Montaigne's method therefore describes a circular movement. His withdrawal into himself is not a retreat into subjectivism because it leads him back into society in full possession of his own individuality.

Diderot's moral ideas and his conception of the self undergo an evolution. In his early works, he expresses a belief in the goodness of human nature : " ' La nature humaine est donc bonne ? ' Oui, mon ami, et très bonne. L'eau, l'air, la terre, le feu, tout est bon dans la nature ; ... ce sont les misérables conventions qui pervertissent l'homme, et non la nature humaine qu'il faut accuser " (*De la poésie dramatique, Œuvres esthétiques*, p. 195)*. This rather idealistic and simplistic view undergoes

rapid modification. Diderot soon begins to see something of the " mixtion humaine " of which Montaigne spoke. He becomes more and more convinced of the physical basis of all our moral ideas : " Il y a un peu de testicule au fond de nos sentiments les plus sublimes et de notre tendresse la plus épurée " (A Damilaville, 3 Nov. 1760, *Corr.*, III, 216). For Diderot, man is complex, contradictory and multivocal : " Un coup d'œil sur les inconséquences et les contradictions des hommes, et l'on voit que la plupart naissent moitié sots et moitié fous " (*Corr.*, III, 97f.). Diversity and contradiction are of the nature of man and of all things :

— Laissons là ce texte inépuisable de nos contradictions et examinons... comment il faut s'y prendre pour circonscrire un sujet.

— Tel par exemple que celui de la diversité de nos jugements ? ... Il est certain que cette diversité a lieu dans tous les hommes et dans toute matière.

— Et par conséquent sous ce point de vue général, c'est l'histoire du monde et de la tête de l'homme. (« De la diversité de nos jugements », A-T, IV, 24.)

Rameau's nephew is such an example of human contradictoriness : " C'est un composé de hauteur et de bassesse, de bon sens et de déraison. ... Rien ne dissemble plus de lui que lui-même " (*Neveu*, ed. Fabre, p. 4). The question asked concerning the character of Monsieur Hardouin, " Est-il bon, est-il méchant ? " receives the answer : " L'un après l'autre. — Comme vous, comme moi, comme tout le monde " (*Est-il bon, est-il méchant ?*, A-T, VIII, 244).

Diderot rings the changes on the theme of human inconstancy in practically every genre : in his correspondence, his speculative works, his art criticism, his dialogues, his theatre. Diderot himself, his fictional characters, his reader, all participate in the " grand branle de la terre ". A key to the theme of the *Neveu de Rameau* is given in the epigraph from Horace : " Vertumnis, quotquot sunt, natus iniquis " (" born under the malignant influence of change "). Rameau embodies malignant change, encompassing all the inconstancy, the contradictions, the pity and wonder, the iniquity of the human personality. In a sense, *Jacques le fataliste* is a set of variations on the theme of inconstancy, epitomized by the lyrical passage which suddenly interrupts the flow of the narrative : " Le premier serment que se firent deux êtres de chair, ce fut au pied d'un rocher qui tombait en poussière ; ils attestèrent de leur constance un ciel qui n'est pas un instant le même ; tout passait en eux et autour d'eux, et ils croyaient leurs cœurs affranchis de vicissitudes. O enfants ! toujours enfants ! " (*Œuvres rom.*, p. 604.) An almost identical passage appears in the *Supplément au voyage de Bougainville*. The moral intent of both passages is clearly to show the absurdity of absolute precepts and the social institutions which depend upon them. Both are incompatible with the law of our nature : inconstancy. The irony implicit in *Jacques le fataliste* is that the novel gives the appearance that nothing in it is fated or of consistent texture.

Diderot's awareness of his own changeability, and the imagery he uses to describe his character, remind us strongly of many passages in

the *Essais* in which Montaigne talks of his inconstancy. The Encyclopedist sometimes found himself " tiraillé par des sentiments bien opposés " (*Corr.*, V, 167). The contradictions of Diderot's thought are not necessarily logical but visceral.[1] His duality is not one of spirit and matter, but of intellect and sensibility—the two poles of man's biologic nature. His life and work were animated by this continual conflict : " J'enrage d'être empêtré d'une diable de philosophie que mon esprit ne peut s'empêcher d'approuver, et mon cœur de démentir " (*Corr.*, IX, 154). Like Montaigne, Diderot viewed himself as *homo duplex*, a unity of contradictions, which confirmed his sense of man's composite nature : " Dire que l'homme est un composé de force et de faiblesse, de lumière et d'aveuglement, de petitesse et de grandeur, ce n'est pas lui faire son procès, c'est le définir " (*Œuvres phil.*, p. 65).

But in spite of this acute awareness of inner flux and doubleness, neither Diderot nor Montaigne abandons himself completely to this incessant mobility. Montaigne tells us that there are two movements to his inner rhythm : " Or la cognoissance de cette mienne volubilité j'ay par accident engendré en moy quelque constance d'opinions, et n'ay guiere alteré les miennes premieres et naturelles. Car, quelque apparence qu'il y ayt en la nouvelleté, je ne change pas aisément, de peur que j'ay de perdre au change. ... Autrement, je ne me sçauroy garder de rouler sans cesse " (*Essais*, II, xii, 641). Elsewhere, especially in Book III, Montaigne has acquired a firmer hold upon himself, a stability of the whole person in possession of itself : " Je fay coustumierement entier ce que je fay, et marche tout d'une piece ; je n'ay guere de mouvement qui se cache et desrobe à ma raison, et qui ne se conduise à peu près par le consentement de toutes mes parties, sans division, sans sedition intestine " (III, ii, 908). In the course of his self-auscultation, Montaigne recognizes in himself a fundamental guiding pattern which abides beyond all diversity and internal contradiction : " Il n'est personne, s'il s'escoute, qui ne descouvre en soy une forme sienne, une forme maistresse, qui luicte contre l'institution, et contre la tempeste des passions qui luy sont contraires " (*Essais*, III, ii, 907).

Likewise Diderot, while he prizes his mobile sensibility, recognizes a certain constancy in himself :

Je suis constant dans mes goûts. Ce qui m'a plu une fois me plaît toujours, parce que mon choix m'est toujours motivé. Que je haïsse ou que j'aime, je sais pourquoi. Il est vrai que je suis porté naturellement à négliger les défauts et à m'enthousiasmer des qualités. Je suis plus affecté des charmes de la vertu que de la difformité du vice. Je me détourne doucement des méchants, et je vole au-devant des bons. S'il y a dans un tableau, dans une statue, un bel endroit, c'est là que mes yeux s'arrêtent. Je ne vois que cela ; je ne me souviens que de cela. Le reste est presque oublié. (*Corr.*, II, 208.)

Diderot discovers that his " forme maistresse ", his natural disposition, leans towards virtue rather than towards vice. This propensity

---

[1] Vernière terms Diderot's dual nature a " bipolarité physiologique " based in the brain and the nervous system (ed. *Œuvres phil.*, p. xxii).

leads Diderot to attempt to reconcile materialist determinism with morality.

In his study of Diderot's moral ideas, Pierre Hermand does not find Montaigne's influence more than of slight importance.[1] Jean Thomas, on the other hand, views Diderot as the authentic descendant of the great Renaissance humanist.[2] According to Thomas, Diderot followed Montaigne's footsteps in creating a set of values in an age of crisis and disorder : values emanating from a conception of man as a psycho-physical unity rather than as an abstraction. He suggests that Diderot was inspired by Montaigne's " experimental " method, by which he means chiefly Montaigne's self-analysis and self-portraiture. Erich Auerbach also terms Montaigne's method " experimental " from the fact that he uses " his own random life in its totality as a point of departure for moral philosophy ".[3] Now, Diderot does not use his own random life as his point of departure ; he does not begin by examining himself. On the contrary, we would be tempted to say that Diderot's method is the inverse of Montaigne's. He is led continually out of himself ; it is only towards the end of his life that he is drawn to introspection.

In the following addition to the *Lettre sur les sourds et muets*, Diderot considered introspection impossible :

Plusieurs fois, dans le dessein d'examiner ce qui se passait dans ma tête, et de *prendre mon esprit* sur le fait, je me suis jeté dans la méditation la plus profonde, me retirant en moi-même avec toute la contention dont je suis capable ; mais ces efforts n'ont rien produit. Il m'a semblé qu'il faudrait être tout à la fois au dedans et hors de soi ; et faire en même temps le rôle d'observateur et celui de la machine observée. Mais il en est de l'esprit comme de l'œil ; il ne se voit pas. (A-T, I, 402 ; *Corr.*, I, 121.)

It would be incorrect to take this passage as Diderot's definitive statement on the question of introspection. It must be taken into account that this work is one of Diderot's earliest attempts to theorize on these phenomena, and in his later works we find statements which, it seems to me, contradict the ideas expressed in the above passage. The reason that Diderot gives here for the impossibility of introspection is that he conceives it to be impossible for one mind to play two roles (" faire en même temps le rôle d'observateur et celui de la machine observée ").

Later in his life, however, the notion of dual functions evolves into the concept of *dédoublement*. For example, *Moi* and *Lui* in the *Neveu de Rameau*, and Jacques and his master in *Jacques le fataliste*, may be considered objectivizations of Diderot himself. In the *Paradoxe sur le comédien*, he conceives of the actor's art as a *dédoublement*, a division of the self into two principles : passion and control. If Diderot is unable

---

[1] *Les Idées morales de Diderot* (Paris, 1923), p. 12.

[2] *L'Humanisme de Diderot, passim.*

[3] *Mimesis* (New York, 1957), p. 262.

to be objective with himself using the procedures of introspection and self-analysis, he can do so by means of the techniques of fiction and the theatre. In Diderot, increased self-awareness leads to multiplication of the self, division of the self into diverse voices which combat and contradict one another like comedians playing their roles. Self-knowledge consists, perhaps, in precisely this awareness of the self's diversity.

What is the connection, if any, between Montaigne and Diderot in regard to self-study and self-portraiture? Pierre Villey, in his appendix to the 1930-31 Alcan edition of the *Essais*, relates a passage from Diderot's *Correspondance* to one from the *Essais* to which it bears resemblance. The Diderot passage is the following : " Vous faites trop d'honneur à ma pénétration. Quand on a un peu l'habitude de lire dans son propre cœur, on est bien savant sur ce qui se passe dans le cœur des autres " (à Sophie Volland, 20 Dec. 1765, *Corr.*, V, 228). The passage in the *Essais* reads thus : " Cette longue attention que j'employe à me considérer me dresse à juger aussi passablement des autres, et est peu de choses dequoy je parle plus heureusement et excusablement " (III, xiii, 1208). Indeed, Villey might have mentioned another similar passage in Diderot's works : " Celui qui se sera étudié lui-même, sera bien avancé dans la connaissance des autres, s'il n'y a, comme je le pense, ni vertu qui soit étrangère au méchant, ni vice qui soit étranger au bon " (A-T, III, 193). It may well be that this notion of knowing others through knowing oneself is an idea that Diderot gets directly from Montaigne. In the second Diderot passage quoted above, an additional reason is given for the efficacy of self-study ; we recognize it at once to be Montaigne's " mixtion humaine ".

Diderot speaks often in his correspondence, especially in his letters to Sophie Volland, of the need and the desire to study oneself. At the age of 49, he wrote to Mlle. Volland :

Comment, un astronome passe trente ans de sa vie au haut d'un observatoire, l'œil appliqué le jour et la nuit à l'extrémité d'un télescope, pour déterminer les mouvements d'un astre, et personne ne s'étudiera soi-même, n'aura le courage de nous tenir registre exact de toutes les pensées de son esprit, de tous les mouvements de son cœur, de toutes ses peines, de tous ses plaisirs ; et des siècles innombrables se passeront sans qu'on sache si la vie est une bonne ou une mauvaise chose, si la nature humaine est bonne ou méchante, ce qui fait notre bonheur et notre malheur. Mais il faudra bien du courage pour ne rien celer. (*Corr.*, III, 39.)

Certainly it is no longer a question in Diderot's mind whether introspection is possible, but only whether it is possible for *him*. It is difficult, and it demands courage and sincerity. This passage expresses glimmers of doubt concerning the value of scientific knowledge. Perhaps Diderot feels his life slipping away from him and that the drudgery of the *Encyclopédie* is keeping him from investigating what is most important of all : himself and his destiny. After over a dozen years of work on the project, perhaps Diderot is beginning to question its fruitfulness in the context of his own existence.

He appears to believe with Montaigne that an exact and sincere study of an individual will disclose secrets about the value of human existence, but he realizes that the obstacles to self-study are enormous :

On s'accuserait peut-être plus aisément du projet d'un grand crime que d'un petit sentiment obscur, vil et bas. Il en coûterait peut-être moins pour écrire sur son registre : « J'ai désiré le trône aux dépens de la vie de celui qui l'occupe », que pour écrire : « Un jour que j'étais au bain parmi un grand nombre de jeunes gens, j'en remarquai un d'une beauté surprenante, et je ne pus jamais m'empêcher de m'approcher de lui. » Cette espèce d'examen ne serait pas non plus sans utilité pour soi. Je suis sûr qu'on serait jaloux à la longue de n'avoir à porter en compte le soir que des choses honnêtes. Je vous demanderais, à vous : « Diriez-vous tout ? » Faites un peu la même question à Uranie ; car il faudrait absolument renoncer à un projet de sincé-rité qui vous effrayerait. Pour moi, dans l'éloignement où je suis de vous, je ne sache rien qui vous rapproche de moi, comme de vous dire tout et de vous rendre présente à mes actions par mon récit. (*Corr.*, IV, 39f.)

Indeed, his letters to Sophie Volland assume the character of a diary : " Mes lettres sont une histoire assez fidèle de la vie." And again : " Vous voyez que je suis toujours le plan que je me suis fait de ne vous laisser ignorer aucun des instants de ma vie " (*Corr.*, V, 225). Yet it is not only for Mlle. Volland that Diderot keeps his epistolary journal. For in addition to bringing his loved one closer to him, this record satisfies a deeper need. He requires others with whom to communicate : " Un plaisir, qui n'est que pour moi, me touche faiblement et dure peu. C'est pour moi et mes amis que je lis, que je réfléchis, que j'écris, que je médite, que j'entends, que je regarde, que je sens " (A-T, XI, 115).[1] For Diderot, self-study and self-portraiture are inseparable from his need for relationships with his contemporaries and ultimately with posterity. Like Montaigne, Diderot discovers that self-study is only possible through self-portraiture, which in turn demands an audience, whether it be interlocutor, correspondent or reader.

Diderot is wary, however, of using self-study as a basis for ethical philosophy. It is for this reason that he is dissatisfied with Helvétius' portrait of man : " Et voilà la véritable histoire de la vie, et non toutes ces suppositions sophistiques où je remarque beaucoup de sagacité sans nulle vérité ; des détails charmants et des conséquences absurdes ; et toujours le portrait de l'auteur proposé comme le portrait de l'homme " (A-T, II, 312).[2] Helvétius' application of Montaigne's method leads to

---

[1] Montaigne described a rather similar need. Cf. *Essais*, III, ix, 1105f. : " Nul plaisir n'a goust pour moy sans communication. Il ne me vient pas seulement une gaillarde pensée en l'ame qu'il ne me fache de l'avoir produite seul, et n'ayant à qui l'offrir."

[2] Diderot's comment is echoed by Gustave Lanson, who applies this critique to the moral philosophy of both Helvétius and Montaigne : " Je ne sais si on l'a assez remarqué ; les plus fragiles ou fausses morales ont toujours été proposées par de très honnêtes gens qui ont pris dans l'instinct et dans le plaisir la règle fondamentale de la vie, parce que leur instinct et leur plaisir ne les écartaient pas sensiblement des actions sans lesquelles

false conclusions about the nature of man. His reduction of man to his physical organization does not follow from Montaigne's experiential method. Montaigne's essay " De l'experience " is an unsystematic but highly sophisticated statement on the unsophisticated, non-intellectual nature of living ; yet it does not reduce experience to pleasure and pain. Diderot sees what is lacking in Helvétius' portrait of man. It is at the same time a grotesque over-simplification of the complexities of human reality and a distortion of what Montaigne had meant when he called for the union of mind and matter.

In his rejection of Helvétian materialism, Diderot marshalls Montaigne and the whole humanistic tradition. In spite of the fact that Diderot's materialism is itself empirical, deterministic, and insists upon the psychophysical unity of mental and bodily experience, it nevertheless seeks to preserve individuality and morality. Yet Diderot is mistrustful of subjectivity as the ultimate source of ethics. This is why he proposes an " experimental method " which may serve as a control and a test of subjectivity.

The *Neveu de Rameau* is an example of such an " expérience ".[1] The procedure of " dédoublement " is the corrective for introspection. The opposing voices of *Moi* and *Lui* submit Montaigne's natural ethic to dialectical examination. But " nature " itself is ambivalent. It provides us with one instinct designed for the preservation of the individual, and another aimed at the preservation of the species. Thus the difficulty of formulating an ethic founded on " nature ". " Following nature " may lead, on the one hand, to the benefit of the individual at the expense of society ; or on the other hand, it may lead to quite the reverse. In the *Neveu de Rameau*, Diderot explores the possible consequences of an ethic such as Montaigne's—an individualist, naturalist ethic—put into practice by a man such as Rameau who is endowed with a very different character and " complexion ". For Rameau, " following nature " means obeying instinct and the laws of his physical organization. The individualist ethic of a man of the Renaissance, when transposed to the shifting society of eighteenth-century Paris, becomes not ethic but amorality.[2]

Diderot's redefinition of subjectivity

In Diderot's opinion, the doctrine of Helvétius is anti-humanist since it fails to provide for the richness and variety of human experience :

---

il n'y a plus de morale, partant plus de société : ainsi Helvétius, ainsi Montaigne " (*Histoire de la littérature française*, ed. remaniée et complétée par Paul Tuffrau [Paris, 1951], p. 332).

[1] Lester Crocker has termed *Jacques le fataliste* and all of Diderot's fictional works " expériences morales " (" *Jacques le fataliste*, an ' expérience morale ' ", in *Diderot Studies III*, ed. Otis Fellows and Gita May [Geneva, 1961], p. 373).

[2] For a fuller treatment of the *Neveu de Rameau*, See above, pp. 44-48.

" Vous n'admettez que des plaisirs et des douleurs corporelles, et j'en ai éprouvé d'autres " (*Œuvres phil.*, p. 568). Diderot learns from the method of Montaigne, who rejected any and all conceptual definitions of man : " Les autres forment l'homme ; je le récite." The important point to observe is that Diderot's materialism makes an attempt to provide a biological basis for a new humanism. That is to say, Diderot's humanism is not opposed to materialism, but it transcends mechanistic determinism because it emerges even from within the materialist picture of man.

Let us first consider the question of man's physical organization. The organism is controlled by two centers : the brain (" l'origine du faisceau ") and the nervous system (" les filets du réseau "). According to a sensationalist view, human existence is determined from the impingement of exterior forces upon the sense organs, which then transmit these events to the brain, the *sensorium commune*. Such a view considers man as externally determined ; the system works from the outside. But surely, Diderot asks himself, this is not the whole of human experience ! Surely all men by their organization are not equally susceptible to the same external influences. There must be an internal determinism as well, which disposes differently of individual propensities. In modern terms, all is not due to environment to the exclusion of heredity. Character is not merely the result of training. Men are, by their physical make-up, through heredity (" la molécule paternelle " which Rameau blames for his failures), disposed either towards virtue or towards vice. Determinism is thus a two-edged sword. Likewise, the physical organization of man is ambivalent. What if it were possible for the pathways between the sense organs and the brain to serve equally well an opposite movement, from the brain to the sense organs ? Dr. Bordeu, in the *Rêve de d'Alembert*, speculates that there is a physiological basis for the concentration of existence which Diderot speaks of elsewhere as the purest form of happiness :

> Si l'origine du faisceau rappelle toutes les forces à lui, si le système entier se meut pour ainsi dire à rebours, comme je crois qu'il arrive dans l'homme qui médite profondément, dans le fanatique qui voit les cieux ouverts, dans le sauvage qui chante au milieu des flammes, dans l'extase, dans l'aliénation volontaire ou involontaire... eh bien, l'animal se rend impassible, il n'existe qu'en un point. (*Œuvres phil.*, p. 349.)

Physical organization is thus both passive and active. The intimate relationship between morality and physical organization, which is an idea Diderot expresses as early as the *Lettre sur les aveugles*, is also twofold. Not only are our ideas derived from our bodies, but the force of our ideas may exert itself upon our bodies as well. The brain, " l'origine du faisceau ", is the seat of memory ; this is its passive function. But it does not merely receive and record sense impressions ; nor is it determined solely by external forces. It has an active function as well : it is a force that can determine itself and the outside world.

112

Diderot conceives of a kind of happiness which would exist in a total release from time. Perfect happiness would be a state of delicious immobility :

Il ne lui restait dans ce moment d'enchantement et de faiblesse, ni mémoire du passé, ni désir de l'avenir, ni inquiétude sur le présent. Le temps avait cessé de couler pour lui, parce qu'il existait tout en lui-même ; le sentiment de son bonheur ne s'affaiblissait qu'avec celui de son existence. Il passait par un mouvement imperceptible de la veille au sommeil ; mais sur ce passage imperceptible, au milieu de la défaillance de toutes ses facultés, il veillait encore assez, sinon pour penser à quelque chose de distinct, du moins pour sentir toute la douceur de son existence : mais il en jouissait d'une jouissance tout-à-fait passive, sans y être attaché, sans y réfléchir. Si l'on pouvait fixer par la pensée cette situation de pur sentiment, où toutes les facultés du corps et de l'âme sont vivantes sans être agissantes, et attacher à ce quiétisme *délicieux* l'idée d'immutabilité, on se formerait la notion du bonheur le plus grand et le plus pur que l'homme puisse imaginer. (*Encyclopédie*, art. « Délicieux », A-T, XIV, 277f.)

Such a state of *ataraxia*, the pure sentiment of one's existence, is an extreme condition of the unity of the self. There is no longer any conflict between matter and mind, no duality of sensation and reflection. The supreme happiness would be this reintegration of *homo duplex*, a reduction of dichotomy to unity. This delicious state, in which time stands still, represents for Diderot not only the unity of the self, but that supreme union of the self with the world in which the whole universe is concentrated in the self. It is a state of which Diderot must have had an inkling at rare moments : " J'en étais là de ma rêverie, nonchalamment étendu dans un fauteuil, laissant errer mon esprit à son gré, état délicieux, où l'âme est honnête sans réflexion, l'esprit juste et délicat sans effort ; où l'idée, le sentiment semble naître en nous de lui-même comme d'un sol heureux " (A-T, XI, 113). Such an existence would be divine : " S'il est un Dieu, c'est ainsi qu'il est. Il jouit de lui-même " *(ibid.).* It is, however, not so much a realizable human happiness, but the nostalgia for an idea of self-transcendence which Diderot knows is quite impossible, though it may perhaps be glimpsed now and then in certain privileged moments of repose. Diderot cherishes these moments in which the self is pure, disembodied and replete withit self : " Je vous jure que je ne suis nulle part heureux, qu'à la condition de jouir de mon âme, d'être moi, moi tout pur " (*Corr.*, VII, 171).

Happiness then, consists in this concentration of one's existence which results in the alienation of the self from physical surroundings, from others, and from time. But such a definition of the self and its proper happiness is perhaps a chimera. Diderot considers the self rather in its relations with others ;[1] its proper happiness is defined also in terms of others, that is, as an expansion rather than a concentration of existence.

In his discussion with Falconet on the respect for posterity, Diderot formulates a definition of man based on his temporal expansiveness. The

---

[1] See above, pp. 110.

Falconet correspondence develops the idea that posterity satisfies man's desire for immortality, for the infinite extension of his brief terrestrial existence :

La sphère qui nous environne et où l'on nous admire, la durée pendant laquelle nous existons et nous entendons la louange, le nombre de ceux qui nous adressent directement l'éloge que nous avons mérité d'eux, tout cela est trop petit pour la capacité de notre âme ambitieuse. ... Il n'y a que cette foule d'adorateurs illimitée qui puisse satisfaire un esprit dont les élans sont toujours vers l'infini. (*Corr.*, V, 208.)

The difference between man and beast is this capacity to extend one's existence in all directions : " Celui qui concentrerait toute son existence dans un instant différerait peu de la brute ; ... il est de la nature de l'homme de s'entretenir du passé et de l'avenir " (*Corr.*, VI, 267). The position of those who have no regard for the future " confond l'homme dont la pente invincible est d'étendre son existence en tout sens, avec la brute qui n'existe que dans un point et dans un instant " (*ibid.*, p. 257). The animal exists only in the moment ; it sees nothing beyond. Man lives " dans le passé pour s'instruire ; dans le présent pour jouir ; dans l'avenir pour se le préparer glorieux à lui-même et aux siens. Il est de sa nature d'étendre son existence par des vues, des projets, des attentes de toute espèce " (*ibid.*, p. 259). The greatness of human activity consists in the widening of the arc of human existence as far as possible back into the past and forward into the future. Such is the life rhythm of " *l'homme pendule* " :

Ce présent est un point indivisible et fluant sur lequel l'homme ne peut non plus se tenir que sur la pointe d'une aiguille. Sa nature est d'osciller sans cesse sur ce *fulcrum* de son existence. Il se balance sur ce petit point d'appui, se ramenant en arrière ou se portant en avant à des distances proportionnées à l'énergie de son âme. Les limites de ses oscillations ne se renferment ni dans la courte durée de sa vie, ni dans le petit arc de sa sphère. (*Ibid.*, p. 86.)

As we have already seen,[1] Diderot involves Montaigne in his defense of " la gloire ", and quotes from the essay of that name (II, xvi). He strongly disagrees with the essayist on the question of the role of " gloire " as a spur to virtuous action. Montaigne, it will be remembered, contends that virtue is its own reward, although the judgment of posterity may be a useful lie serving to foster virtue. A concern for posterity, according to Montaigne, is merely an expression of human vanity. He, too, recognizes man's infinite aspirations, but he rejects them as folly.[2] It is only to God that glory and honor belong. Diderot could not be further

---

[1] See above, p. 42f.

[2] " Nous ne sommes jamais chez nous, nous sommes tousjours au delà. La crainte, le desir, l'esperance nous eslancent vers l'advenir, et nous desrobent le sentiment et la consideration de ce qui est, pour nous amuser à ce qui sera, voire quand nous ne serons plus " (*Essais*, I, iii, 35).

from the essayist here; the respect for posterity, far from being an example of vanity, is endowed by him with divine attributes. He utters a prayer to this object of his devotion; " O Postérité sainte et sacrée, soutien du malheureux qu'on opprime; toi qui es juste, toi qu'on ne corrompt point, qui venges l'homme de bien, qui démasques l'hypocrite, qui flétris le tyran; idée sûre, idée consolante, ne m'abandonne jamais " (*Corr.*, VI, 67). Posterity offers for Diderot the transcendence he rejects as an atheist. It offers immortality to the creative genius and ultimate justice to the righteous: " La postérité pour le philosophe, c'est l'autre monde de l'homme religieux " (*ibid.*). The judgment of posterity becomes the absolute which serves as the standard of moral action.

The faculty responsible for awareness of time is memory. It is the basis of Diderot's concept of the self: " Des sensations continues sans mémoire donneraient la conscience interrompue de son existence; elles ne produiraient nulle conscience du soi " (A-T, IX, 362). Without memory, one would only have awareness of discrete moments of existence and no consciousness of the self's unity: " L'animal est un tout, un, et c'est peut-être cette unité qui consitue l'âme, le soi, la conscience, à l'aide de la mémoire " (*ibid.*, p. 379). Indeed, the self consists in the consciousness of unity, made possible by " la mémoire immense ": " La mémoire immense ou totale est un état d'unité complet. ... C'est la liaison de tout ce qu'on a été dans un instant à tout ce qu'on a été dans l'instant suivant; états qui, liés par l'acte, rappelleront à un homme tout ce qu'il a senti toute sa vie " (*ibid.*, p. 370). In this manner, the individual is not merely the sum of his experiences. In man, there is an accretion of experience; in animals, only succession. Man absorbs each event, digests it, envelops it through the act of memory. Each event becomes fused into the totality of the individual's experience, is at his disposal, can be combined with other events, so that the individual at any given moment is not merely the result of the last event which occurred but of the totality of those events which exist in him all at once.

" La mémoire immense " is the memory of every sensation and thought the individual has ever experienced. It resembles what is called in modern terms the " subconscious ":

Je suis porté à croire que tout ce que nous avons vu, connu, aperçu, entendu; jusqu'aux arbres d'une longue forêt, que dis-je? jusqu'à la disposition des branches, à la forme des feuilles et à la variété des couleurs, des verts et des lumières; jusqu'à l'aspect des grains de sable du rivage de la mer, aux inégalités de la surface des flots soit agités par un souffle léger, soit écumeux et soulevés par les vents de la tempête; jusqu'à la multitude des voix humaines, des cris animaux et des bruits physiques, à la mélodie et à l'harmonie de tous les airs, de toutes les pièces de musique, de tous les concerts que nous avons entendus, tout cela existe en nous à notre insu. (*Eléments de physiologie*, A-T, IX, 366f.)

The individual's entire past remains in a constant state of immanent resurrection. Anticipating Proust, Diderot suggests a theory of in-

115

voluntary memory : " Un son de voix, la présence d'un objet, un certain lieu... et voilà un objet, que dis-je ? un long intervalle de ma vie rappelé. ... Me voilà plongé dans le plaisir, le regret ou l'affliction " (ibid., pp. 369f.). Human existence is distinguished then by the temporal unity of the self.

For Diderot, at the center of the world lies consciousness.[1] It has a dual aspect : it means consciousness of the self's unity and identity ; and it means the process by which the exterior world is interiorized. " Nous sommes toujours nous et pas une minute les mêmes " (Œuvres phil., p. 619). According to Ian Alexander, Diderot is describing the rhythm of human consciousness in the following passage : " Tout se réduit à revenir des sens à la réflexion, et de la réflexion aux sens : rentrer en soi et en sortir sans cesse, c'est le travail de l'abeille " (Œuvres phil., p. 185). Diderot seeks to " delimit the sphere and ascertain the specific qualities and status of the subject or reflective self within the objective and non-reflective, although living, world ".[2]   The originality of Diderot's materialism consists in his recognition of the reciprocal action of sensation and reflection, the " dehors " and " dedans ", and the importance which he gives to subjective values. Against a materialist objectivism may be juxtaposed as corrective the subjectivism of Montaigne. Diderot's own position, however, is rather a synthesis of the two extremes. In contrast to Montaigne, Diderot does not conceive of the self as pure subject cut off from objective reality. He is therefore not interested primarily in self-study per se, but in the interplay of subject and object which takes place in the mind.

We observe in Diderot's lifetime a gradual leaning towards the principle of control over impulse. Early in his career, he is the enthusiast of passion and sensibility.[3] Later, however, he is convinced that extreme sensibility is the mark of mediocrity,[4] while the mark of genius is the proper balance between passion and the controlling power of intellect. Diderot's materialism evolves and leads to a concept of the self that transcends mechanism. Rather than being subject to chance and the inexorable unfolding of the chain of events, the self becomes a center of energy capable of changing itself and the world. The self becomes a cause and an initiator of value.[5]

Let us examine the progressive development of Diderot's ideas on free-will and determinism. In the Lettre à Landois (1756), Diderot presents the following picture of man subjected to the determinism of external mechanism :

---

[1] See Ian W. ALEXANDER, " Philosophy of Organism and Philosophy of Consciousness in Diderot's Speculative Thought ", in Studies in Romance Philology and French Literature Presented to John Orr (Manchester, 1953).

[2] ALEXANDER, p. 2.

[3] Pensées philosophiques, Entretiens avec Dorval.

[4] Rêve de d'Alembert, Paradoxe sur le comédien.

[5] ALEXANDER, op. cit., p. 6.

116

Regardez-y de près et vous verrez que le mot *liberté* est un mot vide de sens ; qu'il n'y a point, et qu'il ne peut y avoir d'êtres libres ; que nous ne sommes que ce qui convient à l'ordre général, à l'organisation, à l'éducation, et à la chaîne des événements. Voilà ce qui dispose de nous invinciblement. On ne conçoit non plus qu'un être agisse sans motif, qu'un des bras d'une balance agisse sans l'action d'un poids ; et le motif nous est toujours extérieur, étranger, attaché ou par une nature ou par une cause quelconque, qui n'est pas nous. Ce qui nous trompe, c'est la prodigieuse variété de nos actions, jointe à l'habitude que nous avons prise tout en naissant de confondre le volontaire avec le libre. Nous avons tant loué, tant repris, nous l'avons été tant de fois, que c'est un préjugé bien vieux que celui de croire que nous et les autres voulons, agissons librement. (*Corr.*, I, 213f.)

The important thing to notice is that Diderot at this point has merely accepted the dogmas of a rigid determinism which presents but one half of the picture. He speaks of " l'ordre général ", " l'organisation ", " l'éducation ", " la chaîne des événements ". The motive of action is always " extérieur, étranger, attaché ou par une nature ou par une cause quelconque, qui n'est pas nous ". Such a description takes into account only physical, external events. It is impossible to accept such a crude schematization as identical with Diderot's mature thought, as many critics have done.[1] Indeed, in the *Rêve de d'Alembert*, Diderot's statement of the question of free-will is considered from an opposite point of view. He still denies the gratuitous act and insists on necessary causes, but now he speaks almost exclusively of *internal* causes : " Est-ce qu'on veut, de soi ? La volonté naît toujours de quelque motif intérieur ou extérieur, de quelque impression présente, de quelque réminiscence du passé, de quelque passion, de quelque projet dans l'avenir " (*Œuvres phil.*, p. 363). Diderot, in 1769, has seen that a determinist doctrine must take into account the phenomena of subjectivity, the complex inner world of human experience. He no longer categorically denies the existence of free-will. But now, he defines it in terms of necessity :

Après cela je ne vous dirai de la liberté qu'un mot, c'est que la dernière de nos actions est l'effet nécessaire d'une cause une : nous, très compliquée, mais une. — Nécessaire ? — Sans doute. Tâchez de concevoir la production d'une autre action, en supposant que l'être agissant soit le même. — Il a raison. Puisque c'est moi qui agis ainsi, celui qui peut agir autrement n'est plus moi ; et assurer qu'au moment ou je fais ou dis une chose, j'en puis dire ou faire une autre, c'est assurer que je suis moi et que je suis un autre. (*Ibid.*)

Free-will is thus not sacrificed to an external physical determinism, but is the expression of an internal physical determinism. Yet it is no less a determinism, one will say. This is true. Indeed, in this fact consists Diderot's synthesis of materialism and humanism ; free-will and determinism are no longer in contradiction because Diderot does not

---

[1] As, for example, Vernière, Roth, Guyot *et al.*

conceive them as distinct hypostatized abstractions; on the contrary, they are intimately conjoined in reality. The result is not a denial of freedom but a functional definition of free-will which at the same time encompasses individuality and subjective experience.

It is indeed paradoxical to define freedom in terms of necessity and determinism in terms of subjectivity. But then, this is the supreme paradox of the *Rêve de d'Alembert*. We shall examine this question in the following chapter when we discuss the structure of the *Rêve*. For the problem of reconciling materialism and humanism has become a problem of literary form.

V. LITERARY FORM AND THE ASSOCIATIVE MIND

> Every truly original spiritual form creates
> its proper linguistic form.
>
> Ernst CASSIRER [1]

Essay and dialogue

We have stated that the comprehension of reality depends on the
investigation of the processes of consciousness.   Diderot, among the
other *philosophes* of the eighteenth century, was fascinated by the mind
and the attempt to explain its workings.   Montaigne's method of self-
study—that is, the investigation of the nature of man and his mind
through the observation of direct experience, the immediate apprehension of a phenomenological existence—is translated by Diderot into
somewhat more theoretical terms.

For Diderot, the *Essais* are the " image fidèle des contradictions de
l'entendement humain ".   His appreciation of their disorderly composition is nothing less than a defense of the human mind.   What
Diderot really means is that the *Essais* are the faithful image of consciousness and its links with the world : " Montaigne suit sans art
l'enchaînement de ses idées ; il lui importe fort peu d'où il parte,
comment il aille, ni où il aboutisse. La chose qu'il dit, c'est celle qui
l'affecte dans le moment " (A-T, XVI, 485).   The foregoing passage
from the article " Pyrrhonienne " is central to the understanding both
of Diderot's appreciation of the *Essais* and of his analysis of consciousness.   Montaigne's book is, for Diderot, paradigmatic of the relationship
between the self and the world.   Montaigne changes from moment to
moment.   Each instant of time embodies within it the three modes of
time (implicit in Diderot's phrase " d'où il parte, comment il aille, où
il aboutisse ") ; that is, each instant involves the total temporal unity

---

[1] *The Philosophy of Symbolic Forms, Vol. I: Language* (New Haven,
1953), p. 141.

of Montaigne's existence, seen, however, from a different aspect. Each moment represents to consciousness a changed world, but consciousness remains one and establishes and preserves the continuity of these successive momentary worlds. Consciousness effectuates, through the process of sensation and reflective thought, the union of object and subject, the " dehors " and the " dedans ". Memory, as one of the constituent faculties of consciousness, is the repository of sensation and reflection and is responsible for the awareness of that unity in multiplicity which we call the self. The " liaisons nécessaires " are thus not mechanical but organic, involving a synthesis between thought and the world, between spirit and matter.

In the " Pyrrhonienne " article, Diderot implies that Montaigne was " artless ", that he was merely led by his ideas and that the *Essais* are a sort of naïve record. Nowhere in the article does Diderot suggest that Montaigne consciously knew what he was about when he composed the *Essais*. Montaigne himself tells us repeatedly that his manner in the *Essais* is the result of conscious choice. Scattered throughout his book are remarks which indicate that Montaigne was his own self-conscious observer. It is obvious, of course, that Montaigne was the first to know the special nature of his composition. Like Diderot, Montaigne early realizes that his mind suffers under protracted concentration :

> Je cognois, par experience, cette condition de nature, qui ne peut soustenir une vehemente premeditation et laborieuse. Si elle ne va gayement et librement elle ne va rien qui vaille. ... Elle veut estre eschaufée et reveillée par les occasions estrangeres, presentes et fortuites. Si elle va toute seule, elle ne fait que trainer et languir. L'agitation est sa vie et sa grace. (*Essais*, I, x, 60.)

He even speaks of *enchaînement*, that concept so dear to Diderot and the eighteenth century : " Tout argument m'est egallement fertile. Je les prens sur une mouche ; et Dieu veuille que celuy que j'ay icy en main n'ait pas esté pris par le commendement d'une volonté autant volage ! Que je commence par celle qu'il me plaira, car les matieres se tiennent toutes enchesnées les unes aux autres " (III, v, 981). Montaigne defends himself in advance against the charge of incoherence : " Je prononce ma sentence par articles descousus ainsi que de chose qui ne se peut dire à la fois et en bloc " (III, xiii, 1209) ; and in " De la vanité ", he justifies his digressions since his thoughts are all related : " Je m'esgare, mais plustot par licence que par mesgarde. Mes fantasies se suyvent, mais par fois c'est de loing, et se regardent, mais d'une veuë oblique " (III, ix, 1115). Well aware of the unusual disorder of the essay, Montaigne turns to Plato's *Phaedrus* as a precedent for his own licence :

> J'ay passé les yeux sur tel dialogue de Platon mi party d'une fantastique bigarrure, le devant à l'amour, tout le bas à la rhetorique. Ils ne creignent point ces muances, et ont une merveilleuse grace à se laisser ainsi rouler au vent, ou à le sembler. Les noms de mes chapitres n'en embrassent pas tousjours la matiere ; souvent ils la denotent seulement par quelque marque.

... J'ayme l'alleure poetique, à sauts et à gambades. C'est une art, comme dict Platon, legere, volage, demoniacle. ... O Dieu, que ces gaillardes escapades, que cette variation a de beauté, et plus lors que plus elle retire au nonchalant et fortuite. C'est l'indiligent lecteur qui pert mon subject, non pas moy. *(Ibid.)*

Expecting the reader to supply the missing transitions, Montaigne refuses to bend and twist his mobile mind to the demands of rhetoric and the patterns of discursive thought. " Mon stile et mon esprit vont vagabondant de mesme " (*ibid.*, p. 1116).

These statements regarding his style are twofold. Montaigne implies that his style is the faithful interpreter of the pathways of his mind, that he has not taken any care to put order into his book—to which he often refers in low comic style : " ce fagotage de tant de diverses pieces ", " ce fricassé que je barbouille icy ", " ce sont icy... des excremens d'un vieil esprit ". His detachment from his book reflects, in part, his aristocratic disdain for pedantry and the literary metier. He wishes to give the appearance of improvisation : " Mon dessein est de representer en parlant une profonde nonchalance et des mouvemens fortuites et impremeditez, comme naissans des occasions presentes " (III, ix, 1077).

Yet at the same time that Montaigne disclaims any artistic pretensions or method, these very disclaimers represent an *apologia pro domo*. The " accidental ", " unpremeditated " tone of the *Essais* results partly from the fact that the mind " est un mouvement irregulier, perpetuel, sans patron, et sans but " (III, xiii, 1199), but also from conscious choice. Montaigne's taste for improvisation, his refusal to adhere strictly to form or plan, his opposition to the tedious syllogizing of Scholastic doctors, amount to an aesthetic at the opposite pole from what may be termed classicism. Montaigne's aesthetic is subjective rather than objective, dynamic rather than static, open rather than closed.

Diderot inherits this aesthetic and contributes to the history of its development. In *De l'Interprétation de la nature* he warns the reader in advance that he is not dealing with a systematic treatise : " Je laisserai les pensées se succéder sous ma plume, dans l'ordre même selon lequel les objets se sont offerts à ma réflexion ; parce qu'elles n'en représenteront que mieux les mouvements et la marche de mon esprit " (A-T, II, 9). In the *Essai sur les règnes de Claude et de Néron*, Diderot writes : " Je ne compose point, je ne suis point auteur ; je lis ou je converse, j'interroge ou je réponds " (A-T, III, 10). Thus, Diderot too prefers the unsystematic, the accidental ; he insists that his style represents the movement of his thought ; and he rejects the role of professional author. In all this, he is in the tradition of Montaigne.

But it is none the less true, although less obvious, that Montaigne's apparent unconcern for method is deceptive. He is not as unsystematic as he claims. The " Apologie de Raimond Sebond " is far from being an unsystematic work. However, as Diderot realizes, Montaigne's

" method " is of a different order. Diderot speaks of Montaigne's " art " while comparing the essayist with Helvétius in his *Réflexions sur le livre de l'Esprit:*

[Helvétius] est très méthodique ; et c'est un de ses défauts principaux : premièrement, parce que la méthode, quand elle est d'appareil, refroidit, appesantit et ralentit ; secondement, parce qu'elle ôte à tout l'air de liberté et de génie ; troisièmement, parce qu'elle a l'aspect d'argumentation ; quatrièmement, et cette raison est particulière à l'ouvrage, c'est qu'il n'y a rien qui veuille être prouvé avec moins d'affectation, plus dérobé, moins annoncé qu'un paradoxe. Un auteur paradoxal ne doit jamais dire son mot, mais toujours ses preuves : il doit entrer furtivement dans l'âme de son lecteur, et non de vive force. C'est le grand art de Montaigne, qui ne veut jamais prouver, et qui va toujours prouvant, et me ballottant du blanc au noir, et du noir au blanc. D'ailleurs, l'appareil de la méthode ressemble à l'échafaud qu'on laisserait toujours subsister après que le bâtiment est élevé. C'est une chose nécessaire pour travailler, mais qu'on ne doit plus apercevoir quand l'ouvrage est fini. Elle marque un esprit trop tranquille, trop maître de lui-même. L'esprit d'invention s'agite, se meut, se remue d'une manière déréglée ; il cherche. L'esprit de méthode arrange, ordonne et suppose que tout est trouvé. ... Si tout ce que l'auteur a écrit eût été entassé comme pêle-mêle, qu'il n'y eût eu que dans l'esprit de l'auteur un ordre sourd, son livre eût été infiniment plus agréable, et, sans le paraître, infiniment plus dangereux. ... Ajoutez à cela qu'il est rempli d'historiettes : or les historiettes vont à merveille dans la bouche et dans l'écrit d'un homme qui semble n'avoir aucun but, et marche en dandinant et nigaudant ; au lieu que ces historiettes n'étant que des faits particuliers, on exige de l'auteur méthodique des raisons en abondance et des faits avec sobriété. (A-T, II, 272f.)

Montaigne's " art " consists in his very ability to dissimulate his method, to remove the scaffolding from the structure of his thought, so that his book reflects only the " ordre sourd " in his mind—the underlying order which is responsible for the inherent coherence of his ideas. Method, when it is a superstructure and not an organic necessity, stifles the mind's mobility ; it is a mark of a mind " trop maître de lui-même ". Here again we note Diderot's ideal of liberty. He attaches the notion of freedom to the idea of genius, imagination, and invention ; while method, argumentation, and order are associated in his mind with constraint, authority, prejudice.

The mobile mind, the " esprit primesautier ", is endowed with an astonishing rapidity of movement ; it is able to take sudden and soaring flight, to take enormous leaps from one idea to another, combining them not by methodical progression but in the perception of heretofore unsuspected relationships :

Le génie hâte... les progrès de la philosophie par les découvertes les plus heureuses et les moins attendues : il s'élève d'un vol d'aigle vers une vérité lumineuse, source de mille vérités auxquelles parviendra dans la suite en rampant la foule timide des sages observateurs. Mais à côté de cette vérité lumineuse, il placera les ouvrages de son imagination : incapable de marcher

dans la carrière, et de parcourir successivement les intervalles, il part d'un point et s'élance vers le but ; il tire un principe fécond des ténèbres : il est rare qu'il suive la chaîne des conséquences ; il est *primesautier,* pour me servir de l'expression de Montaigne. Il imagine plus qu'il n'a vu ; il produit plus qu'il ne conduit. (Art. « Génie », *Œuvres esth.,* p. 14.) [1]

It is this quality of mind that leads to the procedures of digression and dialogue in Diderot's works. He allows himself to be borne away by the winds of circumstance to unexpected regions, and enjoys being taken by surprise by his own mind. Infinitely rich, always in process of self-creation, bursting with energy, his mind is never at rest. Yet paradoxically, Diderot finds relaxation in digression ; it is his re-creation : " Et puis, encore une petite digression, s'il vous plaît. ... Cette contention me fatigue, et la digression me repose " (*Corr.,* IV, 264). He is aware that digression as a literary procedure is commonly considered the recourse of an inferior, superficial intellect unable to bear the concentrated attention that close reasoning requires. Yet his frequent justification of his *écarts* is not indicative of a need to make excuses for any lack of order. On the contrary, it shows that he was well aware of the demands of methodical procedure, and that every time he departs from a systematic presentation it is because his method demands that he do so : " — Et vous voilà, après une assez longue excursion, revenu au point d'où vous êtes parti. — C'est que, dans la science ainsi que dans la nature, tout se tient ; et qu'une idée stérile et un phénomène isolé sont deux impossibilités " (*Corr.,* VII, 261).

Diderot's " libertinage d'esprit " is couched in a picturesque image in the prologue to the *Neveu de Rameau:*

Je m'entretiens avec moi-même... ; j'abandonne mon esprit à tout son libertinage. Je le laisse maître de suivre la première idée sage ou folle qui se présente, comme on voit dans l'allée de Foy nos jeunes dissolus marcher sur les pas d'une courtisane à l'air éventé, au visage riant, à l'œil vif, au nez retroussé, quitter celle-ci pour une autre, les attaquant toutes et ne s'attachant à aucune. Mes pensées, ce sont mes catins. (Ed. Fabre, p. 3.) [2]

The mind must consciously abandon itself, allow itself to be led by ideas which have an existence all their own. The mind is paradoxically both free and not-free. In freeing itself from the constraints of system

---

[1] It is with due reservations that we present this passage from the article " Génie " which most Diderot scholars now agree to be the work of St. Lambert. (For a detailed account of the evidence leading to this conclusion, see Herbert DIECKMANN, " Diderot's Conception of Genius ", *Journal of the History of Ideas,* II [April 1941], 151-182.) Paul Vernière, however, includes it in his edition of Diderot's *Œuvres esthétiques* because he is convinced that Diderot had a hand in its composition (*Œuvres esthétiques,* p. 15). Cf. Montaigne : " J'ay un esprit primsautier. Ce que je ne voy de la premiere charge, je le voy moins en m'y obstinant " (*Essais,* II, xii, 556).

[2] The reader easily recognizes similarities in this passage to Montaigne's manner, to the self-dialogue, the free-association, the caprice of the *Essais.*

and method, it becomes fascinated by its own wanderings and is led further and further out into the world. Yet Diderot's mind appears to consist of a willing self (" Je "), quite apart from his thought. The mind maintains its independence from its ideas and from the *enchaînement* of phenomenological experience.

In the *Encyclopédie* article " Distraction ", Diderot explains further what he means by " libertinage d'esprit " and its origin in the mind's associative faculty :

> La distraction a sa source dans une excellente qualité de l'entendement, une extrême facilité dans les idées de se réveiller les unes les autres. C'est l'opposé de la stupidité qui reste sur une même idée. L'homme distrait les suit toutes indistinctement à mesure qu'elles se montrent ; elles l'entraînent et l'écartent de son but : celui qui au contraire est maître de son esprit jette un coup d'œil sur les idées étrangères à son objet, et ne s'attache qu'à celles qui lui sont propres. ... On peut, avec un peu d'attention sur soi-même, se garantir de ce libertinage d'esprit. (A-T, XIV, 287.)

Clearly, Diderot considers the wandering of the mind fruitful only insofar as the conscious will is in the ascendancy. It is certainly not a question of limitless free-association or " stream-of-consciousness ".

The late Renaissance and the late eighteenth century are periods of transition, in which modes of thought are undergoing transformation. Just as Montaigne had to evolve a form suitable to his own mind and temperament, so does Diderot have to arrive at a means of expression that corresponds to his own dynamic philosophy. As we have earlier remarked, Diderot allows his ideas to generate themselves, and in so doing they create their own form : " Je jette mes idées sur le papier et elles deviennent ce qu'elles peuvent " (*Corr.*, I, 125). In a fragment " Sur la diversité de nos jugements ", Diderot uses the imagery of the chase, Montaigne's particular favorite, and expresses his preference for the essay over the treatise : " J'aime mieux laisser courir mon homme à toutes jambes que de l'arrêter par une interruption qui le détourne de sa route. J'aime mieux un essai qu'un traité ; un essai où l'on me jette quelques idées de génie, presque isolées, qu'un traité où ces germes précieux sont étouffés sous un amas de redites " (A-T, IV, 23). Diderot exhibits a predilection for such forms as the *pensée*, the letter, and the *entretien*. The letter and the *pensée détachée* are free forms which allow a wide latitude of expression ; the letter and the *entretien* reproduce the give-and-take of conversation.

Diderot defends the freedom of the letter as a literary form as follows : " Quant à la multitude des objets sur lesquels je me plais à voltiger, sachez, et apprenez à ceux qui vous conseillent, que ce n'est point un défaut dans une lettre, où l'on est censé converser librement, et où le dernier mot d'une phrase est une transition suffisante " (*Corr.*, I, 101). And again : " J'aurai de l'indulgence pour le style épistolaire, je conviendrai que la familiarité de ce genre admet des pensées et des expressions qu'on s'interdirait dans un autre " (A-T, III, 194). The letter is eminently suited to capturing the rapidity of thought in flight, its

informality liberating the writer from the labored steps of methodical progression, allowing him to give free rein to the natural heat of his ideas. Montaigne also was fond of the free expansiveness of the letter :

J'escris mes lettres tousjours en poste, et si precipiteusement que, quoy que je peigne insupportablement mal, j'ayme mieux escrire de ma main que d'y employer un'autre, car je n'en trouve poinct qui me puisse suyvre, et ne les transcris jamais. ... Celles qui me coustent le plus sont celles qui valent le moins : depuis que je les traine, c'est signe que je n'y suis pas. Je commence volontiers sans project ; le premier traict produict le second. (*Essais*, I, xl, 292.)

Both writers thus share this ideal of a natural form of expression which does not seek to be exhaustive in its treatment of ideas, but rather tries to elicit in the mind of the reader his participation in the movement of thought. By means of suggestion, of sudden and unexpected turns as in animated conversation, by merely sketching in, as it were, the bare outlines of an idea and its implications, it extends the range of ideas into the unknown region of the reader's mind.

Related to this is the distinction Diderot makes between the qualities of the sketch and the finished oil painting :

Les esquisses ont communément un feu que le tableau n'a pas. C'est le moment de chaleur de l'artiste, la verve pure, sans aucun mélange de l'apprêt que la réflexion met à tout ; c'est l'âme du peintre qui se répand librement sur la toile. La plume du poète, le crayon du dessinateur habile, ont l'air de courir et de se jouer. La pensée rapide caractérise d'un trait ; or, plus l'expression des arts est vague, plus l'imagination est à l'aise. (A-T, X, 351f.)

Pourquoi une belle esquisse nous plaît-elle plus qu'un beau tableau ? c'est qu'il y a plus de vie et moins de formes. A mesure qu'on introduit les formes, la vie disparaît... l'esquisse est l'ouvrage de la chaleur et du génie. (A-T, XI, 245.)

L'esquisse ne nous attache peut-être si fort, que parce qu'étant indéterminée, elle laisse plus de liberté à notre imagination, qui y voit tout ce qu'il lui plaît. (*Ibid.*, p. 246.)

In graphic art, it is the sketch that accommodates both the natural expression of the artist's genius and the free play of the observer's imagination. In his mind's eye, the observer transforms the delicate line, the patch of white paper, into the full-bodied forms which emerge from this partnership between the artist and himself. The sketch represents for Diderot the form of expression most suited to his conception of the nature of genius.

The qualities of incompleteness and suggestivity, which are characteristic of the sketch, are qualities which Montaigne himself observed in the *Essais:*

Je sçay bien, quand j'oy quelqu'un qui s'arreste au langage des Essais, que j'aimeroye mieux qu'il s'en teust. Ce n'est pas tant eslever les mots, comme c'est deprimer le sens, d'autant plus picquamment que plus obliquement. Si suis je trompé, si guere d'autres donnent plus à prendre en la

matiere ; et, comment que ce soit, mal ou bien, si nul escrivain l'a semée ny
guere plus materielle ny au moins plus drue en son papier. Pour en ranger
davantage, je n'en entasse que les testes. Que j'y attache leur suitte, je
multiplieray plusieurs fois ce volume. Et combien y ay-je espandu d'histoires
qui ne disent mot, les quelles qui voudra esplucher un peu ingenieusement,
en produira infinis Essais. (I, xl, 289.)

The *Essais* have the power of infinite expansion in the reader's imagination :

Ny elles, ny mes allegations ne servent pas tousjours simplement
d'exemple, d'authorité ou d'ornement. Je ne les regarde pas seulement par
l'usage que j'en tire. Elles portent souvent, hors de mon propos, la semence
d'une matiere plus riche et plus hardie, et sonnent à gauche un ton plus
delicat, et pour moy qui n'en veux exprimer d'avantage, et pour ceux qui
rencontreront mon air. *(Ibid.)*

In the same essay (" Consideration sur Ciceron "), Montaigne makes the
following addition on the subject of letters, which throws further light
on the form of the *Essais:*

Et eusse prins plus volontiers ceste forme à publier mes verves, si j'eusse
eu à qui parler. Il me falloit, comme je l'ay eu autrefois, un certain commerce
qui m'attirast, qui me soustinst et souslevast. Car de negocier au vent,
comme d'autres, je ne sçauroy que de songes, ny forger des vains noms à
entretenir en chose serieuse : ennemy juré de toute falsification. J'eusse
esté plus attentif et plus seur, ayant une addresse forte et amie, que je ne
suis, regardant les divers visages d'un peuple. Et suis deceu, s'il ne m'eust
mieux succedé. *(Ibid.,* pp. 290f.)

That is to say, if Etienne de La Boétie had not died, Montaigne would
perhaps have published his Correspondence. Montaigne needs an
interlocutor ; his thought thrives on conflict, argument, contradiction :
" Les contradictions donc des jugemens ne m'offensent ny m'alterent ;
elles m'esveillent seulement et m'exercent " (*Essais*, III, viii, 1034).
The letter is, after all, but one half of a dialogue. Montaigne had to
evolve a literary form which embodied aspects of the letter and the
dialogue. This is precisely what he does in the *Essais.* His tone is that
of free-and-easy, intimate conversation. We recall Auerbach's feeling
on reading the *Essais*, that he thought he could hear Montaigne speak
and see his gestures.[1] The formulations of the author of *Mimesis* are
striking to anyone who has read enough of Diderot to feel at home with
him. This propensity to reproduce the tone of conversation leads both
authors to use the device of dialogue, which for Diderot is the preferred
form.

---

[1] Erich AUERBACH, *Mimesis* (New York, 1957), p. 254. Auerbach
characterizes Montaigne's tone as " a lively but unexcited and very richly
nuanced conversation. We can hardly call it a monologue for we constantly
get the impression that he is talking to someone " (p. 271).

In recent years, scholars have remarked Montaigne's fondness for the dialogue form.[1] He did not, of course, practice the dialogue as a literary genre. What is interesting, however, is that it is incipient throughout the *Essais*. He did not appropriate the dialogue form as it was practiced in Antiquity or by his contemporaries such as Jean Tahureau. He required a much less rigid form for the presentation of his " niaiseries ". The essay, as Montaigne created it, is a form open to continual addition, growing and developing as a living organism existing in time. It is not static but mobile, never in a state of being but in continual passage. Similarly, Diderot's use of the dialogue is different from the prevailing eighteenth-century practice. For him the dialogue form is not a classical genre ready-made as a vehicle for the expression of his ideas. It is a form which Diderot evolves and shapes to his own temperament and to the character of his thought. He discovers the dialogue progressively. His early works are not dialogues, though they may contain dialogue. Niklaus has pointed out, for example, that the apparent lack of composition in the *Pensées philosophiques* is explained by the fact that it is in reality a dialogue, in which only the external formal trappings and the names of the speakers are missing.[2] Diderot thus listens early to the voices arguing within him, but it is not until later that the dialogue form comes to full bloom in such works as the *Rêve de d'Alembert*, the *Neveu de Rameau* and *Jacques le fataliste*.[3] Diderot's method of *dédoublement*, by which his own conflicting ideas are lodged in the mouths of interlocutors, can be observed to some extent in Montaigne.

Montaigne's use of dialogue proceeds from his habit of self-auscultation. Floyd Gray, in his study of Montaigne's style, tells us that Montaigne engages in dialogue with himself, with his book, with personages of Antiquity and with imaginary interlocutors, but that in spite of this " dialogue perpétuel " there is very little conversation in the *Essais*. He points out that Montaigne, although he is a gifted story-teller, does not have the novelist's ability to project outside of himself characters endowed with an existence independent of their creator.[4] This is, of course, to be expected in a writer who is not interested in the study of character, but who is interested above all in himself. If the

---

[1] See F. GRAY, *Le Style de Montaigne* (Paris, 1958), pp. 241-244 ; also D. M. FRAME, " What Next in Montaigne Studies ? " *French Review*, XXXVI (May 1963), 578.

[2] *Pensées philosophiques*, ed. Niklaus, p. xx. " Les *Pensées* sont pour une bonne part une sorte de conversation entre un athée, un superstitieux et un déiste. ... Diderot laisse parler les différents interlocuteurs pour approfondir sa pensée, pour éviter de construire un système dogmatique, et partir en quête de découvertes nouvelles " *(ibid.)*.

[3] Diderot's use of dialogue is a subject beyond the scope of this study. (See on this matter Roland MORTIER, " Diderot et le problème de l'expressivité : de la pensée au dialogue heuristique ", *CAIEF*, XIII [Juin 1961].) We discuss it only insofar as it bears relation to Montaigne, whose use of dialogue is less well-known.

[4] GRAY, *op. cit.*, p. 206.

Essais be compared with the novel, it is a precursor of the ironic philosophical novel (such as *Jacques le fataliste*), or the novel of the hero's search for himself. In the *Essais*, dialogue serves the functions both of expressing the multiple dimensions of Montaigne's mind and of waging the battle of ideas.

Montaigne is constantly aware of his merits and his faults, always listening to his other self, the criticizing, evaluating self. His two inner voices are in continual contradiction, and his irony results from this internal combat. His ironic " doubleness " is thus very close to Diderot's dialogue. Montaigne often makes diametrically opposed statements in various parts of the *Essais*. This is partly because the *Essais* are a record of change, but the answer does not entirely lie there. Why indeed does Montaigne change so often, if not for the reason that this very variation is caused by the rhythm of his opposing selves? It is now one voice that is in the ascendancy, now another; now the voice of reason, now that of feeling; now that of the ego, now that of conscience. There is the Montaigne who speaks disparagingly of himself, of his position in society, of his memory, of his book; and there is the Montaigne who is smug, self-satisfied, and vain. In the effort to see clear within himself, he has great difficulty in sorting and separating the contradictions of his nature. Hence, the ambiguity and " slipperiness " of his style.

The rambling monologue that is the *Essais* seems always on the verge of erupting spontaneously into dialogue, and indeed it often does. Among the brief outbursts is the tripartite self-dialogue in " Du parler prompt ou tardif " : " J'aurai eslancé quelque subtilité en escrivant. (J'enten bien : mornée pour un autre, affilée pour moy. Laissons toutes ces honnetetez. Cela se dit par chacun selon sa force)..." (I, x, 60). The honest conscience attempts to temper apparent vanity with modesty, but is itself interrupted and effectively silenced by a third voice speaking in the name of a deeper honesty which rejects false modesty. Other examples are Montaigne's defense of his style in " Sur des vers de Virgile " :

Quand on m'a dit ou que moy-mesme me suis dict : Tu es trop espais en figures. Voilà un mot du creu de Gascoingne. Voilà une frase dangereuse (je n'en refuis aucune de celles qui s'usent emmy les rues françoises ; ceux qui veulent combatre l'usage par la grammaire se moquent). Voilà un discours ignorant. Voilà un discours paradoxe. En voilà un trop fol. Tu te joues souvent ; on estimera que tu dies à droit, ce que dis à feinte. — Oui, fais-je ; mais je corrige les fautes d'inadvertence, non celles de coustume. Est-ce pas ainsi que je parle partout ? me represente-je pas vivement ? Suffit ! (III, v, 979.)

and the passage late in " De l'experience " :

Nous sommes de grands fols : Il a passé sa vie en oisiveté, disons nous ; je n'ay rien faict d'aujourd'huy. — Quoy, avez vous pas vescu ? C'est non seulement la fondamentale mais la plus illustre de vos occupations. — Si on m'eust mis au propre des grands maniements, j'eusse montré ce que je

sçavoy faire. — Avez vous sceu mediter et manier vostre vie? vous avez faict la plus grande besoigne de toutes. (III, xiii, 1247.)

It is especially evident in this last example that Montaigne, through the use of an imaginary interlocutor, not only addresses himself to the reader but actually envelops him in his book. He invents, as it were, a character to play the role of reader, using a device for which Diderot had a marked predilection.[1]

Montaigne also uses the dialogue as an implicit structural principle, creating whole chapters in the form of a debate. Gray, in his all too brief discussion of the composition of " Coustume de l'isle de Cea ", is content merely to say that the whole essay " suit le même schème, et a un ordre intérieur ",[2] the scheme being a reflection on suicide as a means of avoiding an uncertain death. He seems not to have noticed the antithetical structure of the essay. This is especially surprising since he states three pages later that antithesis is a constant element of Montaigne's composition.[3]

The essay is a full-scale debate for and against the right of an individual to take his own life. Nevertheless it is not precisely correct to say, with Friedrich, that it " wanders back and forth between for and against ".[4] The essay has a clearly marked scheme and the argument proceeds in a definitely ordered manner. It begins with an introductory paragraph which presents Montaigne's detached, skeptical point of view: " Si philosopher c'est douter, comme ils disent, à plus forte raison niaiser et fantastiquer, comme je fais, doit estre doubter. Car c'est aux apprentifs à enquerir et à debatre, et au cathedrant de resoudre. Mon cathedrant, c'est l'authorité de la volonté divine, qui nous reigle sans contredit et qui a son rang au dessus de ces humaines et vaines contestations " (II, iii, 385). Then follow two pages, more or less paraphrased from Seneca's *Letters*, presenting the Stoical attitude towards suicide. The Stoic's chief argument appears to be the aesthetic superiority of suicide: " La plus volontaire mort, c'est la plus belle " (*ibid.*, p. 386). Now, the second part of the essay, the presentation of the opposing arguments, follows immediately after Montaigne's comment: " Cecy ne s'en va pas sans contraste " (p. 387). Among the first reasons Montaigne gives against suicide are the arguments of Christianity and social responsibility; further, it is not virtuous but cowardly to rush into the tomb in order to avoid the strokes of Fortune. Finally, and this is the most telling argument, stoical suicide is absurd and unnatural:

Et l'opinion qui desdaigne nostre vie, elle est ridicule. Car en fin c'est notre estre, c'est nostre tout... c'est contre nature que nous nous mesprisons

---

[1] Cf. DIDEROT, *Ceci n'est pas un conte*, *Œuvres rom.*, p. 793. See also, H. DIECKMANN, " Diderot et son lecteur ", *Cinq Leçons sur Diderot*, pp. 17-39.

[2] GRAY, *op. cit.*, p. 206.

[3] *Ibid.*, p. 209.

[4] FRIEDRICH, *Montaigne*, p. 337.

et mettons nous mesmes à nonchaloir ; c'est une maladie particuliere, et qui ne se voie en aucune autre creature, de se hayr et desdeigner. C'est de pareille vanité que nous desirons estre autre chose que ce que nous sommes. (P. 389.)

The second part of this quotation (" c'est une maladie... sommes ") resembles the tone of the " Apologie ", while the opening lines fore-shadow the life-oriented attitude of Book III.

The third part of the essay, the examination of particular cases, is the concluding and necessary stage of Montaigne's dialectic. It is introduced by the sentence : " Entre ceux du premier advis, il y a eu grand doute sur ce : Quelles occasions sont assez justes pour faire entrer un homme en ce party de se tuer ? " (P. 390.) From the application of the criteria used by the ancients to specific examples, Montaigne arrives at his conclusion which is in general a rejection of suicide, although he does grant that there may be mitigating circumstances such as unbearable pain and a certain and more painful death (p. 399).

The essay " De la cruauté " provides another example of Montaigne's penchant for debate. The first half of the essay is a discussion of the nature of virtue. Montaigne begins by distinguishing between virtue and natural goodness. It seems to him that virtue presupposes difficulty and the overcoming of contrary appetites. After two pages in this vein, he suddenly pulls the reader up short : " Je suis venu jusques icy bien à mon aise. Mais, au bout de ce discours, il me tombe en fantasie que l'ame de Socrates, qui est la plus parfaicte qui soit venue à ma connoissance, seroit, à mon compte, une ame de peu de recommandation : car je ne puis concevoir en ce personnage là aucun effort de vitieuse concupiscence " (II, xi, 466). Thus, Montaigne's preliminary definition of virtue leads to a paradox : Socrates, the paragon of men, cannot be considered virtuous. Montaigne sees that his initial notion of virtue is inadequate because it defines virtue only with respect to vice : " Si la vertu ne peut luire que par le combat des appetits contraires, dirons nous donq qu'elle ne se puisse passer de l'assistance du vice, et qu'elle luy doive cela, d'en estre mise en credit et en honneur ? " (Ibid.) Such a definition would not account for the serene and dispassionately beautiful death of Socrates or of Cato, for the ease with which they faced death in no way detracts from their virtue. Montaigne concludes from this that the finest form of virtue is that exemplified by Socrates and Cato who by dint of the highest resolution so formed themselves in the habits of virtue that they rooted out the seeds of vice within them. The virtue which involves a victory of reason over passion is less noble, although it remains superior to that innocence which is purely fortuitous and closer to weakness than to strength. It is in this last category that Montaigne places his own virtue, and the essay then passes into a discussion of his character.

It is significant that these examples of Montaigne's structural use of dialogue occur in two essays which were written at approximately the same time (1573-74), and which immediately precede the composition of the " Apologie " (1576). We have already noted the keynote sentence

of " Coustume de l'isle de Cea " : " Si philosopher c'est douter, comme ils disent, à plus forte raison niaiser et fantastiquer, comme je fais, doit estre doubter." Philosophizing is no longer learning how to die, but doubting, and doubting involves inquiry, debate, and spontaneity. The dialogic structure of the two essays we have just examined is thus particularly appropriate to Montaigne's growing skepticism and criticism of his former attitudes.

In the " Apologie ", Montaigne describes the mental processes which are at work in his composition :

En mes escris mesmes je ne retrouve pas tousjours l'air de ma premiere imagination : je ne sçay ce que j'ay voulu dire, et m'eschaude souvent à corriger et y mettre un nouveau sens, pour avoir perdu le premier, qui valloit mieux. Je ne fay qu'aller et venir : mon jugement ne tire pas tousjours en avant ; il flotte, il vague. ... Maintes fois... ayant pris pour exercice et pour esbat à maintenir une contraire opinion à la mienne, mon esprit, s'applicant et tournant de ce costé là, m'y attache si bien que je ne trouve plus la raison de mon premier advis, et m'en despars. Je m'entraine quasi où je penche, comment que ce soit, et m'emporte de mon pois. (*Essais*, II, xii, 636.)

At this point in his intellectual development, as his mind gropingly seeks its way, Montaigne uses the essay heuristically. In the late essays of Book III, where he is no longer searching for answers, the technique of debate is no longer necessary or fitting. Having arrived at order and unity, his tone tends more and more to the didactic and formulaic. Diderot, in his works, never reaches this final degree of serenity and certainty. To the end, his mind continues its inner dialogue.

Analogy and dream

As we recall, Diderot justifies the " disorderly " composition of the *Essais* by a law of association of ideas :

Montaigne suit sans art l'enchaînement de ses idées. ... Il n'est ni plus lié, ni plus décousu en écrivant qu'en pensant ou en rêvant ; or il est impossible que l'homme qui pense ou qui rêve soit tout à fait décousu. ... Il y a une liaison nécessaire entre les deux pensées les plus disparates. ... C'est une règle à laquelle les fous même sont assujettis dans leur plus grand désordre de raison. (A-T, XVI, 485f.)

For Diderot, the associative faculty of the mind is at work in the dreamer, the philosopher, the poet and the madman. It is governed by the principle of analogy, which is the fundamental principle of intellectual activity. Abstractions must depend ultimately upon analogy : " Nous ne parvenons à attacher une idée à quantité de termes qui ne peuvent être représentés par des objets sensibles, et qui, pour ainsi dire, n'ont point de corps, que par une suite de combinaisons fines et profondes des analogies que nous remarquons entre ces objets non sensibles et les idées qu'ils excitent " (*Lettre sur les aveugles, Œuvres phil.*, p. 91).

131

The incoherence of madness, dream, and conversation results from the laws of analogy:

Une seule qualité physique peut conduire l'esprit qui s'en occupe à une infinité de choses diverses. Prenons une couleur, le jaune, par exemple. L'or est jaune, la soie est jaune, le souci est jaune, le bile est jaune, la lumière est jaune, la paille est jaune ; à combien d'autres fils, ce fil ne répond-il pas ? La folie, le rêve, le décousu de la conversation consistent à passer d'un objet à un autre par l'entremise d'une qualité commune. (A Sophie Volland, 20 Oct. 1760, *Corr.*, III, 173.)

In the course of his ramblings to Mlle. Volland, Diderot thus explains the anomalies of the mind as well as its noblest inventions. For underlying the principle of analogy is man's symbol-making capacity, to which is owed the existence of language itself.

Critics have noted the prefigurement in the above-quoted passage of Baudelaire's *correspondances* and the whole theory of Symbolist poetry.[1] The idea is not, of course, original with Diderot ; it goes at least as far back as Aristotle.[2] Image, allegory, symbol, metaphor—all depend upon the suggestivity of analogy.

The perception of *rapports* and the combining power of analogies may also lead the philosopher to the discovery of truth. We recall the passage from *De l'Interprétation de la nature* in which Diderot compares the intuition of the experimental philosopher to a " spirit of divination " which, unlike the *daimon* of Socrates, may be communicated to others : " C'est une facilité de supposer ou d'apercevoir des oppositions ou des analogies, qui a sa source dans une connaissance pratique des qualités physique des êtres considérés solitairement, ou de leurs effets réciproques, quand on les considère en combinaison " (*Œuvres phil.*, p. 197). It is important, however, to make the distinction Diderot himself makes between analogy considered as a logical principle, and analogy as an intuitive, poetic avenue to truth. Diderot is aware that analogical reasoning is uncertain and leads only to greater or lesser *probability*, according to the number of experiments one has made.[3]

Diderot's classic statement on the functioning of the mind is surely the *Rêve de d'Alembert*. Here he himself employs an analogy in order

---

[1] See Margaret GILMAN, *The Idea of Poetry in France* (Cambridge, Mass., 1958), p. 77.

[2] " By far the greatest thing for a poet is to be a master of metaphor. ... It is a mark of genius, for to be good at metaphor is to be intuitively aware of hidden resemblances " (*Poetics*, xxii).

[3] *Encyclopédie*, Art. " Induction ", A-T, XV, 216. According to Jacques Proust (*Diderot et l'Encyclopédie*), this article is anonymous and may not be attributed with certainty to Diderot, since it does not bear an asterisk in the *Encyclopédie*. This, however, does not eliminate the possibility that he may well have been its author. The article is in accord with numerous passages in Diderot's works in which he expresses doubt concerning the inductive method because of this complex interrelatedness of phenomena. Without *all* of the facts, we can not be certain of truth, and how can we ever be certain of possessing *all* of the facts?

to portray the principles by which ideas are aroused in the mind. In an attempt to explain mental phenomena in material terms, he compares the " fibres " of which the brain is composed to vibrating strings :

La corde vibrante sensible, oscille, résonne longtemps encore après qu'on l'a pincée. C'est cette oscillation, cette espèce de résonance nécessaire qui tient l'objet présent, tandis que l'entendement s'occupe de la qualité qui lui convient. Mais les cordes vibrantes ont encore une autre propriété, c'est d'en faire frémir d'autres ; et c'est ainsi qu'une première idée en rappelle une seconde, ces deux-là une troisième, toutes les trois une quatrième, et ainsi de suite, sans qu'on puisse fixer la limite des idées réveillées, enchaînées, du philosophe qui médite ou qui s'écoute dans le silence et l'obscurité. Cet instrument a des sauts étonnants, et une idée réveillée va faire quelquefois frémir une harmonique qui en est à un intervalle incompréhensible. (*Œuvres phil.*, p. 271f.)

The analogy between thought and vibrating strings and the physical phenomenon of enharmonic resonance serves to explain how it is possible for us to think of two or more things at the same time. Analogy is a rule of three performed within the sensitive instrument :

Si tel phénomène connu en nature est suivi de tel autre phénomène connu en nature, quel sera le quatrième phénomène conséquent à un troisième, ou donné par la nature, ou imaginé à l'imitation de la nature? ... C'est une quatrième corde harmonique et proportionnelle à trois autres dont l'animal attend la résonance qui se fait toujours en lui-même, mais qui ne se fait pas toujours en nature. Peu importe au poète, il n'en est pas moins vrai. C'est autre chose pour le philosophe ; il faut qu'il interroge ensuite la nature qui, lui donnant souvent un phénomène tout à fait différent de celui qu'il avait présumé, alors il s'aperçoit que l'analogie l'a séduit. (*Ibid.*, p. 280f.)

There is thus a difference between the use a poet makes of the analogical principle and its application in philosophy. For the poet, it affords a means of expressing a personal vision of the world which may or may not correspond to objective reality. For the empirical philosopher, however, whose goal is not subjective truth but the truth of exterior phenomena, analogies are not valid if they are not in accord with observations.

Yet the analogies of the oneiric imagination may incarnate truths which have objective validity. For Diderot the processes of the mind are unified, and thus arises the ambiguity of the dream and the waking state, which he explores in the *Rêve de d'Alembert*.[1]

Montaigne had, of course, been sensitive to the ambiguity of reality and dream. How fine is the dividing line between them ! Consciousness is, in a sense, no less dream-like than dream, while dreams, on the other hand, seem very real to us : " Ceux qui ont apparié nostre vie à un songe, ont eu de la raison, à l'avanture plus qu'ils ne pensoyent.

---

[1] See below, pp. 137-141.

Quand nous songeons, nostre ame vit, agit, exerce toutes ses facultez, ne plus ne moins que quand elle veille '' (*Essais*, II, xii, 673). Our existence is in suspension in a vague limbo somewhere between sleep and waking :

Nous veillons dormants, et veillants dormons. Je ne vois pas si clair dans le sommeil ; mais, quand au veiller, je ne le trouve jamais assez pur et sans nuage. ... Nostre raison et nostre ame, recevant les fantasies et opinions qui luy naissent en dormant, et authorisant les actions de nos songes de pareille approbation qu'elle faict celles du jour, pourquoy ne mettons nous en doubte si nostre penser, nostre agir, n'est pas un autre songer, et nostre veiller quelque espece de dormir? *(Ibid.)*

Montaigne's purpose here, however, is to aid his humbling of reason. It is to him supremely ironical that man's moments of greatest insight and inspiration often occur when the conscious intellect is not in control :

N'y a il point de la hardiesse à la philosophie d'estimer des hommes qu'ils produisent leurs plus grands effects et plus approchans de la divinité, quand ils sont hors d'eux et furieux et insensez? Nous nous amendons par la privation de nostre raison et son assoupissement. Les deux voies naturelles pour entrer au cabinet des Dieux et y preveoir le cours des destinées sont la fureur et le sommeil. (*Essais*, II, xii, 639.) [1]

Montaigne is fascinated by the paradox that philosophers are sometimes led to place greater value on the irrational than on the rational :

Cecy est plaisant à considerer : par la dislocation que les passions apportent à nostre raison, nous devenons vertueux ; par son extirpation que la fureur ou l'image de la mort apporte, nous devenons prophetes et divins. Jamais plus volontiers je ne l'en creus. C'est un pur enthousiasme que la saincte verité a inspiré en l'esprit philosophique, qui luy arrache, contre sa proposition, que l'estat tranquille de nostre ame, l'estat rassis, l'estat plus sain que la philosophie luy puisse acquerir n'est pas son meilleur estat. Nostre veillée est plus endormie que le dormir ; nostre sagesse, moins sage que la folie, noz songes vallent mieux que noz discours ; la pire place que nous puissions prendre, c'est en nous. *(Ibid.)*

The admission on the part of philosophy that tranquillity of soul is not necessarily the greatest of goods, wrested from it by the spirit of divine truth, leads Montaigne to a final paradox :

Mais pense elle [la philosophie] pas que nous ayons l'advisement de remarquer que la voix qui faict l'esprit, quand il est despris de l'homme, si clair-voyant, si grand, si parfaict et, pendant qu'il est en l'homme, si terrestre, ignorant et tenebreux, c'est une voix partant de l'esprit qui est partie de l'homme terrestre, ignorant et tenebreux, et à cette cause voix infiable et incroyable? *(Ibid.)*

---

[1] The passages in the " Apologie " concerning the ambiguity between dream and the waking state were inserted after 1588, and are not part of Montaigne's original indictment of reason and knowledge derived from the senses.

Montaigne thus remains skeptical of the value attached to dreams and other analogous states of mental alienation. He is aware, however, that the conscious mind is not always capable of equalling the products of the unconscious. He would like to gain control of this elusive part of himself :

Mais mon ame me desplait de ce qu'elle produict ordinairement ses plus profondes resveries, plus folles et qui me plaisent le mieux, à l'im-prouveu et lors que je les cerche moins ; lesquelles s'esvanouissent soudain. ... Il m'en advient comme de mes songes : en songeant, je les recommande à ma memoire (car je songe volontiers que je songe), mais le lendemain je me presente bien leur couleur comme elle estoit, ou gaye, ou triste, ou estrange ; mais quels ils estoient au reste, plus j'ahane à le trouver, plus je l'enfonce en l'oubliance. Aussi de ces discours fortuites qui me tombent en fantaisie, il ne m'en reste en memoire qu'une vaine image. (*Essais*, III, v, 981.)

In the final essay, Montaigne speaks again of dreams :

Je n'ay poinct à me plaindre de mon imagination : j'ay eu peu de pensées en ma vie qui m'ayent seulement interrompu le cours de mon sommeil, si elles n'ont esté du desir, qui m'esveillat sans m'affliger. Je songe peu souvent ; et lors c'est des choses fantastiques et des chimeres produictes communément de pensées plaisantes, plustost ridicules que tristes. Et tiens qu'il est vray que les songes sont loyaux interpretes de nos inclinations mais il y a de l'art à les assortir et entendre. (III, xiii, 1235.)

Skeptical of an occult quality in dreams, Montaigne might, however, have become interested in the interpretation of dreams as an aid in self-analysis. The chief significance, however, of the dream in the *Essais*, is the use Montaigne makes of the ambiguity between sleep and wake as evidence of the mind's inability to be absolutely sure of anything. He is acutely aware of an unbreachable discontinuity between ourselves as perceiving individuals and the objects of our perception. We are isolated from everything but our own bodies.

Diderot had expressed an interest in dreams as early as the *Bijoux indiscrets*.[1] In the *Salon de 1767*, he is intrigued by the ambiguity of dream and consciousness :

J'ai passé la nuit la plus agitée. C'est un état bien singulier que celui du rêve. Aucun philosophe que je connaisse n'a encore assigné la vraie différence de la veille et du rêve. Veillé-je, quand je crois rêver ? rêvé-je, quand je crois veiller ? Qui m'a dit que le voile ne se déchirerait pas un jour, et que je ne resterais pas convaincu que j'ai rêvé tout ce que j'ai fait, et fait réellement tout ce que j'ai rêvé ? Les eaux, les arbres, les forêts que j'ai vus en nature, m'ont certainement fait une impression moins forte que les mêmes objets en rêve. (A-T, XI, 143.)

Diderot has the capacity to abandon himself completely to his dreams, to the point where he is more acutely struck by what he sees in dreams

---

[1] " Rêve de Mangogul " (A-T, IV, 255-259) ; also IV, 303-305.

than what he sees in reality, or at least he thinks so. Madame Geoffrin confirms Diderot's own characterization of himself : " Il a la tête si mauvaise et il est si mal organisé qu'il ne voit ni n'entend rien de ce qu'il voit ni de ce qu'il entend tel que cela était. Il est toujours comme un homme qui rêve et qui croit réel tout ce qu'il a rêvé." [1] It is in sleep that the distinction between the real and the unreal falls away. In dream, each object possesses equal importance, equal validity ; reality and fiction, the bizarre and the profound—all blend to form an ambiguous world :

Le sommeil, cet état où... comme dans la maladie, chaque filet du réseau s'agite, se meut, transmet à l'origine commune une foule de sensations souvent disparates, décousues, troublées ; d'autres fois si liées, si suivies, si bien ordonnées que l'homme éveillé n'aurait ni plus de raison, ni plus d'éloquence, ni plus d'imagination ; quelquefois si violentes, si vives, que l'homme éveillé reste incertain sur la réalité de la chose. (*Rêve de d'Alembert, Œuvres phil.*, p. 360.)

But, in spite of these statements, it must not be forgotten that Diderot was a rationalist who believed in the efficacy of reason to comprehend the world. He does not believe that intellectual understanding is possible in dream.[2] In Georges May's recently published edition of Diderot's commentary on Hemsterhuis, we find an interesting remark by Diderot on the dream, which corresponds in part to statements we find elsewhere in his works. The importance of this new text is that it makes clear the fact that Diderot never believed in the dream as a direct means of understanding :

Je ne crois pas qu'aucune découverte géométrique ait été faite en rêve ; ni qu'il s'en fasse jamais aucune. Le rêve ne reproduit que les images de la veille, images tantôt successives et sans liaison, plus souvent liées. Il y a bien de la ressemblance entre le rêve et la folie. Un homme qui ne sortirait point de l'état de rêve serait un fou.[3]

---

[1] *Correspondance inédite*, ed. Charles Morny, p. 466 ; cited in DIDEROT, *Corr.*, VII, 132, n. 11.

[2] Cf. Dieckmann's statement on the significance for Diderot of the dream as a mode of knowledge : " Pour Diderot... le rêve représentait un ordre de connaissance, et le mouvement de la pensée tel que nous l'observons dans le rêve correspond à beaucoup d'égards à certains modes de pensée de l'état de veille " (*Cinq Leçons sur Diderot*, p. 84).

[3] F. HEMSTERHUIS, *Lettre sur l'homme et ses rapports, avec le commentaire inédit de Diderot*, ed. Georges May (New Haven, 1964), p. 91. Cf. the following passage from the *Bijoux indiscrets:* " Nos rêves ne sont que des jugements précipités qui se succèdent avec une rapidité incroyable, et qui, rapprochant des objets qui ne se tiennent que par des qualités fort éloignées, en composent un tout bizarre. — Oh ! que je vous entends bien, dit Mirzoza ; et c'est un ouvrage en marqueterie, dont les pièces rapportées sont plus ou moins nombreuses, plus ou moins régulièrement placées, selon qu'on a l'esprit plus vif, l'imagination plus rapide et la mémoire plus fidèle : ne serait-ce pas même en cela que consisterait la folie?... — Vous y êtes, madame ; oui, si l'on examine bien les fous, on sera convaincu que leur état n'est qu'un rêve continu " (A-T, IV, 303).

Thus, although dream, madness, and genius are very closely related, nevertheless dream is more akin to madness than to a mode of thought. In his notes to Hemsterhuis, Diderot remarks that the dreamer " peut voir plus vivement; pour raisonner plus juste, je n'en crois rien ".[1]

In view of the foregoing considerations, therefore, it would be inaccurate, it seems to me, to qualify the dream as a mode of knowledge. Diderot's choice of the dream as a literary vehicle and its particular expressivity in the *Rêve de d'Alembert* needs, therefore, to be further clarified.[2] It is not merely a question of the ambiguity of reality and illusion as a philosophic problem to which Diderot has given concrete form. Nor is Diderot's interest in dream " pre-Freudian " in the sense that dream may reveal the secrets of the subconscious. Why should Diderot have chosen the dream as the form in which to cloak his most lucid exposition of materialism? Actually, it is probably more accurate to say that the very nature of the speculations in the *Rêve* engendered the form of the dialogues.

It is in the structure of the *Rêve* and the relationship between the first two dialogues of the trilogy—the *Entretien entre d'Alembert et Diderot* and the *Rêve de d'Alembert* proper—that one can discern the close unity between the ideas expressed in the work and its form. The difference between the two dialogues is not contained in the doctrine each presents but in the change of tone. The *Entretien* is a fairly conventional dialogue in which Diderot lays a basis for a monistsic materialism and d'Alembert argues from a dualist position representative of the deism of the *philosophes*. The tone of the dialogue is that of sober, reasoned discourse. It ends inconclusively, for Diderot has been unable to persuade d'Alembert by rational means of the truth of his speculations, and the dialogue closes with d'Alembert affirming his skepticism : " Sceptique je me serai couché, sceptique je me lèverai " (*Œuvres phil.*, p. 281). The *Entretien*, which had proceeded so seriously, ends in total irony : d'Alembert agreeing patronizingly with Diderot, who, in turn, subjects the former to the irony which becomes immediately clear in the second dialogue.

Now, Diderot himself reveals in his correspondence with Sophie Volland some essential facts about the genesis of the *Rêve:*

J'ai fait un dialogue entre d'Alembert et moi. Nous y causons assez gaiement, et même assez clairement, malgré la sécheresse et l'obscurité du sujet. A ce dialogue il en succède un second, beaucoup plus étendu, qui sert d'éclaircissement au premier. Celui-ci est intitulé le *Rêve de d'Alembert*. Les interlocuteurs sont d'Alembert rêvant, Mlle de Lespinasse, l'amie de d'Alembert, et le docteur Bordeu. Si j'avais voulu sacrifier la richesse du fond à la noblesse du ton, Démocrite, Hippocrate et Leucippe auraient été

---

[1] *Op. cit.*, p. 93.

[2] On this subject, see for example Paul Vernière's *édition critique* and Eleanor M. Walker's illuminating study (" Diderot's *Rêve de d'Alembert* " [unpubl. diss., Columbia University, 1952]). In my own discussion, I am indebted on a few points to Professor Aram Vartanian who spoke at New York University (Dec. 1964) on " Diderot and the Dream ".

mes personnages ; mais la vraisemblance m'aurait renfermé dans les bornes étroites de la philosophie ancienne, et j'y aurais trop perdu. Cela est de la plus haute extravagance et tout à la fois de la philosophie la plus profonde. Il y a quelque adresse à avoir mis mes idées dans la bouche d'un homme qui rêve. Il faut souvent donner à la sagesse l'air de la folie, afin de lui procurer ses entrées. J'aime mieux qu'on dise : « Mais cela n'est pas si insensé qu'on croirait bien », que de dire : « Ecoutez-moi, voilà des choses très sages. » (31 Août 1769, *Corr.*, p. 126f.)

Je crois vous avoir dit que j'avais fait un dialogue entre d'Alembert et moi. En le relisant, il m'a pris une fantaisie d'en faire un second, et il a été fait. Les interlocuteurs sont d'Alembert qui rêve, Bordeu et l'amie de d'Alembert, Mlle de Lespinasse. Il est intitulé le *Rêve de d'Alembert*. Il n'est pas possible d'être plus profond et plus fou. (11 Sept. 1769, *ibid.*, IX, 140.)

We may draw the following conclusions from Diderot's own remarks : although the *Entretien* was written first, it was not entirely replaced by the much longer second dialogue which Diderot felt was needed as a further clarification ; his intention, upon completing the second dialogue, was to keep them side by side, although the later dialogue presents no essentially new ideas. Why did he not simply discard the first dialogue as a first draft of the second ? What purpose is served by their juxtaposition, which might only result in a certain redundancy ? The answers to these questions seem implicit in Diderot's own statements. Diderot is well aware that it was something of a brilliant stroke to have put his ideas in the mouth of the dreaming d'Alembert. But its force would be considerably weakened without the first dialogue. The importance of the *Entretien* is that it lays the *conceptual* foundation, with the presentation of arguments pro and con, for the following dialogue. This rational basis, however, serves a double purpose. First, it establishes Diderot's identity as the author of the ideas and enables him to present the opposing position representative of contemporary intellectual opinion. But second, this display of reason is in itself a critique of reason, for reason is unable to arrive at a conclusion. It does not possess the total evidence required to establish truth, and even if it did have all the facts, reason is often unable to combat the force of prejudice and the weight of an intellectual tradition. Therefore, the conceptual function of the *Entretien* needs to be supplemented by the *visionary* function of the *Rêve*. The fact that the vision is ostensibly d'Alembert's and not Diderot's is, of course, the irony generated by the succession of the two dialogues. D'Alembert, in the *Rêve*, espouses the doctrine he had opposed in the *Entretien*, but it is not the result of rational persuasion. It is not external ; it springs from deep within his being.

Let us now turn to a consideration of the structure of the central dialogue of the trilogy, the *Rêve de d'Alembert* proper. The most significant feature of the dialogue, from the point of view of structure, is that the dream is not narrated directly. D'Alembert's dreaming —the outward signs of which have disquieted Mlle. de Lespinasse— becomes the occasion for her having sent for Dr. Bordeu, whose arrival

triggers the opening of the conversation. On Dr. Bordeu's arrival, d'Alembert is still asleep. The major part of his dream has already taken place before the start of the dialogue. Now it is significant that d'Alembert's dream is not a personal vision; it is not solipsistic. He had communicated it in his delirium to Mlle. de Lespinasse, who took notes. It is these notes which she reads to Dr. Bordeu. What we have is a kind of double indirect discourse reminiscent of the structure of Plato's *Symposium*, in which all of the speeches are reported indirectly.

There are thus in the *Rêve* five levels of discourse upon which the dialogue is constructed.[1] We might term zero degree the point of view of Diderot, the author; in contrast to the *Entretien*, he is conspicuously absent from the *Rêve*, although we might consider that he distributes himself amongst his three interlocutors. The other levels are as follows:

1st degree : the direct discourse of the interlocutors speaking to each other in their conscious waking state.

2nd degree : the continuation of d'Alembert's delirium as he reports his dream to Mlle. de Lespinasse and Dr. Bordeu.

3rd degree : Mlle. de Lespinasse's report of the first part of the dream to Dr. Bordeu.

4th degree : D'Alembert's report of his dream to Mlle. de Lespinasse (before the dialogue began).

Now, the first degree appears throughout the dialogue in the conversation between Mlle. de Lespinasse and the doctor. D'Alembert, however, moves successively from fourth degree (before the start of the dialogue) through third, second and finally first degree in the latter part of the dialogue, after he has awakened from sleep. What happens in the *Rêve*, therefore, is the gradual return of d'Alembert to consciousness. The effect of this process is heightened by the use of the successive degrees of directness just outlined, which might also be termed degrees of the dream's proximity to the reader.

Because of these various levels of indirect discourse, the reader never enters the mind of the dreaming d'Alembert. It is not the pure subjectivity of the dream with which Diderot is concerned. On the contrary, throughout the dialogue d'Alembert's dream is an object of discussion and explication. It is, however, for d'Alembert, a hiatus in his awareness of self and of the world. D'Alembert's insistence that he would go to bed a skeptic and get up still a skeptic is borne out by the conclusion of the dialogue when he has no memory or comprehension of what he had dreamt. This discontinuity between d'Alembert's consciousness and his dream is, however, transformed for the reader into a continuity by means of the dialogue's structure. What the structure of the dialogue also achieves is the continuity of subjectivity and objecti-

---

[1] The following analysis was suggested in part by Robert Mauzi's treatment of the structure of *Jacques le fataliste* ("La Parodie romanesque dans *Jacques le fataliste*", *Diderot Studies VI*, ed. Otis Fellows [Geneva, 1964]).

vity, the union of the processes of inner experience and knowledge of the exterior world, and, above all, the union of mental and physical processes.

At the close of the *Rêve*, once d'Alembert has returned to consciousness, the three interlocutors analyze the dream as a psychophysical phenomenon. The ambiguity of dream and wake results from the continuity of psychophysical processes and the identity of the raw material available to consciousness and sleep :

Dans la veille le réseau obéit aux impressions de l'objet extérieur. Dans le sommeil, c'est de l'exercice de sa propre sensibilité qu'émane tout ce qui se passe en lui. Il n'y a point de distraction dans le rêve ; de là sa vivacité : c'est presque toujours la suite d'un éréthisme, un accès passager de maladie. L'origine du réseau y est alternativement active et passive d'une infinité de manières : de là son désordre. Les concepts y sont quelquefois aussi liés, aussi distincts que dans l'animal exposé au spectacle de la nature. Ce n'est que le tableau de ce spectacle réexcité : de là sa vérité, de là l'impossibilité de le discerner de l'état de veille ; nulle probabilité d'un de ces états plutôt que de l'autre ; nul moyen de reconnaître l'erreur que l'expérience. (*Œuvres phil.*, p. 361.)

The dream is thus subjective without being solipsistic. The dreamer selects and recombines elements from his conscious experience of the world. He does not invent. His subjective experience is correlated to the objective world.

This is the innovation of Diderot's humanistic materialism, which is so well put into concrete form in the *Rêve de d'Alembert* : the world of human experience is placed within the context of material reality, according to which human events are explained as physical events. But this is, after all, the principle underlying materialism. What Diderot does in the *Rêve* is to present his speculations on the nature of the physical world in the context of subjective human experience, namely the dream. But he does not therefore contradict the materialist premise and retreat into subjectivism. The dream itself is an object observed and explained in material terms by Dr. Bordeu and submitted to an empirical test.

There is irony contained in this juxtaposition of reason and vision, in Diderot's belief that " il faut souvent donner à la sagesse l'air de la folie, afin de lui procurer ses entrées ". Like his ancestors, Plato and Montaigne, Diderot accepted this maxim as a principle of method. But to imply that they placed greater value on irrationality would be erroneous. Like Plato, Diderot realized the power of images to woo and subdue the recalcitrant intellect, especially when sufficient proof to convince by rational means is lacking. Furthermore, the mind that can fabricate syllogistic proofs is also capable of forging potent analogies which image forth truths about reality : images which straddle the realms of science and poetry.

The profoundest irony of the *Rêve de d'Alembert* is the choice of the most subjective of human experiences for the exposition of an objective

140

materialism whose tenets tend to deny the value of individualism. The ambiguity of dream and consciousness serves as the artistic means by which Diderot hoped to effect a synthesis of scientific determinism and the humanist tradition. The value of individualism and subjectivity, which Diderot inherited from Montaigne but for which he sought to find a new and meaningful context in a God-less world ruled by un-mindful Nature, is one of the poles of Diderot's dialectic. The *Réfutation d'Helvétius* makes clear Diderot's defense of humanism in the face of an anti-humanist materialism. Through the medium of literary form, Diderot was able to reconcile otherwise irreconcilable ideas.

Montaigne and Diderot, in the search for adequate expression of their complex, multivocal ideas, have ultimate recourse to a poetic principle. Thought engenders form. The unity of idea and structure is the aesthetic foundation of a humanism. Montaigne, in the *Essais*, recreates the plenitude of his self-consciousness, and thus reintegrates the self and the world. Similarly, Diderot sees the possibility of resolving in literary terms the contradictions of his philosophy.

CONCLUSION

> Après un long pèlerinage à la recherche de la vérité, Diderot rejoint Montaigne et porte le regard sur soi aussi bien qu'en dehors de soi, s'efforçant comme Montaigne l'avait fait de rétablir le sentiment de l'harmonie intérieure qui existe entre l'homme et l'univers.[1]

Montaigne and Diderot have led us along paths which diverge and meet again. We have found it difficult always to differentiate between influence and affinity, for the two processes often merge and become indistinguishable. Indeed, the strongest influence of one mind upon another is frequently manifested, not in resemblance, but in reaction. Diderot's relationship to Montaigne displays this complexity.

We have not attempted to provide an exhaustive catalogue of all the possible points of contact between the essayist and the Encyclopedist. In view of the diffuseness of both writers, such a task would have seemed out of all proportion to the end to be served. We have chosen, rather, to be guided by certain leading ideas suggested by Diderot's own statements about Montaigne. These have seemed to me to fall under the general headings of skepticism, naturalism, subjectivism, and literary form. Common to all these terms is the intuition of mobility shared by both Montaigne and Diderot. For each, the cosmos reflects the perpetual flux of the human consciousness.

In spite of the flux of the phenomenological world, Montaigne finds stability in himself emerging paradoxically from the flux of his phenomenological self. He is led further into the self as the final fount of knowledge as well as a degree of certainty. Although he may doubt the reliability of his sense organs to give him a true report of exterior reality, he does not doubt the validity of his body's perception of itself. Montaigne does not retreat into solipsism. He maintains his links with

---

[1] Robert NIKLAUS, " Présence de Diderot ", *Diderot Studies VI*, ed. Otis Fellows, p. 28.

142

the world, his consciousness mirroring the world in itself. "Chaque homme porte la forme entiere de l'humaine condition" (*Essais*, III, ii, 900). Montaigne learns that the path to truth involves a journey inward ; he arrives at knowledge of the world through knowing himself.

Diderot is the inheritor of Montaigne's naturalism. His skepticism, however, although it is founded in his awareness of the mutability and complexity of nature and thus of the difficulty of all man's attempts to arrive at truth, ultimately leads to a position very different from that of Montaigne. Diderot does not move deeper and deeper into himself to find stability, but out into the world. It is the concept of unity and continuity which is the counterpoise to flux. He is thus led out of the self and towards a position of positivism. For him also, bodily experience is a unity of sensation and reflection, or in modern terms, of perception and apperception, enabling the mind to probe deeper into the nature of external reality. For Diderot, to know the world is to know ourselves.

Diderot shares with Montaigne the fundamental conviction that all knowledge rests on man's knowledge of himself. Thus, although Diderot rejects the prejudice of anthropocentrism in natural philosophy, his cosmology abandoning man to chance and the blind combinations of matter in movement, Diderot the moralist and humanist never dislodges man from the center of his thought, for human consciousness is still at the center of the universe :

Une considération surtout qu'il ne faut point perdre de vue, c'est que si l'on bannit l'homme ou l'être pensant et contemplateur de dessus la surface de la terre, ce spectacle pathétique et sublime de la nature n'est plus qu'une scène triste et muette. L'univers se tait ; le silence et la nuit s'en emparent. Tout se change en une vaste solitude où les phénomènes inobservés se passent d'une manière obscure et sourde. C'est la présence de l'homme qui rend l'existence des êtres intéressante ; et que peut-on se proposer de mieux dans l'histoire de ces êtres, que de se soumettre à cette considération ? Pourquoi n'introduirons-nous pas l'homme dans notre ouvrage, comme il est placé dans l'univers ? Pourquoi n'en ferons-nous pas un centre commun ? ... L'homme est le terme unique d'où il faut partir, et auquel il faut tout ramener, si l'on veut plaire, intéresser, toucher jusque dans les considérations les plus arides et les détails les plus secs. Abstraction faite de mon existence et du bonheur de mes semblables, que m'importe le reste de la nature ? (A-T, XIV, 453.)

Diderot realizes that the advent of science, in changing man's position with respect to the universe, creates a situation of crisis in humanist thought. It calls into question the very possibility of a humanism, since a materialist view subjects man to the mechanisms of nature, and renders urgent the desire, by a renewal of the premises of humanism, to make it consistent with science and not in contradiction to it. Diderot's attempt to continue and revitalize the humanist tradition is based on a fundamentally Montaignean principle. The philosophic, aesthetic, ethical, and political ideas of which such a humanism is composed must not be absolutes applied to man ; they must originate

from an experiential knowledge of what man is : " Quelle notion précise peut-on avoir du mal, du beau et du laid, du bon et du mauvais, du vrai et du faux, sans une notion préliminaire de l'homme ? " (A-T, XI, 124.) Such a definition must be of man's biologic nature, based upon the investigation of his physical organization. But the springs of human behavior are so complex that they present perhaps insuperable barriers to our understanding. If such be the case, if we can arrive at no comprehension of man, " si l'homme ne se peut définir... tout est perdu " *(ibid.)*.

Diderot understands the crux of the problem. How is it possible to reconcile a scientific view which subjects man to a mechanistic materialism with a humanism which assumes that man is free to work out his own destiny? On the face of it, they are in absolute contradiction.[1] The biological necessities of human existence are inescapable objective facts, but they do not explain the whole of human reality. What Diderot seeks is not only a scientific realism with respect to inanimate matter, but a full integration of man into his conception of the world. Considering the state of scientific knowledge and technology in his time, the range of his intellectual striving is truly staggering. It is small wonder that the twentieth century recognizes in Diderot a kindred spirit, for his concern—the future of humanism—is ours.

---

[1] See Alfred North Whitehead, who characterized as follows the " radical inconsistency at the basis of modern thought " : " a scientific realism, based on mechanism, is conjoined with an unwavering belief in the world of men and of the higher animals as being composed of self-determining organisms " (*Science and the Modern World* [New York, 1925], p. 110). Diderot saw the inconsistency and sought a means of resolving it. Ironically, Diderot, who is absent from Whitehead's account of eighteenth-century science, has recently been viewed as a precursor of Whitehead's own philosophy of organic mechanism.

APPENDIX

The following symbols are used for the references in the Index Locorum :

A-T   DIDEROT, *Œuvres complètes*. Ed. J. Assézat et M. Tourneux. 20 vols. Paris, 1875-77.

Br.   DIDEROT, *Œuvres*. Ed. J. L. J. Brière. 21 vols. Paris, 1821-23.

Corr.   DIDEROT, *Correspondance*. Ed. Georges Roth. 12 vols. published. Paris, 1955-.

Fab.   DIDEROT, *Le Neveu de Rameau*. Ed. critique par Jean Fabre. Genève-Lille, 1950.

OE   DIDEROT, *Œuvres esthétiques*. Ed. Paul Vernière. Paris, 1959.

OP   DIDEROT, *Œuvres philosophiques*. Ed. Paul Vernière. Paris, 1956.

OR   DIDEROT, *Œuvres romanesques*. Ed. Henri Bénac. Paris, 1959.

INDEX LOCORUM

This is a list of the passages in Diderot's works in which he mentions Montaigne by name, or quotes, paraphrases or alludes to the *Essais*. The references are followed by quoted key phrases, or a brief descriptive sentence or paraphrase. Where Diderot's authorship is uncertain, the entire entry is placed in parentheses.

Bijoux indiscrets

A-T, IV, 224. M.'s imagination.

Correspondance

Corr., I, 78. " Le monde est un esteuf... à peloter aux philosophes."
Corr., IV, 154 ; V, 119 ; V, 134. " Tête bien faite."
Corr., V, 228. Self-study basis for studying others.
Corr., VI, 253, 256, 296 : Brief imitations of M.'s expressions.
Corr., VI, 257. Virtue is its own reward vs. respect for posterity.
Corr., VI, 257-258. M. and glory.
Corr., IX, 94. Reminiscence of the essay " Des coches ".
A-T, XIX, 69. M. affords a useful and lasting pleasure.

Eloge de Richardson

OE, p. 29. Richardson put M.'s maxims into action.

Encyclopédie

A-T, XIII, 370f. " Art." M.'s conservative attitude towards firearms.
(A-T, XIV, 28. " Caraïbes, ou Cannibales." M. on polygamy.)
A-T, XIV, 263. " Cyniques." Praise and paraphrase of M.'s energetic and original style.
A-T, XIV, 440. " Encyclopédie." Imitation of M's "low and trivial" style.
A-T, XV, 66. " Grecs." M. on Aristotle.
A-T, XV, 189. " Imposture." Indictment of charlatans.
(A-T, XVI, 148f. " Nonchalance." Nonchalance in the *Essais*.)

(Br., XVIII, 22f. " Ondoyant." Use of M.'s word.)

(A-T, XVI, 294. " Pire." Reminiscence of passage from " Apologie de Raimond Sebond".)

(A-T, XVI, 342. " Politique." M.'s judgment of Jean Bodin.)

A-T, XVI, 485-486. " Pyrrhonienne." D. justifies M.'s manner of composition.

(Br., XIX, 173f. " Recueil." Sample entry from M.'s essay " De l'art de conférer".)

(Br., XX, 350. " Vigueur." The vigor of M.'s style.)

Entretien d'un père avec ses enfants

OP, p. 436. " Doux et mol chevet."

Essai sur le mérite et la vertu

A-T, I, 9f. or *Corr.*, I, 51. Religious fanaticism and literary censorship.

A-T, I, 19n. Rebuke of weak-willed atheists.

A-T, I, 37, n. 2. M.'s account of the growth of superstition.

Essai sur les règnes de Claude et de Néron

A-T, III, 66, 187. Mentions that M. is *not* his source.

A-T, III, 120. Presents passage in which M. defends Seneca against Dio.

A-T, III, 193. Self-study basis for studying others.

A-T, III, 196ff. Honesty in borrowing from other authors.

A-T, III, 204. " C'est alors que j'étais lui, qu'il était moi."

A-T, III, 233f. D. defends M.'s preference of Seneca to Cicero.

A-T, III, 234. The *Essais*, the " bréviaire des honnêtes gents "

A-T, III, 235. M. familiar with language and literature of Antiquity.

A-T, III, 235. In defense of M.'s taste.

A-T, III, 235. M. on death.

A-T, III, 236. In praise of M.'s literary taste.

A-T, III, 236. Praise and example of M.'s lively style.

A-T, III, 240, 384. Many words in *Essais* have fallen into disuse.

A-T, III, 267, 401. M. among other defenders of Seneca.

(Extrait d'un ouvrage anglais sur la peinture)

(A-T, XIII, 37. " Sans y penser, je mesure mon enjambée, dirait Montaigne, à celle de mon compagnon de voyage.")

Interprétation de la nature

OP, p. 185f. Vanity of an editor of the *Essais*.

Jacques le fataliste

OR, p. 715. M.'s critique of prudishness.

Lettre sur les aveugles

OP, p. 140. Places himself in relation to Condillac, as Charron is to M.

OP, p. 146. D. not far from taking up M.'s motto.

147

Lettre sur les sourds et muets

    A-T, I, 379. M. as precedent for digression.
    A-T, I, 388. M.'s enrichment of language.

Mémoires sur différents sujets de mathématiques

    A-T, IX, 79. M. among other satirists.

Neveu de Rameau

    Fab., p. 103, 104. M.'s expression " perché sur l'épicycle de Mercure ".

Pensées philosophiques

    OP, p. 21f. Paraphrase of Cicero passage. (Via M. ?)
    OP, p. 24, 26. Paraphrase of M.'s critique of dogmatism.
    OP, p. 26. Paraphrase of M.'s " doux et mol chevet ". (Via Pascal.)
    OP, p. 41. " Cette aventure se calfeutra... d'un si grand nombre de pièces."
    OP, p. 46. M. among those damned by the devout.

Plan d'une université

    A-T, III, 492. M. among the moralists.

Promenade du sceptique

    A-T, I, 185. M. among other skeptics, satirists and critics.
    A-T, I, 216f. M., standard-bearer of the Pyrrhonists.

Réflexions sur le livre de l'Esprit

    A-T, II, 272f. M. an " auteur paradoxal ".

Réfutation du livre d'Helvétius intitulé l'Homme

    A-T, II, 290. M. compared with Helvétius.
    A-T, II, 394. Helvétius more methodical than M.

Spéculations utiles et maximes instructives

    A-T, IV, 90. M.'s pessimism.

Salon de 1767

    A-T, XI, 56. " C'est celle qui fait tous les matins son oraison dans Montaigne, et qui a appris de lui, bien ou mal apropos, à voir plus de malhonnêteté dans les choses que dans les mots."
    A-T, XI, 58. Use of M.'s " pelotons " image.

Sur Térence

    OE, p. 60. On literary immortality.
    OE, p. 62. The love song from M.'s essay " Des cannibales ".

A SELECTED BIBLIOGRAPHY

The following is a list of all works cited in the notes as well as a few others which proved to have a bearing on the present study. Those works consulted which were not found to be directly relevant have been omitted.

ALEXANDER, Ian W. " Philosophy of Organism and Philosophy of Consciousness in Diderot's Speculative Thought ", in *Studies in Romance Philology and French Literature Presented to John Orr*. Manchester, 1953.

AUERBACH, Erich. *Mimesis: The Representation of Reality in Western Literature*. Trans. Willard Trask. New York, 1957. (First German edition published in Berne, 1946.)

BESPALOFF, Rachel. " L'Instant et la liberté chez Montaigne ", *Deucalion*, XXX (1950), 65-107.

BESSE, Guy. " Observations sur la Réfutation d'Helvétius par Diderot ", *Diderot Studies VI*, ed. Otis Fellows (Geneva, 1964).

BOASE, Alan M. *The Fortunes of Montaigne: A History of the Essays in France, 1580-1669*. London, 1935.

BURNET, John. *Early Greek Philosophy*. New York, 1957. (Reprint of 4th edition, 1930. First edition, 1892.)

CASSIRER, Ernst. *The Individual and the Cosmos in Renaissance Philosophy*. Trans. Mario Domandi. New York, 1964. (First German edition, Leipzig and Berlin, 1927.)

— *The Philosophy of the Enlightenment*. Trans. Fritz C. A. Koelln and James P. Pettegrove. Boston, 1955. (First German edition, Tubigen, 1932.)

— *The Philosophy of Symbolic Forms, Vol. I: Language*. Trans. Ralph Manheim. New Haven, 1953. (First German edition, Berlin, 1923.)

CHINARD, Gilbert. *L'Exotisme américain dans la littérature française du seizième siècle*. Paris, 1911.

CROCKER, Lester G. *An Age of Crisis: Man and World in Eighteenth-Century French Thought.* Baltimore, 1959.

— " *Jacques le fataliste,* an ' expérience morale ' ", *Diderot Studies III,* ed. Otis Fellows and Gita May. Geneva, 1961.

— *Two Diderot Studies: Ethics and Esthetics.* Baltimore, 1952.

CRU, R. Loyalty. *Diderot as a Disciple of English Thought.* New York, 1913.

CURTIUS, Ernst Robert. " Diderot and Horace ", in *European Literature and the Latin Middle Ages.* Trans. Willard Trask. New York, 1953. (First German edition, Berne, 1948.)

DIDEROT, Denis. *Correspondance.* Ed. Georges Roth. 12 vols. published. Paris, 1955—.

— (ed.). *Encyclopédie, ou Dictionnaire raisonné des sciences, des arts et des métiers,* par une société de gens de lettres. 17 vols. Paris, 1751-1765.

— *Lettre sur les aveugles.* Ed. critique par Robert Niklaus. Genève, 1951.

— *Lettres à Sophie Volland.* Ed. A. Babelon. 3 vols. Paris, 1930.

— *Le Neveu de Rameau.* Ed. critique par Jean Fabre. Genève-Lille, 1950.

— *Œuvres.* Ed. J. L. J. Brière. 21 vols. Paris, 1821-23.

— *Œuvres complètes.* Ed. J. Assézat et M. Tourneux. 20 vols. Paris, 1875-77.

— *Œuvres esthétiques.* Ed. Paul Vernière. Paris, 1959.

— *Œuvres philosophiques.* Ed. Paul Vernière. Paris, 1956.

— *Œuvres politiques.* Ed. Paul Vernière. Paris, 1963.

— *Œuves romanesques.* Ed. Henri Bénac. Paris, 1959.

— *Pensées philosophiques.* Ed. Robert Niklaus. Genève-Paris, 1957.

— *Le Rêve de d'Alembert.* Ed. critique par Paul Vernière. Paris, 1951.

— *Supplément au voyage de Bougainville.* Ed. G. Chinard. Baltimore, 1935.

— *Supplément au voyage de Bougainville.* Ed. critique par Herbert Dieckmann. Genève-Lille, 1955.

DIECKMANN, Herbert. *Cinq Leçons sur Diderot.* Genève-Paris, 1959.

— " Diderot's Conception of Genius ", *Journal of the History of Ideas,* II (April 1941), 151-182.

— " Diderot : *Sur Térence,* le texte du manuscrit autographe ", *Studia Philologica et litteraria in honorem L. Spitzer.* Berne, 1958.

— *Inventaire du fonds Vandeul et inédits de Diderot.* Genève-Lille, 1951.

— " Manuscrits de Diderot conservés en Russie ", *Diderot Studies IV,* ed. Otis Fellows (Geneva, 1963), pp. 53-57.

DOW, Neal. *The Concept and Term " Nature " in Montaigne's Essays.* Philadelphia, 1940.

DREANO, Maturin. *La Renommée de Montaigne en France au dix-huitième siècle, 1677-1801*. Angers, 1952.

DUCROS, Louis. *Les Encyclopédistes*. Paris, 1900.

ETIEMBLE, R. *L'Orient philosophique au dix-huitième siècle*. 2 vols. Paris, 1956-57.

FAGUET, Emile. *Seizième siècle: Etudes littéraires*. Paris, n.d.

FELLOWS, Otis. " The Theme of Genius in Diderot's *Neveu de Rameau* ", *Diderot Studies II*, ed. Otis Fellows and Norman Torrey (Syracuse, 1952), 168-199.

— and Norman TORREY (eds.). *The Age of Enlightenment*. New York, 1942.

FRAME, Donald M. " Did Montaigne Betray Sebond ? " *Romanic Review*, XXXVIII (Dec. 1947).

— *Montaigne in France, 1812-1852*. New York, 1940.

— *Montaigne's Discovery of Man*. New York, 1955.

— " What Next in Montaigne Studies ? " *French Review*, XXXVI (May 1963).

FREDMAN, Alice Green. *Diderot and Sterne*. New York, 1955.

FRIEDRICH, Hugo. *Montaigne*. Berne, 1949.

GILLOT, Hubert. *Denis Diderot: L'Homme, ses idées philosophiques, esthétiques et littéraires*. Paris, 1937.

GILMAN, Margaret. *The Idea of Poetry in France*. Cambridge, Mass., 1958.

GORDON, Douglas H. and Norman L. TORREY. *The Censoring of Diderot's Encyclopédie and the Re-Established Text*. New York, 1947.

GRAVA, Arnolds. " Diderot and Recent Philosophical Trends ", *Diderot Studies IV*, ed. Otis Fellows (Geneva, 1963), 73-103.

GRAY, Floyd. *Le Style de Montaigne*. Paris, 1958.

GUYOT, Charly. *Diderot par lui-même*. Paris, 1957.

HEMSTERHUIS, François. *Lettre sur l'homme et ses rapports, avec le commentaire inédit de Diderot*. Ed. Georges May. New Haven, 1964.

HERMAND, Pierre. *Les Idées morales de Diderot*. Paris, 1923.

KRAKEUR [Crocker], Lester G. *La Correspondance de Diderot, son intérêt documentaire, psychologique et littéraire*. New York, 1939.

LANSON, Gustave. *Les Essais de Montaigne, étude et analyse*. Paris, 1929.

— *Histoire de la littérature française*. Remaniée et complétée par Paul Tuffrau. Paris, 1951. (First edition, 1894.)

LEFEBVRE, Henri. *Diderot*. Paris, 1949.

LIOUBLINSKI, V. S. " Sur la trace des livres lus par Diderot ", *Europe* (Jan.-Feb. 1963), 276-290.

LIPMAN, Wynona Moore. " Attitudes of Diderot Toward Primitivism ". Unpublished dissertation, Columbia University, 1953.

LOVEJOY, A. O. *The Great Chain of Being*. Cambridge, Mass., 1936.

— and G. BOAS. *Primitivism and Related Ideas in Antiquity*. Baltimore, 1935.

Loy, J. Robert. *Diderot's Determined Fatalist*. New York, 1950.

— " L'Essai sur les règnes de Claude et de Néron ", *Cahiers de l'Association Internationale des Etudes Françaises*, XIII (juin 1961), 239-254.

— " Nature, Reason, Enlightenment ", *Studies on Voltaire and the Eighteenth Century*, XXVI, ed. Theodore Besterman (Geneva, 1963).

Luppol, I. K. *Diderot, ses idées philosophiques*. Paris, 1936.

Mauzi, Robert. " Diderot et le bonheur ", *Diderot Studies III*, ed. Otis Fellows and Gita May (Geneva, 1961).

— *L'Idée du bonheur en France au dix-huitième siècle*. Paris, 1960.

— " La Parodie romanesque dans *Jacques le fataliste* ", *Diderot Studies VI*, ed. Otis Fellows (Geneva, 1964).

May, Georges. *Quatre Visages de Denis Diderot*. Paris, 1951.

May, Gita. *Diderot et Baudelaire, critiques d'art*. Genève-Paris, 1957.

Mayer, Jean. *Diderot, homme de science*. Rennes, 1959.

Mesnard, Pierre. *Le Cas Diderot, essai de caractérologie littéraire*. Paris, 1952.

Montaigne, Michel de. *Essais*. Ed. Pierre Coste. Paris, 1725.

— *Les Essais*. Ed. F. Strowski, P. Villey *et al.* 5 vols. Bordeaux, 1906-1933. (Known as the *Edition Municipale*.)

— *Essais*. Ed. Albert Thibaudet. Paris, 1950. (2nd Pléiade ed.)

— *Essais*. Ed. Pierre Villey. 3 vols. Paris, 1930-31.

— *Essays*. Trans. and ed. Jacob Zeitlin. 3 vols. New York, 1934-36.

— *Œuvres complètes*. Ed. A. Armaingaud. 12 vols. Paris, 1924-41.

Moore, Will G. " Montaigne's Notion of Experience ", in *The French Mind: Studies in honour of Gustave Rudler*. Ed. Will Moore, Rhoda Sutherland, Enid Starkie. Oxford, 1952. Pp. 34-52.

Moreau, Pierre. *Montaigne*. Paris, 1958.

Mornet, Daniel. " La Véritable Signification du *Neveu de Rameau* ", *Revue des Deux Mondes* (15 août 1927), 881-908.

Mortier, Roland. " Diderot et le problème de l'expressivité : de la pensée au dialogue heuristique ", *Cahiers de l'Association Internationale des Etudes Françaises*, XIII (juin 1961), 283-298.

Naigeon, Jacques-André. *Encyclopédie méthodique (Philosophie ancienne et moderne)*. Vol. II. Paris, 1792.

— *Mémoires historiques et philosophiques sur la vie et les ouvrages de Denis Diderot*. Paris, 1821.

Niklaus, Robert. " Diderot et le conte philosophique ", *Cahiers de l'Association Internationale des Etudes Françaises*, XIII (juin 1961), 299-316.

— " Présence de Diderot ", *Diderot Studies VI*, ed. Otis Fellows (Geneva, 1964).

Perkins, Jean A. " Diderot's Concept of Virtue ", in *Studies on Voltaire and the Eighteenth Century*, XXIII, ed. Theodore Besterman (Geneva, 1963), 77-91.

PEYRE, Henri. *Literature and Sincerity.* New Haven, 1963.

POMMIER, Jean. *Diderot avant Vincennes.* Paris, 1939.

POPKIN, Richard H. " Scepticism in the Enlightenment ", in *Studies on Voltaire and the Eighteenth Century,* XXVI, ed. Theodore Besterman (Geneva, 1963), 1321-1345.

POULET, Georges. *Etudes sur le temps humain.* Paris, 1950.

PROUST, Jacques. *Diderot et l'Encyclopédie.* Paris, 1962.

— " La Bibliothèque de Diderot ", *Revue des Sciences Humaines,* fasc. 90 (avril-juin, 1958).

VON RORETZ, Karl. *Diderots Weltanschauung.* Vienna, 1914.

SAINTE-BEUVE, Charles-Augustin. *Port-Royal.* 2nd ed. Vol. II. Paris, 1860.

SCHALK, Fritz. " Einleitung in die Encyclopädie der Französischen Aufklärung ", *Münchner Romanistische Arbeiten,* VI (München, 1936).

SEILLIÈRE, Ernest. *Le Naturisme de Montaigne et autres essais.* Paris, 1938.

SPITZER, Leo. *Linguistics and Literary History.* Princeton, 1948.

STEEL, Eric M. *Diderot's Imagery.* New York, 1941.

THIELEMANN, Leland. " Diderot and Hobbes ", *Diderot Studies II,* ed. Otis Fellows and Norman Torrey (Syracuse, 1952), 221-278.

THOMAS, Jean. *L'Humanisme de Diderot.* 2nd ed. Paris, 1938.

VARTANIAN, Aram. *Diderot and Descartes.* Princeton, 1953.

— " From Deist to Atheist, Diderot's Philosophical Orientation 1746-1749 ", *Diderot Studies I,* ed. Otis Fellows and Norman Torrey (Syracuse, 1949), 46-63.

VENTURI, Franco. *Jeunesse de Diderot, 1713-1753.* Trans. Juliette Bertrand. Paris, 1939.

VERNIÈRE, Paul. *Spinoza et la pensée française avant la Révolution.* 2 vols. Paris, 1954.

VILLEY, Pierre. *Les Essais de Montaigne.* Paris, 1932.

— *Montaigne devant la postérité.* Paris, 1935.

— *Les Sources et l'évolution des Essais de Montaigne.* 2 vols. Paris, 1908.

WALKER, Eleanor M. " Diderot's *Rêve de d'Alembert* : The Literary and the Scientific Imagination." Unpublished dissertation, Columbia University, 1952.

WHITEHEAD, Alfred North. *Science and the Modern World.* New York, 1925.

WILSON, Arthur M. *Diderot: The Testing Years, 1713-1759.* New York, 1957.

— " Leningrad, 1957 : Diderot and Voltaire Gleanings ", *French Review,* XXXI (1957-58), 351-363.

INDEX

Printed in Switzerland

TO THE MEMORY
OF MY PARENTS

JEROME SCHWARTZ

DIDEROT AND MONTAIGNE

THE *ESSAIS* AND THE SHAPING
OF DIDEROT'S HUMANISM

GENÈVE

LIBRAIRIE DROZ

11, rue Massot

1966

DIDEROT
AND MONTAIGNE

THE *ESSAIS* AND THE SHAPING
OF DIDEROT'S HUMANISM

WITHDRAWN